FEATURE AND MAGAZINE WRITING

FEATURE & MAGAZINE WRITING

David E. Sumner and Holly G. Miller

ACTION, ANGLE
AND ANECDOTES
THIRD EDITION

WILEY-BLACKWELL

A John Wiley & Sons, Ltd., Publication

This third edition first published 2013
© 2013 David E. Sumner and Holly G. Miller

Edition history: Blackwell Publishing Ltd (1e, 2005; 2e, 2009)

Wiley-Blackwell is an imprint of John Wiley & Sons, formed by the merger of Wiley's global Scientific, Technical and Medical business with Blackwell Publishing.

Registered Office
John Wiley & Sons Ltd, The Atrium, Southern Gate, Chichester, West Sussex, PO19 8SQ, UK

Editorial Offices
350 Main Street, Malden, MA 02148-5020, USA
9600 Garsington Road, Oxford, OX4 2DQ, UK
The Atrium, Southern Gate, Chichester, West Sussex, PO19 8SQ, UK

For details of our global editorial offices, for customer services, and for information about how to apply for permission to reuse the copyright material in this book please see our website at www.wiley.com/wiley-blackwell.

The right of David E. Sumner and Holly G. Miller to be identified as the authors of this work has been asserted in accordance with the UK Copyright, Designs and Patents Act 1988.

Wiley also publishes its books in a variety of electronic formats. Some content that appears in print may not be available in electronic books.

Designations used by companies to distinguish their products are often claimed as trademarks. All brand names and product names used in this book are trade names, service marks, trademarks or registered trademarks of their respective owners. The publisher is not associated with any product or vendor mentioned in this book. This publication is designed to provide accurate and authoritative information in regard to the subject matter covered. It is sold on the understanding that the publisher is not engaged in rendering professional services. If professional advice or other expert assistance is required, the services of a competent professional should be sought.

Library of Congress Cataloging-in-Publication Data
Sumner, David E., 1946– author.
    Feature and magazine writing : action, angle, and anecdotes / David E. Sumner and Holly G. Miller. – Third Edition.
        pages   cm
    Includes bibliographical references and index.
    ISBN 978-1-118-30513-3 (pbk.)
    1. Feature writing.   2. Journalism–Authorship.   I. Miller, Holly G., author.   II. Sumner, David E., 1946– Feature & magazine writing.   III. Title.
    PN4784.F37S86 2013
    808.06'607–dc23
                                                2012037005

A catalogue record for this book is available from the British Library.

Cover image: Glowing mobile phone standing on digital pads © CLIPAREA / Custom media; Sprinter getting ready to start the race © Peter Bernik; Public safety patrol on the street © SVLuma; Man holding object © Adchariyaphoto; Business collage made of 225 business pictures © Maksim Shmeljov
Cover design by RBDA

Set in 10.5/13 pt Minion by Toppan Best-set Premedia Limited
Printed and bound in Malaysia by Vivar Printing Sdn Bhd

3   2013

CONTENTS

PREFACE

FEATURE WRITING IN A DIGITAL ERA

The success of the second edition of *Feature and Magazine Writing: Action, Angle and Anecdotes* led the publisher to ask us to write a new and updated edition. The second edition's adoption by dozens of universities in the United States and its substantial sales in Europe, Africa, the Middle East and Asia have made us recognize we write for readers worldwide. Yet, in the past five years, the breathtaking changes in delivery technology have erased geographical boundaries. Distinctions in "feature writing" for newspapers, magazines and online media have blurred and even disappeared as the mass media have developed applications to enable instant access to their content anytime, anywhere. While we continue to offer a focus on writing for magazines, we have expanded the definition of content to include feature writing for all media forms.

The power of magazines has always been the personal identity that they convey as well as their color, design and editorial tone. Magazines are the most intimate form of media because they establish a relationship with their readers unequalled by newspapers, television or radio. A magazine becomes a friend—a reflection of and integral part of the reader's personal and professional life. While print magazine circulation has declined by 5 to 10 percent in the past 10 years, it has not declined as substantially as that of newspapers. Many top consumer magazines have reported healthy gains in digital-only subscribers. *Cosmopolitan*, for example, which has the highest newsstand circulation of any American magazine, was the first to reach a milestone: 100,000 paid digital subscriptions in 2012. Condé Nast Publishing hit the 500,000 digital subscription mark among eight of its publications a few months earlier.

"A couple of years ago, the big question was what's going to happen to magazines like *Cosmo* in the future?" Kate White, the magazine's editor-in-chief, told *Ad Age*. "There was a little bit of anxiety. What this has done is say that our content will rule and will thrive. Women want our content, and they'll get it on a variety of platforms."

Content remains king in any medium.

Because we're convinced that every good product can be better, we've updated this third edition with fresh facts and examples, and we've integrated ideas and suggestions gleaned from teachers, students, professional writers and editors. Most chapters have been strengthened with new facts and fresh examples, and we've added two new chapters.

"Building a Story Blog" (Chapter 17) explores how writers can create a digital presence around a story or collection of stories that extend the writing beyond the article. It examines excellent magazine writer blogs, analyzes the kinds of blogs a writer may want to build, discusses how to manage the digital community and explains how to balance long-form writing with short-form blogging and community management.

"Long-Form Digital Storytelling" (Chapter 18) explains what's required to tell long-form stories within a tablet environment. It covers the magazine environment on the iPad and long-form writing with tablets and other digital readers. It explains the skills required to conceptualize and create this kind of story. We invited our tech-savvy colleague Brad King to share his expertise in these two chapters.

Storytelling has created universal bonds between people in all cultures and all ages. Editors will always seek original stories that inform, inspire and entertain, whether in print or online. This book is based on that long-time formula for successful feature writing: provide stories and information that readers can't get anywhere else. Between the covers of this textbook we explain the entire process—from identifying a good idea to creating an original angle, and from finding primary sources to constructing a final draft. We focus on a basic principle: telling stories about people and putting people into every story.

Our joint experiences outside the classroom include overseeing the lifestyle section of a daily newspaper, serving as editors of an online magazine and print magazines, supervising *Ball Bearings*, an award-winning campus magazine, fulfilling hundreds of freelance feature assignments, and writing books. The chapters in this book are based on our professional experience as well as our experience teaching feature and magazine writing classes for more than 25 years. Yet writing is an indomitable challenge. The goal of this book is to equip the next generation of feature writers with the tools to meet those challenges of writing in any medium for people anywhere.

David E. Sumner
Holly G. Miller
August 2012

ABOUT THE AUTHORS

David E. Sumner is a professor of journalism and head of the magazine journalism program at Ball State University, U.S.A. He received his Ph.D. from the University of Tennessee and is a former "Magazine Educator of the Year" in recognition of his contribution to journalism teaching. He has given papers and talks about magazines and magazine writing from Turkey to Honduras and throughout the United States. His books include *The Magazine Century: American Magazines Since 1900* (2010) and *Magazines: A Complete Guide to the Industry* (2006).

Holly G. Miller is a working journalist and communications consultant with bylines in numerous publications including *Reader's Digest*, *TV Guide* and *Indianapolis Monthly*. She has degrees from Indiana University and Ball State University, U.S.A., and teaches advanced feature-writing classes across America. In addition to writing, ghost-writing and co-authoring more than a dozen books, she has won awards from the Associated Press, the Society of American Travel Writers and the Evangelical Press Association.

PART I

READING, WRITING AND RELEVANCE

"Ninety-eight percent of the people who get the magazine say they read the cartoons first—and the other 2 percent are lying."

David Remnick, editor
The New Yorker

The challenge of every feature writer is to find a topic that is so relevant and riveting that readers tune out all distractions—regardless how entertaining—and concentrate on the article's content. The process begins with knowing where to look for such topics, understanding the audience that the publication serves and conducting in-depth research.

WHAT MAKES A STORY INTERESTING?

KEY POINTS

- Why action, angle and anecdotes matter
- What makes a story interesting?
- Understanding readers and reader demographics
- Five mistakes of beginning writers

"*Sálvame, por favor. Sálvame. Save me. Please save me,*" he prays to Our Lady of Guadalupe. In the chilly, early morning hours of March 24, 2009, 57-year-old José Arias fights for his life, floating in the water 66 miles from Cape May. The nearest lights are from another fishing vessel, which does not see him, anchored less than a half-mile away. A little farther out, a mammoth container ship steams toward Philadelphia. Although Arias does not know it yet, all six of his friends and fellow fishermen are dead, and the red-hulled scalloper, the Lady Mary, is resting, right-side up, on the sandy bottom of the Atlantic.

Thus begins "The Wreck of the Lady Mary," a story that won the Pulitzer Prize in feature writing for Newark *Star-Ledger* reporter Amy Ellis Nutt. She reported a deeply probing story of the mysterious sinking of a commercial fishing boat that drowned six men in the Atlantic Ocean.[1]

"The Man the White House Wakes Up To," in the *New York Times Magazine*, profiled Mike Allen, publisher of the daily e-mail newsletter *Playbook*, which thousands of the nation's most influential political leaders, media

Feature and Magazine Writing: Action, Angle and Anecdotes, Third Edition.
David E. Sumner and Holly G. Miller.
© 2013 David E. Sumner and Holly G. Miller. Published 2013 by John Wiley & Sons, Inc.

executives and journalists read daily for their "insider" news about politics.[2] The profile, which won a National Magazine Award, told this anecdote about Allen:

> In 1993, Allen was covering a trial in Richmond, Va., for *The New York Times* (as a stringer) and *The Richmond Times-Dispatch* (which employed him). He found a pay phone, darted into the street and got whacked by a car. Allen composed himself, filed stories for both papers and then found his way to the hospital with a broken elbow. This is one of the many "Mikey Stories" that Washingtonians share with awe and some concern.

"You Have Thousands of Angels Around You," from *Atlanta Magazine*, told a heart-tugging story about Cynthia Siyomvo, a 17-year-old refugee from Burundi who, after arriving in Atlanta without any family, faced the threat of deportation. But soon she discovered a circle of new friends who helped her find a home, and she began pursuing a biology degree and a career in medicine.[3]

These stories, all of which won either the National Magazine Award or the Pulitzer Prize, offer rich examples of *action, angle* and *anecdotes*, the three primary ingredients of *interesting* writing. "There is a principle of writing so important, so fundamental that it can be appropriately called the First Law of Journalism and it is simply this: be interesting," wrote Benton Patterson, a former *Guideposts* editor and author of *Write To Be Read*.[4] The book you are holding includes "*Action, Angle and Anecdotes*" as a subtitle because we believe that lively action, a fresh, creative angle and lots of anecdotes characterize interesting writing that keeps readers reading.

Action. These stories tell about a mysterious sinking of a commercial fishing boat that the U.S. Coast Guard spent months investigating, a high-profile political reporter who talks daily with senior officials in the White House and Congress and a Burundi teenage girl who discovered a new circle of friends and support from a southern American city.

"Readers love action, any kind of action, and the story that does not move, that just sits there stalled while people declaim, explain, elaborate and suck their thumbs is justly labeled by some editors as MEGO—My Eyes Glaze Over," wrote William Blundell in *The Art and Craft of Feature Writing*.[5]

Angle. These stories offer an angle on specific people who have experiences to share that illuminate larger issues. An angle makes a story interesting because it provides enough detail about a subject to give the reader some fresh, original information. Broad subjects are vague, fuzzy and boring. Fresh angles give insight into old topics. You have to discover a tiny slice that no one has yet cut from a broad topic to make a compelling and publishable story.

For example, in the *Good Housekeeping* feature "The (Surprising) Truth About Salt," a National Magazine Award finalist, writer Rachael Moeller Gorman, tackled the unusual angle that salt is not necessarily "bad" for everyone. She interviewed doctors and medical researchers who said that, while it makes sense for some people with high blood pressure to lower their salt intake, current science shows that most people will reap little, if any, benefit from reducing their salt intake.[6]

Anecdotes. "The Wreck of the Lady Mary," "The Man the White House Wakes Up To" and "You Have Thousands of Angels Around You" tell *specific* stories about *specific* people doing *specific* things at *specific* times and in *specific* places. Anecdotes make articles interesting by telling true stories about people doing things. Many articles begin with an anecdote for a good reason: anecdotes tell a story—a tiny tale that draws us into the larger one. They illustrate the meaning of the information that follows. Nothing is more involving or revealing than human drama, and anecdotes capture drama with impact.

Feature stories are sometimes called "human-interest stories." Good writers know people as well as they know language. They are sensitive, socially connected individuals who have a talent for finding and writing stories that interest people. The more you talk to people, the more you understand what people are interested in hearing and discussing.

Successful salespersons nurture relationships with their customers. Likewise, successful writers nurture relationships with their readers. Good writers need to develop two personalities as they write. The first is the sensitive creator of words and eloquent ideas. The second is the critical editor, acting on behalf of the reader, who savagely scours the page looking for mistakes and unnecessary content. The editor part of your mind must demand perfection.

When you write, always ask yourself: "How will the reader react to this? Will this sentence cause the reader to laugh or roll his eyes? Will this paragraph fascinate the reader or send her quickly to another article?"

We frequently refer to "the reader" in this book because great writers develop a second-sense about *for whom* and *to whom* they are writing. As you build experience as a writer, you develop a sense of what interests readers and what bores them. Your readers scan their tablet computers and smartphones while they roam supermarket aisles and airport lounges. They browse through cover lines of articles while waiting in line for the checkout or to make their plane connection. If a title attracts their attention, they read it. If it holds their attention, they read to the end. Think about this happening millions of times every week, and you get the picture. Editors are paid, writers are paid, websites stay in business and everyone is happy.

Large publishers hire research companies to determine the characteristics of their readers because advertisers demand it. Known as "demographics," this information includes readers' median ages, household income and gender and race percentages. You can often find this information on a publication's website under links for advertisers. Sidebar 1.1 includes an illustration of the differing reader demographics of *The New Yorker*, *Rolling Stone* and *Lucky*. These magazines' readers differ so much that an article written for one magazine could never be published in the other two.

SIDEBAR 1.1

Demographics of Magazine Readers (2012)

	The New Yorker	Rolling Stone	Lucky
Median age	55	33	35
Median household income	$157,247	$64,160	$82,293
Male	49%	58%	6%
Female	51%	42%	94%
Graduated/ attended college	81%	60%	44%

Source: Magazine websites and MRIPlus.com (Mediamark Research, Inc.).

When most people read an article, they seek diversion, entertainment or information. If a reader doesn't finish an article, you can't blame the reader; blame the author. You can't argue that the reader is too lazy to understand the challenging content. If the reader feels bored, the writers didn't do their jobs. Great writing is all about reaching the reader through the use of compelling action, an original angle and colorful anecdotes.

The best way to develop sensitivity for the reader is to read—a lot. If you are not an avid reader who reads everything you get your hands on, it's doubtful you will ever be a great writer. Read books, blogs, bulletin boards, billboards, menus, manuals, meeting minutes, magazine articles in the doctor's office and online articles anywhere you go. Read the fine print before you "agree" to a download; read the junk mail before you throw it away. Even if you find it boring, you've improved your writing ability because you now possess a better sense of what bores people and what interests them. If you don't read much outside classes, you may not realize that what you consider a groundbreaking idea may have already been written about dozens of times.

Great writers acquire intellectual depth from a huge amount of time spent reading. It's not enough to know the mechanics of writing or how to put together a coherent sentence. Most college students know how to do that. To break out ahead of the journalism pack, you must acquire ideas to write about. You must possess a well of ideas drawn from reading hundreds of books and periodicals.

FIVE MISTAKES OF BEGINNING WRITERS

After reading thousands of student-written articles for more than 35 years, we've created a list of the most common mistakes. We will start by explaining these five common mistakes and tell you how this book will teach you to avoid them.

Staying safe in your own backyard

A newspaper editor once joked to a group of journalists at a workshop that "News is what happens to or near the editor." Many new writers, unfortunately, develop their story ideas based on what happens to or near them. They rely on home-grown situations for article ideas and personal connections for interviews. They write stories about themselves or their parents, brothers and sisters, aunts and uncles, or grandparents. That's a good start. Probably every person has a few good stories that originate among relatives or friends. But, once you've written those stories, your tank is empty. You can't become a successful writer by staying in your own backyard.

The main problem with writing about friends or family members is your lack of objectivity and detachment. For example, what seems fascinating to you about your father may, in fact, be common and bore most readers. The *Model Code of Ethics* published by the Associated Collegiate Press says collegiate journalists "Should not cover . . . or make news judgments about family members or persons with whom they have a financial, adversarial or close sexual or platonic relationship."[7] Another reason to avoid these convenient sources is that they fail to challenge you to venture outside your backyard.

Introduce yourself to a stranger, join a club or listen to a visiting speaker. Visit a museum or browse the stacks in the library for new experiences and ideas. Listen to a politician whose views differ from your own. If you are a Christian, visit a synagogue or mosque. If you are a Muslim, visit a church or synagogue. If you are a Jew, visit a church or mosque. If you are not religious, visit any house of worship.

Call a stranger and ask for an interview. If you can't do that, your future in journalism is doubtful. Meg Grant, an editor for *AARP* magazine, says: "You really have to be fearless about approaching people and getting them to give you what you need. I think they will often give it to you if you ask them." She says that years ago, when she worked for *People* magazine, an editor assigned her to interview the families of three children killed by a drunk driver who was also a celebrity athlete:

> The editor told me, "You have to knock on their door and talk to some of these victims' families. I know you think they don't want to talk to you, but the truth is they do. They want to talk to someone and they want to tell you about their kids." So I had to go bang on those people's doors and say, "Would you talk to me?" And he was right. They did want to talk.[8]

Choosing a broad topic that lacks an angle

Second, beginning writers often want to write about a vague topic without an angle. When we ask students for proposals for story ideas, many come up with a vague topic that interests them—but not a story idea. For example, here are six of the most over-worked topics that students frequently propose:

- getting along with a roommate
- tips for healthy eating
- how to lose weight
- stress prevention for college students
- exercise tips to stay fit
- fashion trends and advice

Besides lacking a specific angle, these topics originate in the "backyard" of college students. Even a more specific topic such as "the benefits of vegetarianism" is too broad. "What can you tell us about this subject that we haven't read before?" and "What is your specific angle?" are always the first questions we ask when someone comes up with an unfocused idea like this. Instead of writing about "the benefits of vegetarianism," we'd rather see a narrower angle on "the best vegetarian choices in fast-food restaurants."

Many magazines and newspapers have published stories about the advantages or disadvantages of alternative medicine. *Cat Fancy* took this same topic and gave it an angle aimed directly at its niche readership: In "Traditional vs. Alternative Medicine: Which Is Best for Your Cat?" the writer wrote, "You might be able to improve your cat's quality of life and hasten recovery from illness by including complementary and alternative medicine."[9]

The prevalence of this second mistake is why we're spending two chapters on developing and focusing ideas. Chapter 2 contains a dozen specific ways to come up with an idea while Chapter 3 gives some suggestions for whittling it down to a publishable angle.

Failing to dig deep

Strong, creative writers dig deep. They aggressively locate experts, request interviews and ask probing questions. Jack Kelley, a former senior editor for *People*, says:

> Many of the best magazine writers liken their work to mining. They chip and chip until they extract a nugget. Then they chip some more. They are not embarrassed to keep asking questions until they hear what they need. Gold is in the details, and compelling color, quote and detail do not simply materialize.[10]

One academic study found that Pulitzer Prize-winning feature stories were, on average, based on interviews with 53 people.

Some articles by beginning writers exhibit a credibility problem. These authors write in their own voices, failing to give any examples, illustrations or quotes. For example, one student wrote about how to use proper nutrition and vitamins to solve common medical problems. Since this college student lacked training in either medicine or nutrition, the reader would have had a problem recognizing her as an authority on the topic. Therefore, the reader wouldn't have been sure whether to trust the information.

If you aren't an expert on the topic you write about, you have to quote experts, as well as give examples and everyday illustrations. You have to interview several people and dig deep to find these expert sources. These people don't just appear in your life or knock on your door. The time to start is when you are doing the research, not after you sit down to write.

Some student writers constantly check the word counts on their computers because their goal is to reach the word count that a professor requires. Professional writers typically have the opposite problem. They do enough research to assemble more than enough good material. Their main problem is "editing down" rather than "pumping up" a manuscript.

Some beginners write articles full of generalizations but lacking in detailed evidence that backs them up. Writing skill, while essential, can never carry the article without strong content. Editors want facts, and they love to break stories with news their competitors have missed. Few writers have opinions or personal experiences that are in great demand.

Digging Deep

Here is an excerpt from the Newark *Star-Ledger*'s published report about how its Pulitzer Prize-winning story, "The Wreck of the Lady Mary," was researched:

> Reporting began in January after the U.S. Coast Guard finished its investigative hearings. For the next seven months, Amy Ellis Nutt made dozens of trips, to Cape May, Philadelphia, Atlantic City and North Carolina. Those interviewed included: the co-owner of the Lady Mary; the boat's sole survivor; family members and friends of the six men who died in the sinking; scallop fishermen, especially those working within six miles of the Lady Mary the night she disappeared; the divers who explored the sunken wreck; officials from the Coast Guard and the rescue crew who saved José Arias; and the dock manager for Hamburg Sud, the shipping company that leases the container ship Cap Beatrice.
>
> Some 800 pages of testimony from Coast Guard hearings were reviewed, navigation and vessel tracking records studied, and nearly two dozen marine experts interviewed, a number of whom had specific training in shipwreck forensics. Two sources with direct access to the investigation also provided documents the Coast Guard refused to make public because it has not yet released its report. In addition to evidence from the sinking of the Lady Mary, the *Star-Ledger* also combed through more than 2,500 Coast Guard incident reports from 2002 through 2007.[11]

SIDEBAR 1.2

Writing without anecdotes

The fourth mistake is failing to use anecdotes. Anecdotes tell true stories that illustrate the writer's main theme. Some editors call them the "chocolate chips" of writing because they whet readers' appetites and keep them reading. Anecdotes add credibility because they give real-life examples to the claims and generalizations made by the writer. The reason that anecdotes and examples increase credibility with readers is that they give true examples of the point you make. They tell a story about a specific person doing a specific thing in a specific place at a specific time.

Anecdotes are so essential and so difficult to find that they deserve their own chapter in this book. Anecdotes come from the people you interview. Chapter 10 explains how to find sources and phrase questions that will bring out the most humorous and compelling anecdotes.

Writing boring articles

Boring, windy articles lacking any action constitute the fifth mistake. We have read dozens of student articles that sound like condensed research papers or encyclopedia articles. Many beginning writers use stiff, bloated content that doesn't fit the tone of today's magazines. Other symptoms of this malady are the use of too many passive-voice verbs, long and convoluted sentences, runaway adjectives and adverbs, and an academic tone.

Editors eagerly look for stories that move, outrage, alarm, delight or inspire readers. They want to make their readers laugh, cry or get angry. They prefer angry letters to the editor than none at all because that means people are at least reading their publication. A plodding, formal style is a turnoff to every editor.

Chapter 9 tells you how to avoid boring stories by building action into characters and content. It shows you how to create action by increasing the use of tension, using people to illustrate abstract ideas and increasing the use of narrative, dialogue, action verbs and active voice.

You will succeed as a writer if you assume that people who might read your work are:

• *Busy.* People are not forced to read magazines, newspapers or Internet content. People use their discretionary time to read feature articles. It's your job to attract their attention and sustain it.

- *Knowledgeable.* People who frequently read books and articles are generally more educated than the general public. Therefore, you must work hard and dig deep to give them information they haven't read before.
- *Easily distracted.* In today's digital world, readers can choose from hundreds of sources of information. You can't assume they will finish reading what they begin. You have to find color and human-interest material to sustain readers to the end.

These characteristics may not describe each reader. If you assume that they do, however, you will work harder and get published more quickly than your peers.

What makes a story interesting? The most interesting stories are original; they captivate the hearts of readers as well as their minds. They tell readers something they've never read before because they have an unusual angle. They sustain the reader's attention because they are full of action and anecdotes.

IN-CLASS ACTIVITIES

Instructor: Ask students to bring a favorite feature article to class. Students: Write a 50-word summary of the article you find the most interesting. Read the summaries in class and discuss the action, angle and anecdotes contained in the stories.

Instructor: Ask each student to recall a humorous or dramatic experience he or she has had during the past five years. Discuss these stories from the perspective of "action, angle and anecdotes" explained in this chapter.

ASSIGNMENTS

Students: Find 10 stories with an anecdotal lead. Remember that an anecdote should tell a story about a specific person at a specific place and time. Explain how each anecdote introduces the angle and main idea of the story that follows.

Students: Interview five random people, asking these two questions and recording the answers: "What characteristics of any article you read make it interesting to you?" and "What characteristics of any article you read make it boring?" Bring the results of your survey to class. In small groups, determine common characteristics of interesting and boring articles.

NOTES

1 Amy Ellis Nutt, "The Wreck of the Lady Mary," Newark *Star-Ledger*, Nov. 21, 2010. www.nj.com/news/index.ssf/2010/11/the_wreck_of_the_lady_mary_cha.html (accessed March 3, 2012).

2 Mark Leibovich, "The Man the White House Wakes Up To," *New York Times Magazine*, April 21, 2010. www.nytimes.com/2010/04/25/magazine/25allen-t.html?pagewanted=1&_r=1 (accessed March 3, 2012).

3 Paige Williams, "You Have Thousands of Angels Around You," *Atlanta Magazine*, Oct. 2007.

4 Benton Rain Patterson, *Write to Be Read* (Ames, Iowa: Iowa State University Press, 1986), 6.

5 William Blundell, *The Art and Craft of Feature Writing* (New York: Penguin Books, 1988), 54.

6 Rachel Moeller Gorman, "The (Surprising) Truth About Salt," *Good Housekeeping*, April 2011. www.goodhousekeeping.com/health/nutrition/truth-about-salt (accessed March 3, 2012).

7 Albert DeLucca and Tom Rolnicki, *Associated College Press Model Code of Ethics for Collegiate Journalists*, 4th ed. (Minneapolis, Minn.: Associated Collegiate Press, 2012), 5.

8 Telephone interview with David E. Sumner, Nov. 29, 2003. Updated correspondence April 16, 2012.

9 Narda G. Robinson, DVM, "Traditional vs. Alternative Medicine: Which Is Best for Your Cat?" *Cat Fancy*, July 2008, 30–33.

10 Telephone interview with David E. Sumner, Jan. 19, 2004. Updated correspondence March 15, 2012.

11 Amy Ellis Nutt, "The Wreck of the Lady Mary," Newark *Star-Ledger*, Nov. 21, 2010. www.nj.com/news/index.ssf/2010/11/the_wreck_of_the_lady_mary_cha.html (accessed March 3, 2012).

2

HOW TO FIND AN ORIGINAL IDEA

KEY POINTS

- Determining your audience
- Determining your angle
- Ten places to find ideas

Most writers naturally start out by wanting to write articles for people like themselves. They stay in their own backyards. College students want to write articles for college students; those interested in fashion want to write about fashion; and those interested in sports want to write for sports fans. As you progress in your writing experience, however, you learn to detach yourself from your personal interests and write articles that will interest people of vastly differing ages, professions and outlooks.

The first step in developing an idea is figuring out for whom you want to write. Beginners often don't try to find an outlet for the article until after they've written it. Student writers, if they consider audience characteristics at all, begin with some vague, amorphous concept of readers exactly like themselves—other college students. In news-writing courses, you learn to write one way for a standard, vaguely defined audience. Among the first tasks when you create a magazine article idea is deciding who your readers are and which magazines or websites you are aiming for. Here are some possible audiences and some sample magazine titles that serve them:

Feature and Magazine Writing: Action, Angle and Anecdotes, Third Edition.
David E. Sumner and Holly G. Miller.
© 2013 David E. Sumner and Holly G. Miller. Published 2013 by John Wiley & Sons, Inc.

- college-aged males (*Maxim*)
- single women (*Cosmopolitan*)
- middle-aged women (*More*)
- business entrepreneurs (*Entrepreneur*)
- pro-football fans (*Pro Football Weekly*)
- turkey hunters (*Turkey and Turkey Hunting*)
- adherents of specific religions and faiths (*U.S. Catholic*)
- managers of printing businesses (*Printing Impressions*)
- restaurant owners and managers (*Nation's Restaurant News*)
- residents of the South or New England (*Southern Living* or *Yankee*)

While the cliché "write what you know" has merit, it only takes you so far and often will fail to pay the bills. Professional writers take assignments on topics in which they have no personal interest. Even professional writers could not write more than a few articles based solely on what they already know. This is part of what we mean when advising you to get outside your own backyard. Not many magazines or websites will pay you for writing about what's in your backyard.

Sidebar 2.1 illustrates how beginning writers differ from professional writers in finding a place to publish their articles. Professional writers typically choose magazines or websites they want to write for. They study the audiences who read those publications, study the guidelines for writers, and come up with ideas that fit those publications and audiences. Beginning writers choose a topic that interests them, write the articles and then hope someone will be interested. Professional writers do enough research to enable them to choose a topic they already know will interest a particular publication or group of readers. They begin and end with the reader in mind.

Notice the basic differences as you progress up the ladder. The beginner writes an article and then tries to figure out where to send it. The professional writer understands a few favorite markets and develops ideas and writes articles based on those markets' needs.

DETERMINE YOUR ANGLE

The most difficult task beginning writers face is finding an original idea with a clearly focused angle. Many can organize words, sentences and

SIDEBAR 2.1

The Ladder of Success for Publishing Magazine Articles

	Step 1	Step 2	Step 3	Step 4	Step 5
The typical beginner	Get an idea	Write the article	Send to favorite magazine or website	Wait	Get rejected
The aspiring writer	Get an idea	Write the article	Study writers' guidelines	Send to more appropriate choice	Probably get rejected
The seasoned novice	Get an idea	Study writers' guidelines and archives of magazines and websites	Write article based on targeted market	Send query letter to targeted choice	Perhaps get your article accepted
The semi-pro	Choose some magazines you want to write for	Study writers' guidelines and archives of magazines and websites	Develop idea based on content and needs of these publications	Send query letter or e-mail to targeted choice	Very likely get your articles accepted
The professional writer	Repeat Step 4 until you find an editor who likes your work	Editor contacts you and gives you assignments	Write the articles	Send the articles in	Cash your checks

paragraphs using good punctuation and grammar. What most struggle with, however, is coming up with a strong angle that has a chance of being published.

Editors today insist on new material because they know their readers don't want a rehash of what's already out there. *Woman's Day* advises prospective writers in its guidelines: "We want fresh articles based on new material—new studies, new statistics, new theories, new insights—especially when the subject itself has received wide coverage. Any article that could have been published three years ago is not for *Woman's Day*."

Ellen Levine, former editor of *Good Housekeeping*, advises writers: "Give readers information unavailable elsewhere" and "strive for exclusive stories."[1] Everything a writer produces needs an original angle supported by information not already in print. Being original means that each article should "smell fresh" when it arrives in front of the reader. It shouldn't sound like it's been pulled from an "article warehouse" shelf somewhere. That's why you can't write an original article simply by regurgitating material from existing online articles.

Let's put it this way: if you don't do any background reading before you develop an idea, you're likely to come up with an unoriginal idea. The best way to find an original idea is to read. If you don't know what's been published in magazines, websites and books, you have no way of recognizing an original idea. Successful feature writers have an insatiable appetite for reading. If you don't, you should question whether journalism right for you.

For example, suppose you're interested in writing an article about the benefits of cat ownership. So you read through some back issues of *Cat Fancy* to get some ideas. In one issue, you find "Clergy Cats: An Exclusive Look into the Lives of Religious Leaders and Their Feline Companions." The writer interviewed a Catholic bishop, a rabbi and two Protestant ministers about their cats.[2] About a year later, the same magazine ran an article titled "The Writer's Muse: Cats Help Inspire Their Owners' Creativity." This writer interviewed two professional writers about their cats and how cats inspire their creativity.[3] These two articles suggest that *Cat Fancy* likes to run articles about how and why people in particular kinds of work like cats. So why not propose a story about "Firefighters and Their Cats" or "Police Officers and Their Cats"?

"The real importance of reading is that it creates an ease and intimacy with the process of writing," wrote Stephen King. "It also offers you a constantly growing knowledge of what has been done and what hasn't, what is trite and what is fresh, what works and what just lies there dying (or dead) on the page."[4]

NINE PLACES TO FIND IDEAS

A few years ago, David E. Sumner interviewed 15 syndicated magazine and newspaper columnists about their craft. Each one was asked: "Where do you get ideas for your columns?" Almost all of them cited "reading" as the most frequent source for new ideas. Anyone who hopes to maintain a

How to Know Whether You Have an Original Article Idea

You should be able to answer "yes" to at least the majority of the following 10 questions:

1 Is this topic so new and original that you can't find any books written on the subject?
2 Will your topic appeal to the special-interest group who read the magazine you are interested in writing for? Or is there a magazine that focuses on what you are interested in writing about?
3 Does this topic deal with fundamental life issues such as death, love, sickness, money, careers, health—issues that affect millions of people?
4 Do you have a strong, central unifying theme?
5 Can you state your theme in one sentence using an action verb?
6 Does your angle allow you to offer intelligent insight—as opposed to saying something that's obvious, that's commonsense or that readers have read about many times?
7 Are there elements of drama or conflict to attract and sustain the reader?
8 Will your topic generate several colorful and compelling anecdotes from your sources? Can you find human-interest stories about it?
9 Does your theme question or contradict what most people think or assume? The best articles question the conventional wisdom about a subject.
10 Do you have access to the sources you need to write this article? These sources should be participants, keen observers or experts on the topic you are writing about.

steady flow of ideas has to read continually, including publications that few others read. Ideas may come from unexpected sources: professional quarterlies, association newsletters, academic journals, annual reports and almanacs. While they seem boring, such sources often contain the most original thinking and latest developments long before they reach the general public. Here are more specific items to read or places to look as you dig for ideas for your feature articles.

1. Yellow Pages of telephone directories

The Yellow Pages of small and large communities offer a plethora of businesses and individuals who can lead you to dozens of ideas. The best place to start is the "A" listings and browse until an inspiration hits you. However, here are some tips:

- Profiles of successful businesses or professionals. Every business, industry and profession has at least one magazine for people who work in that field. These magazines look for profiles of people in their field with unusual accomplishments or innovations.
- Profiles of people engaged in out-of-the-ordinary endeavors. General-interest magazines may have an interest in profiles of practitioners of unusual jobs, such as magicians, horse breeders, dieticians or international trade consultants. Look under "paternity testing and services" and find out why some people need these services.
- Look for practitioners to interview for expert advice for a "how-to" article. For example, you can interview apartment building managers for advice on questions to ask before you sign a lease. You can interview auto dealers for advice on the most reliable used-car models or how to negotiate the best deal. You can interview dermatologists about the dangers and risks of tanning salons.
- Think about "what's up" and "what's down." All business cycles produce winners and losers, and even a dismal economy has some who profit from the downturn. R.V. and luxury car sales suffer with high gasoline prices, while train and bus travel increases. In recessionary times, thrift, discount and second-hand stores do well. Think about trends or cycles in your local economy and write about businesses affected by them in positive or negative ways.
- Look under "social service organizations" for details on groups that serve the underprivileged or engage in humanitarian causes that interest you. Call and ask about notable volunteers or recipients of their services who have inspiring or newsworthy stories. For example, our community has a place called "Stepping Stones for Veterans," which provides a residence for veterans who are unemployed or face substance-abuse problems.

You can also browse through the business directories for any city in the United States through online services such as Switchboard.com,

Yellowpages.com and Yellowbook.com. These are excellent resources for finding ideas and sources for articles outside your immediate geographic area.

2. Small-town newspapers (print and online)

Check local and area newspapers for small news items that you can develop into long feature stories for a magazine. Focus on locally written stories, not Associated Press or national stories. Look for brief articles about people who have received awards. The award itself may simply culminate an interesting series of events or achievements leading up to it. Many of our students have found their story ideas in small-town weekly newspapers. "Newspapers are filled with undeveloped stories, announcements of meetings and events, or tiny clues that could lead to interesting narratives," says Roy Peter Clark, senior scholar at the Poynter Institute for Media Studies.[5]

3. Old magazines and magazine archives

Magazines have certain perennial or evergreen topics that they revisit at least once a year. Look for seasonal articles related to holidays and anniversaries of major events. If you browse through enough issues, you can discover their perennial topics and come up with a fresh angle. Even if you don't think you have a chance of selling that idea to a prestigious magazine, you can send a query on a similar topic to a competing but lesser-known publication.

Remember that you can't copyright the *idea* for an article—only the particular way in which you write it. If you take an article as inspiration and develop it into something else, you haven't committed plagiarism. Plagiarism only occurs when you use words from another article without giving credit.

Editors frequently complain that freelance writers don't study their publications before they submit unsolicited ideas and manuscripts. Experienced freelance writers pick the magazine or group of magazines they want to write for before they decide on an idea for a story. Then they study dozens of back issues at a library or online archive. That's because the best ideas will come from seeing the types of articles that those particular periodicals publish.

Here are some advantages to choosing your target publications first and reading through some of their previous issues:

- You know what topics have been covered and therefore can recognize an original idea when you see it.
- You know about current trends within the field of interest you want to write about and can pick a topic related to one of those trends.
- You become able to recognize the types of articles most frequently published in these magazines. For example, some magazines never publish profiles, poetry or personal experience articles.
- You become familiar with the writing style, tone and "personality" of the magazine (see Chapter 6 for more details).

Another advantage to reading old issues of some of your favorite magazines is that you can discover their evergreen topics. Susan Ungaro, former editor of *Family Circle*, once said:

Certain "evergreen" articles are published in every magazine over and over again. For instance, we constantly tell readers different ways to make the most of their money or to take charge of their health. I do a story every spring and fall on spring-cleaning your house, how to get organized, how to deal with clutter in your life. Romance and marriage secrets—how to make your marriage closer, more intimate, more loving—are probably addressed in every issue of every women's magazine.[6]

4. Bulletin boards

The curious writer never passes a bulletin board without stopping to look at it. Campus bulletin boards contain notices of future events, concerts, speakers or meetings of organizations. Musical performers or nationally known speakers may be visiting your area. You may find them more accessible to an interview than you expect. Visiting performers and speakers may have "down time" before and after their engagements. To obtain an interview, contact the sponsoring group for contact information on people you wish to interview. One advantage to old-fashioned bulletin boards is that they contain "grassroots" information. Accessible to anyone and everyone with their posters and flyers, bulletin boards may lead you to scoops and news tips before they get published anywhere.

5. Events calendars

Most universities, cities, towns and their TV and radio stations publish an online calendar of upcoming events. Websites sponsored by city governments and visitors' bureaus contain the same information. A hobby or trade show, for example, will give you access to dozens of experts. These listings may also publicize meetings of self-help groups and hobby and service clubs, and may include meeting times and contact numbers. For example, support groups exist for families of murder victims, the mentally ill and drug abusers. These groups may allow you to visit if you promise to protect individual identities.

6. Faculty biographies on university websites

Go to any university's website and look for biographical sketches and research interests of faculty members. Colleges are the homes of some the nation's best minds, and the writer who doesn't tap this source of free information will miss a great opportunity. For example, a Florida zoology professor is an expert on alligators and often treks through the state's swamps with a camera and notebook. After getting an idea through reading faculty biographies, you can follow up with a telephone call to the professor. Many professors are nationally known experts in their subject areas and are flattered by requests for interviews. To find them, click on the "academic programs" link on any university's website and then find a department that interests you. Most departmental websites will list the books, articles and accomplishments of their faculty members along with telephone and e-mail addresses.

Look up professors that you know and find out their special expertise and research interests. Some universities have searchable databases for the media to use in finding faculty experts on particular topics.

7. Association directories

The *Encyclopedia of Associations: Regional, State and Local Organizations* contains names, descriptions and contact information for more than 100,000 groups that serve every conceivable occupational and special-interest group. Most academic libraries carry copies of this multivolume annual series. Association directories are a treasure trove for ideas and expert sources. "For every problem you can think of, there is an organization who can guide you to people who have it or have a story to tell. There are support groups for everything you can possibly imagine. There is not a disease or a political cause that is not represented somewhere in some group," says New York-based magazine writer Judith Newman.[7]

Here are some association categories representative of groups with broad types of concerns and interests:

- diseases, disabilities and other consumer medical issues
- political causes, environmental issues or civil rights for various minority groups
- hobbies, leisure pursuits and sports
- religion-based causes and organizations
- professional organizations representing various professions and careers
- fraternal organizations and service clubs, such as Kiwanis or Rotary clubs

You can also browse the association directory at the Internet Public Library (www.ipl.org/div/aon), which is maintained by a consortium of universities with programs in library and information science. In the medical category alone, you will find hundreds of organizations, such as the Association of Suicidology, the National Attention Deficit Disorder Association, Sexual Compulsives Anonymous and the Chronic Fatigue and Immune Dysfunction Syndrome Association. In the entertainment and leisure category, you will find groups such as the American Kitefliers Association, the Unicycling Society of America, the Association of Canadian Mountain Guides, the United Skateboarders Association and the National Woodcarvers Association.

8. *CQ Researcher*

CQ Researcher is often the first source that librarians recommend when researchers are seeking original, comprehensive reporting and analysis on issues in the news. Founded in 1923 as *Editorial Research Reports*, *CQ Researcher* is noted for its in-depth, unbiased coverage of health, social trends, criminal justice, international affairs, education, the environment, technology and the economy. Reports are published weekly by CQ Press. Although not available as a free website, print and electronic editions are available through academic libraries. Each issue of this biweekly resource contains a balanced review with several articles and a bibliography of suggested reading. Recent topics included eating disorders, hydraulic fracturing, the future of labor unions, digital education, Google's dominance and college football scandals.

9. Ask for tips and leads

Experienced reporters and magazine writers "mine" their sources by continually asking people they know for tips and leads for stories and whom to interview. One writer asked an oncologist for an idea for a cancer-related story. Start with the people you know—teachers, librarians, doctors and the people you do business with. You don't get ideas by staring at a keyboard. Visit unfamiliar places and talk to strangers. Get away from the university and ask store clerks what their best-selling items and products are. Listen to their gripes, problems and stories. Go to a political rally for a visiting candidate for office. The more you seek new experiences, the more likely they will offer something to write about.

An editor once told a writer: "Your manuscript is both good and original, but the part that is good is not original and the part that is original is not good." To make it into publication an article must ooze quality, style and freshness. In short, the most successful features inform, provoke thought and introduce the reader to something new.

IN-CLASS ACTIVITIES

Instructor: Give students 45 minutes to do anything they want to find a story idea for the next assignment. Options could include visiting the library, reading bulletin boards, reading telephone book Yellow Pages, browsing a bookstore or calling a friend. At the end of the time limit, ask them to return to class and report their story ideas.

Instructor: Bring to class a variety of brochures, advertisements, academic journals, posters and so on and distribute them in class. Students: Working in pairs, come up with an idea for a timely magazine article based on the item you have received.

ASSIGNMENTS

Students: Use Lexis-Nexis to locate and read 10 magazine articles on a single topic you are interested in writing about. Summarize each article in one sentence and then create a one-sentence idea for an original angle not covered by any of these articles.

Students: Start an "idea brainstorm list" using a small pocket notebook. For one week, create 25 one-sentence ideas from reading bulletin boards, events calendars, faculty biographies and weekly newspapers. Revise and edit the ideas before turning them in.

NOTES

1   Quoted in Sammye Johnson and Patricia Prijatel, *Magazine Publishing* (Lincoln-wood, Ill.: NTC Contemporary Publishing, 2000), 193.
2   Sandy Robins, "Clergy Cats: An Exclusive Look Into the Lives of Religious Leaders and Their Feline Companions," *Cat Fancy*, Dec. 2006, 36–39.
3   Christie Craig, "The Writer's Muse: Cats Help Inspire Their Owners' Creativity," *Cat Fancy*, July 2008, 80–81.
4   Stephen King, *On Writing: A Memoir of the Craft* (New York: Simon & Schuster Pocket Books, 2000), 150.
5   Telephone interview with David E. Sumner, July 21, 2008.
6   Quoted in Judy Mandell (ed.), *Magazine Editors Talk to Writers* (New York: John Wiley & Sons, 1996), 57.
7   Telephone interview with David E. Sumner, Dec. 11, 2003. Updated correspondence May 2, 2012.

3

STRONG ANGLES
AND FOCUSED IDEAS

KEY POINTS

- Big problem: broad ideas
- Summarize your story idea in a single sentence
- Characteristics of a focused angle
- How to know whether your topic is too broad
- How to narrow your topic

The most frequent problem among story ideas from new writers is broad, unfocused ideas. A *Wall Street Journal* editor explains:

> Most of us think too big. We try to embrace the circus fat lady, and only well into the effort do we find there is too much of her and not enough of us. The result is a piece impossibly long, or superficial, the reporter frantically skipping from point to point without dwelling on any of them long enough to illuminate and convince.[1]

Jane Harrigan, former editor of the *Concord (NH) Monitor*, tells a story about a writer friend of hers:

> One day as I was climbing the stairs to her apartment, she yelled down a warning: "Watch out! I'm in the middle of a piece, and the place is a mess." Inside, her writing room looked just like mine, piles of paper covering every horizontal surface. Then something on the windowsill caught my eye. It was an index card with a single sentence written on it.

Feature and Magazine Writing: Action, Angle and Anecdotes, Third Edition.
David E. Sumner and Holly G. Miller.
© 2013 David E. Sumner and Holly G. Miller. Published 2013 by John Wiley & Sons, Inc.

"What's that?" I asked.

"That's the point," Sue replied. "I put it there so I always know where to find it."[2]

SUMMARIZE YOUR STORY IDEA IN A SINGLE SENTENCE

Summarizing a story's central idea in a single sentence is a time-tested principle of writing. It's also a time-tested principle for creating a strong angle. A true theme is a clear, coherent sentence that expresses a single piece of irreducible meaning. Without that sentence, an article has no unifying theme, focus or compelling message. That focus prevents all of the bits and pieces of information you have collected from sprawling into an incoherent mess. Here are three examples of student-written stories that displayed a tight focus in a single-sentence title:

- "World Belly Dance Day Promotes Self-Esteem"
- "Young Artist Makes Noise in the Music Industry"
- "New Treatment Offers Hope to Athletes with Hip Pain"

Some writers come up with vague topics they want to write about (such as physical fitness or a local band) but they don't create story ideas that have any chance of publication. For example, one student wanted to write an article about eating disorders. Her teacher challenged her to come up with a tighter angle on this broad topic. After some conversations with the professor, the student decided to focus on treatment and build her story around the experiences of a young woman who acknowledged her problem and sought help. Still another writer chose a gender angle and explored anorexia among men.

Meg Grant, former West Coast editor for *Reader's Digest*, explains how the magazine's editors narrowed a proposed feature article on foster care for children:

We didn't want to do the same piece everybody is reading in the local papers about how broken the foster care system is. We picked a section of the foster care issue that was a smaller piece to chew on, which was about those kids who spend their whole lives in foster care and never get out of the system. We decided to look at one of the programs, and then we found one kid and told his story.[3]

A limited tale told clearly has more impact than a sweeping story that lacks depth and insight. The more frequently magazines and newspapers cover a given topic, the sharper and fresher the angle must be. Sidebar 3.1 provides examples of how to narrow the angle of some broad and unfocused topics.

How to Give a Tighter Angle to a Broad Topic

Too Broad	Tighter Angle
Losing Weight	Teacher Tells How She Lost 100 Pounds
Quitting Smoking	Can Hypnotism Help You Quit the Habit?
Improving Your Home's Security	An Ex-Burglar Tells How to Burglar-Proof Your Home
Traveling on a Budget	Five Ways to Find Cheap Hotels and Overnight Lodging
Choosing a Smartphone	Don't Buy These Extra Features You Don't Need in a Smartphone

The angle tree

One of the best ways to focus an idea is to use the "angle tree" exercise, which allows you to brainstorm on paper. Start with a broad topic you are interested in covering and write it in a center circle (as shown in Figure 3.1). Then write down four directions or angles you could pursue with that topic. If you try to cover all angles, your article will lack depth; however, you can choose one angle as your main focus and a second angle to explore as a sidebar. After you've decided on your focus, the next step is to determine whom you should interview and what kind of background research you should do.

CHARACTERISTICS OF A FOCUSED ANGLE

A focused angle has unity, action and concreteness. Unity means everything hangs together around a central idea. This central idea creates an

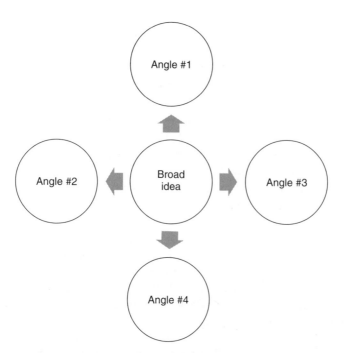

Figure 3.1 This "angle tree" illustrates how to take a broad idea and break it down into four angles.

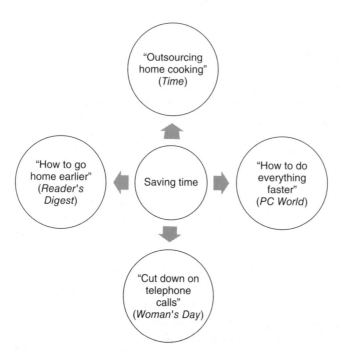

Figure 3.2 This is an example of four angles developed from the broad idea of time management. We chose some real titles that have been published in well-known magazines.

organizing principle to help you determine whom you interview, what to look for in your research, what facts to include and what facts to omit. If you have a sharply focused angle before you begin, you will save dozens of hours in fruitless research that leads you down the wrong path. Sometimes you find a fascinating anecdote and you feel as if you just have to include it. But those paragraphs that interrupt the unity of the article will also jar the reader. So go back and remove them.

William Zinsser, who taught nonfiction writing at Yale for many years, stresses this point in his classic book *On Writing Well*:

> As for what point you want to make, I'll state as a rule of thumb that every successful piece of nonfiction should leave the reader with one provocative thought. . . . Not two thoughts, or five—just one. So try to decide what point you most want to leave in the reader's mind. It will give you a better idea of what route you ought to follow and what destination you hope to reach.[4]

A good, clear focus means that the title and introduction let the readers know exactly where you are going and give them a chance to get off if they don't want to go there. Here's the start of an example of a tightly focused article from *Businessweek*:

Toyota's All-Out Drive to Stay Toyota
How's this for strange? Toyota Motor, the company that has the rest of the auto industry running scared, is worried. As new hires pour in and top executives approach retirement, the company fears it might lose the culture of frugality, discipline, and constant improvement that has been vital to its success. So management has launched a slew of education initiatives, and even uses a business school in Tokyo to teach Toyota to be, well, more like Toyota.[5]

The article can be summarized in this sentence: "Toyota has launched a slew of education initiatives to teach its employees how to maintain its culture of frugality, discipline and improvement." And everything in the story pertains to that central idea.

Unity anchors good writing and assures the reader that you know where you intend to go and what you intend to cover. Unity doesn't trick readers into thinking they will read about one topic only to shift to another and then another along the way. It gives order and structure to your writing and directs the course of your research.

Unity means not only content but also a unified voice, verb tense and mood. As Gary Provost says in *Beyond Style: Mastering the Finer Points of Writing*: "Unity, that quality of oneness in your writing, means that everything you write should look as if it were written at one time, by one person, with one purpose, using one language."[6]

Strong, creative articles contain action. They describe people having fun, helping others, getting a job or making a business succeed. A strong action verb in the title or magazine's cover line attracts the attention of the editor and the reader. Go to a store's magazine display and look at the teasers that are placed above the newspaper's nameplate. Both cover lines and teasers are meant to attract readers, which is why they often contain action verbs.

J.C. Suares, a New York magazine designer, believes that cover lines must contain an action verb. Verb-less cover lines are motionless and boring, he argues:

> There's no such thing as a cover line without a verb. If it doesn't have a verb then it's not a cover line. It's a title. You've got to come up with a sentence with a verb in it. I talk myself blue in the face [to editors] about having a verb in the cover line or headline.[7]

Here are some cover lines from recent magazines. Notice that each one contains at least one action verb.

- "*Hazing* Nightmares: You *Won't Believe* These Shocking Stories" (*Teen People*)
- "What to *Do* When His Crazy 'Ex' Won't *Let Go*" (*Teen People*)
- "*Get* Lean All Over: A New Diet and Workout Plan to *Max* Your Metabolism" (*Shape*)
- "Chill Out—How to *Calm* Your Hot Horse" (*Horse and Rider*)
- "Cool Wedding Trends: What Other Couples are *Doing* Coast to Coast" (*Bride*)
- "How to *Avoid* the Fat Trap in Fast Food Salads" (*Ladies' Home Journal*)

Concreteness is another characteristic of tightly focused angles. Facts and quotes must include the specific dates and places in which they occurred. "Unanchored" articles are vague and make it difficult for the reader to visualize their ideas. If you can't cite specific dates and places in an article, it isn't sufficiently anchored. Tell where your quoted experts are from and who they work for. Avoid the abused words "recent" and "recently" and tell how long ago the interview or event occurred. Even if your story is on some broad "evergreen" topic such as tax-saving tips, you have to anchor it with expert sources and examples that occurred in specific places at specific times.

For example, suppose you traveled to Cleveland and want to write an article about the Rock and Roll Hall of Fame and Museum. What about it? Since hundreds of articles have been written about it, what has happened recently that is newsworthy? Who has been inducted into the Hall of Fame since last year? Remember that a story should be a verb. Give it a specific angle or "news peg."

For example, *Radio and Music* magazine published an article announcing that Guns N' Roses, the Beastie Boys and the Red Hot Chili Peppers were inducted into the museum's 2012 Hall of Fame. A recent news event like this gives the story a news peg that you can use in the title and lead before writing more broadly about the museum or its history.

HOW TO KNOW IF YOUR TOPIC IS TOO BROAD

Following are some guidelines that will help you to determine whether your story idea is too broad. Let's say you're thinking about writing an article on e-mail scams—we will use this as an example.

If you can find a book

Never write a feature article from rehashed book content. Editors demand fresh, original stories. They don't want a repetition of what you've pulled from books, newspapers or Internet articles. A search using the term "e-mail scams" at Amazon.com turns up more than a dozen books on the topic. Here are some examples:

- *The Complete Idiot's Guide to Frauds, Scams, and Cons*
- *A Con Man Reveals the Secrets of the Esoteric Trade of Cheating, Scams, and Hustles*
- *Crimes of Persuasion: Schemes, Scams, Frauds*

- *E-mails From Hell*
- *Phishing Exposed*

Judging by the number of books, "e-mail scams" by itself is definitely too broad a topic for a feature article.

If someone could write a book

If someone could write a book on a subject, they probably have. About 100,000 printed books and 800,000 digital books are published every year in the United States. Feature articles can't cover everything because their length usually ranges between 1,000 and 2,000 words. Each story must focus on a small slice of a huge pie.

If your proposed title has no verbs

We've already discussed the importance of action in an angle. Look at the titles of articles from popular magazines. As mentioned, most will include a verb in the title that describes something happening. The term "e-mail scams," of course, has no verbs, and we've already ruled it out as a topic. So let's look at how five magazines or TV networks covered the topic from five angles:

- "Do Online Banks Facilitate Fraud?" (*The Motley Fool*)
- "Former Congressman Duped by Nigerian Scams" (*ABC News*)
- "How a Massachusetts Psychotherapist Fell for a Nigerian E-Mail Scam" (*The New Yorker*)
- "In Pictures: How to Spot an E-Mail Scam" (*PC World*)
- "Whaling: Latest E-Mail Scam Targets Executives" (*Network World*)

If you want to write an article on e-mail scams, we challenge you to read a dozen articles on the topic before you begin writing or interviewing. Then—and only then—will you know what's been covered, what the issues are, where disagreements exist, which questions remain unanswered and what questions to ask. Then—and only then—will you know how to come up with a fresh and original angle on well-worn topics.

HOW TO NARROW YOUR TOPIC

While reading about your general topic in other publications is the first step, it only helps you to eliminate nonoriginal angles. After that there are no quick and easy steps. The broader your topic, the more likely readers will have read about it before. The narrower you make it, the more likely you will give readers information they have never read or heard about. These five suggestions will point you in the right direction.

Find a news peg

First, ask yourself, "How can I hang this topic on a news peg?" A news peg is a current event or anniversary of a historical event that illustrates the topic you want to write about. For example, the January birthday of Martin Luther King Jr. offers a news peg to write stories related to civil rights or race relations. An election campaign offers a news peg for stories about controversial issues that the candidates are debating. A recent death caused by a drunk driver offers a peg for several possible angles on the subject of alcohol abuse.

"Any time you're fortunate enough to have a news item related to your topic, the battle for your reader's attention if half over," said author Mary S. Schaeffer in an article in *The Writer*.[8] News pegs offer a way to "get into" or develop a lead for a feature story. To get some ideas, simply browse the headlines of newspapers and news websites and see where you can go from there.

"Nationalize" a local topic

Newspaper reporters and editors always try to localize a national story by finding a local source who can give it an angle that's closer to their readers. Magazines sometimes follow the other direction. They write about a story in a small town that illustrates or amplifies an important national issue. *The New Yorker* story mentioned earlier—"How a Massachusetts Psychotherapist Fell for a Nigerian E-Mail Scam"—illustrates this point. The writer found a 57-year-old psychotherapist from Groton, Mass., who lost $600,000 by falling for one of the infamous Nigerian e-mail scams. While telling the psychotherapist's story, the writer offered factual background and context about e-mail scams and showed readers how they could avoid making the same mistake.[9]

Decide what you want to know

Ask yourself, "What would I like to know about this topic?" If you don't know the answers to some of your questions, it's more likely readers will be asking the same questions. Trust your hunch about what angle seems the most interesting. One of the biggest myths about writing is the often-repeated aphorism "write about what you know." If we only wrote about what we knew, none of us would last more than a week in the publishing business.

If a magazine editor asks you "What do you know about _____?" then try this answer: "Well, I'm not an expert, but I want to find some experts and ask them the right questions." In other words, you don't have to be an expert to write a good story. You simply need to know where to go to find the experts.

Find a unique source

Another way of deciding how to focus a topic is by asking, "What unique or primary sources do I have access to?" A person with expertise or unique experiences in a particular area is a primary source. Other primary sources are copies of correspondence or official documents. Maybe you know someone who is newsworthy because of a unique accomplishment. Maybe a friend can help you get an interview with a celebrity.

One student wrote about the lifelong romance of a couple who had been married 65 years. Their romance began with writing love letters to each other while the husband was fighting overseas in World War II. The student obtained copies and quoted the letters the couple wrote to each other during the 1940s, which brought freshness, originality and poignancy to the story.

David E. Sumner wrote a magazine story about a small Florida town's "Kumquat Festival," which attracts 30,000 people every January (a kumquat is a small citrus fruit). His angle was on a Boston TV celebrity who has visited the festival every year since it began. The story idea originated, however, with a conversation with his nephew, who helps organize the festival and who helped him obtain interviews with the TV celebrity and other festival organizers.

Use the funnel of focus

Another way of narrowing an angle is the "funnel of focus" exercise developed by Dr. Gerald Grow, a professor of journalism at Florida Agricultural and Mechanical University.[10] The purpose of this exercise is to begin with a broad topic and narrow it down into a focused angle. Here is an example beginning at the "top" of the funnel and proceeding to the narrow end.

1　Topic big enough to fill a library. Example: "College Education."
2　Topic big enough to fill a book. Example: "Paying for a College Education."
3　Theme topic for one issue of a parenting magazine: Example: "Where to Find Scholarships for Your Children."
4　A single article in the same magazine. Example: "Best Scholarships for Children of Military Veterans."
5　Another article in the same magazine. Example: "Where to Find Scholarships for Journalism Majors."

SUMMARY

An angle takes a specific approach to its subject matter. A strong angle can be summarized in one sentence and displays unity, action and specificity. The cover lines on magazines provide examples of focused angles. You can use the "angle tree" or "funnel of focus" as exercises to narrow your topic. You can narrow your topic by asking yourself what you want to know and what sources you have access to, and by finding a news peg that ties your topic to a current event.

The narrower your angle, the more likely you are write a creative, original article. The narrower your angle, the more likely you will find a "scoop" that no one else has written about. Finally, the narrower your angle, the more likely you will get published. Finding a good angle isn't easy, but the more you read what's already been published the easier it will become.

Writer and movie producer Nora Ephron advises:

> You must come up with some little thing that you know about that others don't. A good journalist figures that out. It means reading everything possible to keep up with what's going on. You can't merely find a subject that may interest a magazine editor. Find a subject on which you have something interesting, surprising or perverse to say.[11]

IN-CLASS ACTIVITIES

Instructor: Display on a screen two feature articles that cover the same topic from a different angle. Discuss these two angles in class. Students: Working in pairs, create two additional angles on this topic for different demographics—for example, one for men and one for women or one for young adults and one for middle-aged adults.

Instructor: Divide students into groups of three or four. Assign each group a broad topic commonly covered in newspapers and magazines. Students: Create four story ideas that bring a more tightly focused angle to that broad topic.

ASSIGNMENTS

Students: Pick a hot topic currently in the news. Do an online search and make a list of 10 articles with different angles on that same topic. Include the author's name, the article title, the publication title, the date and the Web address.

Instructor: Give each student a list of 10 broad topics. Ask the students to do some online research and write a one-sentence angle for a feasible story on each topic.

NOTES

1   William Blundell, *The Art and Craft of Feature Writing* (New York: Penguin Books, 1988), 24.

2   Jane Harrigan, "Organizing Your Material," in *The Complete Book of Feature Writing*, ed. Leonard Witt (Cincinnati, Ohio: Writer's Digest Books, 1991), 100.

3   Telephone interview with David E. Sumner, Nov. 29, 2003. Updated correspondence April 16, 2012.

4   William Zinsser, *On Writing Well: An Information Guide to Writing Nonfiction*, 3rd ed. (San Francisco, Calif.: Harper and Row, 1985), 63.

5   David Welch and Ian Rowley, "Toyota's All-Out Drive to Stay Toyota," *Businessweek*, Nov. 22, 2007. www.businessweek.com/stories/2007-11-21/toyotas-all-out-drive-to-stay-toyotabusinessweek-business-news-stock-market-and-financial-advice (accessed June 18, 2008).

6   Gary Provost, *Beyond Style: Mastering the Finer Points of Writing* (Cincinnati, Ohio: Writer's Digest Books, 1988), 42.

7   Quoted in David E. Sumner, *Magazines: A Complete Guide to the Industry* (New York: Peter Lang, 2006), 52.

8   Mary S. Schaeffer, "Take a Potentially Dry Topic and Spice It Up," *The Writer*, July 2007, 27.

9   Michael Zuckoff, "How a Massachusetts Psychotherapist Fell for a Nigerian E-Mail Scam," *The New Yorker*, May 15, 2006. www.newyorker.com/archive/2006/05/15/060515fa_fact (accessed June 19, 2008).

10 Quoted in Candy Schulman, "The Idea Ideal," in *Handbook of Magazine Article Writing*, ed. Jean M. Fredette (Cincinnati, Ohio: Writer's Digest Books, 1988), 25.

11 Gerald Grow, "The Funnel of Focus." www.longleaf.net/ggrow (accessed Nov. 2, 2008). Reprinted with permission.

4

DIGGING DEEP FOR ORIGINAL STORIES

KEY POINTS

- The "40–40–20" rule of research
- Why you need libraries
- Why interviews are essential
- Primary sources essential for originality
- The Internet: primary or secondary source?
- Copyright and fair use

THE "40–40–20" RULE OF RESEARCH

Some reporters follow the "40–40–20" rule for writing great stories. This means that they spend the first 40 percent of their time doing background research to find a good topic, angle and sources; the next 40 percent doing interviews and background research; and the final 20 percent writing the story. Most feature and magazine writers will agree that the actual writing of a story is the easiest part. They typically spend 80 percent of their time on this "up-front" work so that the writing follows easily.

When faced with the challenge of coming up with an idea for a story assignment, many beginning writers follow the "thumb-sucking" rule. This means that they sit at home and suck their thumb, thinking, "What shall I write about?"

Feature and Magazine Writing: Action, Angle and Anecdotes, Third Edition.
David E. Sumner and Holly G. Miller.
© 2013 David E. Sumner and Holly G. Miller. Published 2013 by John Wiley & Sons, Inc.

The problems with this thumb-sucking approach are, first, that you're not likely to come up with an original idea. You're likely to find only a "backyard topic"—a topic drawn from the narrow perimeters of your personal interests—not one that has any chance of getting published in a national magazine with millions of subscribers.

The most common "backyard topics" for students are male-female relationships, stress, diet, health and fitness, sororities and fraternities, local bands and music, and travel ideas. For example, we've read dozens of student articles on "How to Plan a Spring Break Trip." The first problem with these tired topics is that they've been written about hundreds of times. Finding an original angle is difficult. The second problem with tired topics is that they rarely contain original insight or rise above common-sense information anyone can figure out or find on the Internet.

Beginning with background research offers the best way to narrow your focus. If you have a general idea of what to write about but are puzzled about the angle, then start reading. Read a dozen articles on your chosen topic before doing any interviews. This background research helps you to determine the context, focus and angle for an article. It tells you what's been written, what questions have been asked and—most importantly— what questions haven't been asked or answered. By discovering these gaps and questions, you can come up with a fresh angle on an old topic.

A few years ago, David E. Sumner surveyed 134 journalism professors who taught feature- and magazine-writing courses. He asked them to choose, from a list of 20 common writing mistakes, the ones that occurred most often in their students' work. The biggest mistake? An overwhelming number of these professors ranked number one: "Not reading widely enough to distinguish between original and unoriginal ideas," which confirms a point we made in Chapter 1.

Many comments from these professors in Sumner's survey reflected students' failure to do substantive research or interviewing. "The main problem I've found is lack of depth in reporting," wrote one professor. Students tend to choose topics that affect them personally and then rely on the Internet or "Googling" for most of their research. One professor said, "If the subject has not affected them personally, they have a hard time relating to it." Another added, "Students want to write first-person columns about their personal feelings or interview friends or people they know."

Comments from a professor at the University of Western Sydney in Australia revealed that these problems are not limited to American students. She said, "The problem that troubles me most is the lack of motivation in students to investigate issues. They seem happy to use information that is readily available rather than ask questions or dig deep."

WHY YOU NEED LIBRARIES

Take a few minutes to introduce yourself to a reference librarian. Because librarians enjoy books and reading, they enjoy helping writers and researchers. Explain what you are looking for to a reference librarian and she can send you directly to what you need, saving you hours of research time.

More than two million books (printed and electronic) are published every year around the world. These books range in price from $1 to more than $100 and few, if any, are free on the Internet or electronic readers such as Kindle. Authors who spend their days and weeks doing research, conducting interviews and writing deserve to earn a living like everyone else. So, if you want to read about the most recent breakthrough discoveries, you have to go to a library.

Joe Treen, a former managing editor for *People*, says library resources possess three advantages over the Internet: "First of all, they've got books. Second of all, they've got employees who can help you. Third, they have reliability. I don't always trust stuff I see on the Internet. I think bricks and mortar libraries are not going to go away."[1]

Library books and articles are also more likely to be closely scrutinized and fact-checked by professional editors than material you find elsewhere. Academic journal articles are peer-reviewed, which means that two or three experts in the field review and approve each article before it appears in print.

Libraries have two other advantages not found elsewhere. First, you can browse the magazine stacks and read articles from back issues. Browsing through their article topics will help you create ideas as well as locate target markets for your stories. The biggest complaint editors make about freelance writers is that they don't study their publications before submitting a query letter or article. The library is the only place to study old print issues of target magazines and get a personal "feel" for the kinds of articles they publish.

Second, university libraries subscribe to commercial electronic databases not accessible on the Internet. For example, *Lexis-Nexis News, Access*

World News and *Newspaper Source* are all commercial databases available only through libraries. *Newspaper Source* contains major newspapers, such as *The New York Times* and *The Wall Street Journal*, while *Access World News* includes daily newspapers in smaller cities. You can find the full text of court decisions through *Lexis-Nexis Legal. Science Direct* offers full-text access to 900 scientific journals covering such areas as biotechnology, chemistry, computer technology and more. Large libraries pay more than $100,000 a year to subscribe to these databases but make them free to their patrons. While the databases are always available through in-house terminals, many libraries also make them available through their websites to registered patrons.

WHY INTERVIEWS ARE ESSENTIAL

The most common excuse we hear from students about not getting interviews is, "He never replied to my e-mail." Hello? Just pick up the telephone and call. The best way to obtain an interview is with the telephone. Find the number and call the person you want to interview. A telephone call or voicemail message cannot be ignored as easily as an e-mail message. Many professional people do not answer e-mail from people they do not know or those whom they consider "unimportant."

Feature articles based on e-mail or text interviews often seem flat and uninspiring. The quotes are too precise, mechanical and unemotional to captivate or sustain readers. The words sound like they come from, well, an e-mail message and not a personal conversation. People will more likely tell you what they think you want to hear rather than the spontaneous answers that come in a conversation. We cannot stress these points strongly enough.

While background research adds depth and detail to article writing, personal interviews bring freshness, color and originality. Face-to-face and telephone interviews cover numerous topics in a relatively short period of time. The time required to type on a keyboard slows down communication and discourages your source from giving you as much information as they would in a face-to-face or telephone interview.

"Scary" is how John Brady, a professional-in-residence at Ohio University, describes the prevalence of e-mail interviews and reliance on Internet research among his students. Brady wrote, "Interviewing is the key to effective feature writing. Without enough interviews, reporters are writing on empty. I feel so strongly about this problem, I wrote a book about it."[2] Some students have been known to conduct e-mail interviews with persons who work at the same school that they attend.

Myron Struck, former editor-in-chief of Targeted News Service, says, "Eight of 10 interns who have come to us over the past four years from

Get "Up Close and Personal" with Your Interviews

Face-to-face interviews

When you sit in front of someone, you hear and see (a) words; (b) tone and voice inflection; (c) pauses; (d) facial expressions; (e) dress, physical appearance and mannerisms; (f) room surroundings; and (g) people who live or work nearby. In other words, you get the benefit of the whole context of the interview.

Telephone interviews

When you talk on the phone, you only hear (a) words; (b) tone and voice inflection; and (c) pauses. You don't see facial expressions. You don't get many spontaneous comments. Face-to-face interviews offer facial expressions indicating skepticism, surprise, approval or disapproval that often prompt you to ask follow-up questions. You miss these on the telephone and in e-mail.

E-mail and texting interviews

You see: (a) words. Your interviewee can use carefully chosen words to evade your questions. You can't ask spontaneous follow-up questions. You can't detect the mood or tone of voice. Use e-mail for quotes only when you are looking for brief facts. E-mail can also be useful for verifying facts and quotes from people you have already interviewed.

The *Model Code of Ethics* published by the Associated Collegiate Press says writers should verify an e-mail source's identity with a follow-up telephone call. Telephone or in-person interviews always surpass e-mail interviews in the quality of the information that they produce.

SIDEBAR 4.1

journalism programs do not know how to conduct face-to-face interviews and believe that e-mail and perhaps the telephone are far superior." He advocates that teachers should discourage e-mail interviews and "encourage more practice doing face-to-face interviews."[3]

Some people feel self-conscious about poor grammar or spelling ability and don't reply to nonessential e-mail. Or they only offer terse replies. E-mail also gets lost because of technical problems and disappears when a server is down, a power outage occurs or the sender makes a typographical error in the address.

Sources cannot avoid a telephone call or personal visit like an e-mail message. While they can hit the "delete" key for unwanted e-mail, they have to say something when you appear at their door or reach them on the telephone. It's just harder to say "no." The more distance you put between yourself and a source, the more information you lose. We cover interviewing techniques in Chapter 5.

Gay Talese, Pulitzer Prize-winning reporter, wrote in his memoir, *A Writer's Life*,

> At least half the time I have devoted to this current book, as well as to my earlier ones, has been spent collecting and assembling information that I obtained from libraries, archives, government buildings where public records are kept, and from various individuals whom I have sought out and interviewed. I believe face-to-face contact is necessary because I want not only a dialogue but a visual sense of the interviewee's personal features and mannerisms, as well as the opportunity to describe atmospherically the setting in which the meeting took place.[4]

PRIMARY SOURCES: VITAL FOR ORIGINALITY

A *Reader's Digest* editor once advised his writers:

> Bullet-proof your manuscript. When a story is scheduled, our fact-checking department begins its work. Our fact-checkers are second to none. We don't use secondary sources. You can't quote from newspapers or magazines. You've got to go back to the primary sources to confirm that they weren't misquoted.[5]

The terms "primary source" and "secondary source" distinguish between information that comes from its original creator and that which an intermediary has edited and filtered. A primary source for an interview comes from a person who directly observed an event. A primary source for a document is one that hasn't been published in its original form—such as a letter or report. Articles from existing magazines and newspapers are "secondary" by definition because another writer has already gathered and edited the facts for readers.

Secondary sources aren't necessarily inferior to primary sources. You need them to find ideas, determine the angle and add context and depth to your material. To get an article published, however, you have to interview and use primary sources to get the "scoop."

The Internet creates both a disturbing threat and an unparalleled opportunity for writers. It threatens good reporting because websites offer limitless opportunities for shallow research and plagiarism. You can find hundreds of articles on any topic, rearrange a few facts here, lift a few quotes there and create a 1,500-word article. This patchwork approach to

Subscription Databases Available in Academic Libraries

Academic Search Premier	History Cooperative
America: History and Life	LexisNexis Academic
Biography in Context	McClatchy Tribune Collection
Business Source Premier	Medline
Communication & Mass Media Complete	Military and Intelligence Collection
	Newspaper Source
Company Profiles	Oxford African-American Collection
Contemporary Authors	PubMed Central
CQ Researcher	Reference U.S.A.
CQ Weekly	ScienceDirect
Findarticles.com	Standard Rate and Data Service
Gale Directory Library	Standard and Poor's Net Advantage
GaleVirtual Reference Library	Thomas: Legislative Information on the Internet
Historical Statistics of the U.S.	

SIDEBAR 4.2

Internet research is easy to recognize because it smells stale; it's also dishonest and illegal.

"I can now see how word processors and the Internet make it easy for writers to cut and paste the work of other authors into their own text. At the same time, the Internet also makes it easy for fact-checkers to catch writers in the act," said Lori K. Baker, a former fact-checker at *Arizona Highways*, in an article in *The Writer*.[6]

The Internet offers a tremendous opportunity to writers because it helps to locate expert sources on any topic and makes a great starting point. When properly used, the Internet can offer writers in out-of-the-way places access to nationally known experts. It offers access to millions of government records that used to require a trip to the state capital, U.S. National Archives or Library of Congress. The Internet offers a vast "gateway" to information. But don't do all of your research on the Internet or you will likely end up with stale, outdated information.

THE INTERNET: PRIMARY OR SECONDARY SOURCE?

Articles and documents found on the Internet can be primary sources or secondary sources. If the information comes from an article in an online newspaper or magazine, it's a secondary source. But other types of online information can be used as valuable primary source material. Here are some types of primary source information that you can find online.

Speeches, reports and judicial decisions

Published stories about important speeches summarize and paraphrase that speech. But, if you can find the full text of the original, you have a primary source. The full texts of speeches, agency reports, research reports and judicial decisions give you original information not filtered or interpreted by other writers. Public figures, such as political leaders and company presidents, often place the full text of their speeches on their company or office's website. Professional associations, nonprofit organizations and government agencies may publish the full texts of research reports on the Internet. The full texts of most judicial decisions at the state and national level are available online. If you're writing about a controversial court decision, for example, go to the Internet and find the full text of the decision so you won't have to rely on another writer's interpretation.

Reports from companies, government agencies and nonprofits

A "report" usually results from an in-depth investigation of an issue or problem. Academic scholars, nonprofit foundations and associations and government agencies issue thousands of reports every year on public policy issues. They sometimes contain gems and nuggets of information. Since corporate websites focus on putting a "PR" spin on their company, you will most likely find hard-hitting reports at "edu," "org" and "gov" sites. Some internal documents may not be public knowledge until a writer finds them, combs through them and pulls out the "bombshell" that officials hoped no one would notice.

Original statistical data

Original statistical data also reveal facts and trends that haven't been interpreted or distorted by other writers. When you find the original data, you can report the story using first-hand interpretations.

Statistics add indisputable credibility. They describe a quantitative relationship between phenomena and help you prove the growth, decline or magnitude of any issue you write about. The US government spends millions of taxpayer dollars every year to compile statistics on every aspect of life: economics, transportation, health, crime, public safety, labor, manufacturing, birth and death rates and more. All of these results are available at a website (www.fedstats.gov) described as "the gateway to statistics from over 100 U.S. federal agencies." You can search for statistics by keyword, agency, topic or state. This site also contains an online version of the annual series, the *Statistical Abstract of the United States*. Most libraries also have the most recent print edition of the *Statistical Abstract* in their reference section. Over the years, we have used the *Statistical Abstract* as a research reference more often than any other print publication.

Most journalists dislike numbers, and you may be among them. If you want to gain a competitive edge over your peers, however, learn to summarize and interpret data trends. Today's most successful writers know how to download information into Excel spreadsheets, examine it and find stories. Spreadsheets allow you to take a large list of data—such as regional and national averages on various issues—and alphabetize or sort from highest to lowest. Any writer who can examine a table of numbers and detect a trend or find an unreported scoop has a talent that employers value. For example, original statistical data from the Census Bureau may yield a story around the rapid increase in birth rates in a particular state, increased worker productivity in another state or a population exodus from other states. It's easy to find auto fatality rates by state and determine the most and least dangerous states in which to drive. Or you can find cities with the highest and lowest crime rates and write a story about those in which it's safest to live.

A trend story (see Chapter 16) results when a phenomenon is getting bigger or more popular, or the opposite: getting smaller or losing popularity. For example, these stories may report on birth, marriage or divorce rates; consumer spending habits; lifestyle; or career choices. They originate in statistics you can find at the Census Bureau (www.census.gov) or studies conducted by professional associations that represent these issues.

Academic studies and scholarly journal articles

Scholarly journals containing studies conducted by academic researchers are an exception to the rule that previously published articles are secondary sources. Reports on groundbreaking studies from medical journals are frequently published or broadcast in the media. Don't rely on what a magazine story says about a study from the *New England Journal of Medicine*. Go back and find the original article, which is a primary source. You may find a different angle on the same information. Since scholarly journals usually have low circulations, they offer writers the opportunity to publicize the results of groundbreaking studies to the wider public. Browsing through scholarly journals in psychology, sociology, political science or business may also give you plenty of article ideas. Since most authors are also professors, you can interview them after finding their telephone numbers through university websites.

Congressional reports and testimonies

Because of the volume and complexity of its work, the U.S. Congress divides its tasks between approximately 250 committees and subcommittees. Parliamentary bodies in other countries have similar committees. They conduct thousands of hearings every year on social, economic and political issues that affect everyone. Testimonies at these hearings come from people ranging from victims of crimes or injury to nationally known experts on health and safety issues. For example, we used transcripts from committee hearings on identity theft for a magazine article on that topic. Consult the government documents department of your library or look for the transcripts of most congressional hearings on the U.S. Senate (www.senate.gov) or House of Representatives (www.house.gov) websites.

Correspondence and papers

Original correspondence from well-known people is a wonderful primary source. When famous people die, their papers are often donated to libraries. These "papers" sometimes consist of hundreds of boxes of correspondence and other personal documents. The papers of more recent U.S. presidents are contained at their respective presidential libraries, where anyone may use them. The enormous size of these collections makes it possible for authors to write dozens of books on them, each with a different angle and different sources of information. Many celebrities and public figures donate their papers to the libraries of their alma maters. These papers are contained within a library's special collections department. Your nearest library may be a good place to start to find ideas for stories. Ask about its special collections.

COPYRIGHT AND FAIR USE

Three prominent historians who have written dozens of books and often appeared on television talk shows were charged with plagiarism several years ago. All of them admitted to quoting other authors' material in their books and failing to give proper credit and attribution. While none were taken to court, one was forced to pay an out-of-court settlement with the author she had inadvertently quoted.

While plagiarism can occur unintentionally, it still violates copyright law and its consequences can be just as serious as intentional plagiarism. All three of these historians' reputations were damaged and they received fewer invitations to television talk shows.

"Lifting quotes" is one of the most common forms of unintentional plagiarism. We know of one writer who interviewed a well-known celebrity and published a profile about him in a national magazine. Another writer lifted one of those quotes and used it in his article without giving proper attribution to the first writer. The original writer protested and forced the second magazine to publish a clarification and proper credit in the next issue.

The latest edition of the *MLA Handbook for Writers of Research Papers*, published by the Modern Language Association, has an entire section devoted to unintentional plagiarism: "Plagiarism," it says, "sometimes happens because researchers do not keep precise records of their reading, and by the time they return to their notes, they have forgotten whether their summaries and paraphrases contain quoted material that is poorly marked or unmarked."[7]

Proper Attribution for Secondary Quotes

Since journalistic writers don't use footnotes, you have to give proper credit within the context of the article. If you choose to requote a source from another publication, you should attribute it in this way:

"If we have bad crops, it's going to be a wild ride. There's just no cushion," Joseph Glauber, the Agriculture Department's chief economist, told *The New York Times*.

"He played that record about 10 times, and I said, 'That's it, Wayne; that's the record right there. We hit the lottery,'" said Ronald "Slim" Williams in a *Rolling Stone* article.

"I traveled to Cambodia for the first *Tomb Raider*. I got to this country and expected broken, angry people, and found smiling, kind, warm people," Angelina Jolie told Rich Cohen in a *Vanity Fair* interview.

The *MLA Handbook* goes on to distinguish between three types of plagiarism:

- repeating or paraphrasing a few words without giving credit
- reproducing a particularly apt phrase
- paraphrasing an argument or line of thinking[8]

In each case, the plagiarist misrepresents to readers the intellectual property of others as if it were his or her own.

The purpose of the federal Copyright Act is to protect "original works of authorship." Congress purposely chose the broad term "works of authorship" to avoid having to rewrite the Copyright Act every time a new "medium" was developed. This means the Copyright Act (Title 17, U.S. Code) protects Internet pages and articles, computer software and multimedia CDs, even though these items didn't exist at the time the law was passed in 1976.

The Internet hasn't changed the copyright laws. It has simply made plagiarism easier and more tempting. If you publish an article on the Internet, whether for a personal or commercial Web site, copyright law protects it as soon as it's published regardless of whether the copyright symbol appears or whether the copyright is registered. If someone else copies and publishes your Internet article elsewhere, you can sue for copyright infringement using the same Copyright Act of 1976.

What copyright doesn't protect

One writer sent a query to a newspaper's feature editor that proposed a story about how people celebrate Christmas when they have jobs that require them to work on the holiday—medical and law enforcement personnel, pilots and flight attendants and so forth. The writer never received a reply, but on Christmas day the newspaper published a feature on that identical topic. Of course, the writer was angered, but there was nothing he could do. He later learned this isn't an original idea since many newspapers and magazines publish articles on this topic every Christmas. Even if it was original, he had no grounds for copyright infringement. That's because ideas can't be copyrighted. At least six types of material are generally not protected by copyright. These include:

1 Unpublished works that have not been fixed in a "tangible form of expression." These could include speeches, conversations or performances never written down or recorded.
2 Titles, names, short phrases and slogans; variations of typographic ornamentation; lists of ingredients or contents. This means you can't copyright song titles or titles of articles.

3   Works from the public domain with no original authorship, such as government documents, calendars and telephone directories. After a copyright expires (currently 70 years after the death of the author), the work also falls into the public domain.

4   Press releases. Companies and organizations that send out press releases want their information to be published. They put it in the public domain and allow writers to use anything they want—facts, quotes or anecdotes.

5   Published works of the U.S. government or government employees.

6   Ideas, procedures, methods, processes and concepts.

Number six is particularly important for writers. As we previously noted, you cannot copyright the idea for an article; you can only copyright the particular way in which the idea is expressed and written. This is good news and bad news for writers.

The good news

The good news is you're free to browse through newspapers, magazines and websites and look for ideas you can adapt. Take any idea you find, interview your own sources and write your own article. That's legal. Another "good news" consequence of the dichotomy between ideas and their expression is that copyright offers no protection for basic facts or common knowledge. For example, the BBC, *The Washington Post* and CNN can all write stories about the latest conflict in the Middle East without intruding upon each other's copyright. Copyright does not protect the ideas and facts of any particular news event but only the arrangement of words and phrases in a particular story.

Section 107 of the U.S. Copyright Act covers "Fair Use." In general, the legal term "fair use" means you can use brief quotes from other sources as long as you give proper credit. The law gives permission to build upon the work of others for "purposes such as criticism, comment, news reporting, teaching (including multiple copies for classroom use), scholarship or research."

"The primary objective of copyright is not to reward the labor of authors," wrote Justice Sandra Day O'Connor in a 1991 Supreme Court decision, "but to 'promote the progress of science and useful arts.' To this end, copyright assures authors the right to their original expression, but encourages others to build freely upon the ideas and information conveyed by a work."[9]

The fair use provision doesn't say how many words or how much information you can borrow without permission from the author. Writers generally agree you should not exceed 400 words in any circumstance, sometimes even less. The law gives four general guidelines that determine whether fair use applies to the use of someone else's intellectual property:

1 The purpose and character of the use, including whether such use is of a commercial nature or is for nonprofit educational purposes
2 The nature of the copyrighted work
3 The amount and substantiality of the portion used in relation to the copyrighted work as a whole
4 The effect of the use upon the potential market for or value of the copyrighted work

Plaintiffs file many lawsuits each year over the meaning of "fair use." In general, the courts have ruled that the first criterion (a profit motive for the use) and the fourth (damage to market sales) are the most important. But the courts have also ruled that educational use of copyrighted material doesn't automatically make it "fair use." For example, a state court ruled against a New York school system that made copies and distributed videotapes to avoid purchasing them from the publisher.

If you copy someone else's intellectual property (electronically or manually) without giving credit or paying for it, you are violating fair use. Copying a CD and giving it to a friend so that he doesn't have to buy it is a copyright infringement. Prosecutions can and do occur. Think of how you would feel if someone made a copy of your intellectual work to avoid paying for it.

Plagiarism is not only wrong but bad for your career. To avoid ruining your career, be sure you understand your copyrights and wrongs.

IN-CLASS ACTIVITIES

Instructor: Ask students to go online and locate names, telephone numbers or e-mail addresses of experts on the following topics (or any topics you assign): a syndicated cartoonist who can discuss racial issues in cartoons; a middle-aged woman who has an eating disorder; an expert on DNA identification in criminal cases; an expert on autism; and a parent who has lost a child as the result of an accident caused by a drunk driver.

Instructor: On an overhead screen, review and discuss in class the electronic databases that your library offers its users. See Sidebar 4.2 for examples, such as Academic Search Premier, Biography in Context and Business Source Premier.

ASSIGNMENTS

Students: Using the Internet Public Library's "Associations on the Net" directory (www.ipl.org/div/aon), find the name of a contact person for associations that represent these types of groups or interests: Arab Americans, farmers, magicians, optometrists and those with sleep disorders.

Instructor: Create a separate list of topics representing students' areas of interest and ask them to find associations representing these interests.

Students: Use the Internet to find the following types of primary sources: the full text of a speech, a federal court decision, a set of statistical data, recent legislation and a company's annual report. Summarize the content of each source and choose one to suggest a story idea.

NOTES

1   Telephone interview with David E. Sumner, Nov. 21, 2003.
2   John Brady, *The Interviewer's Handbook: A Guerilla Guide: Techniques & Tactics for Reporters & Writers* (Waukesha, Wis.: The Writer Books, 2004).
3   Telephone interview with David E. Sumner, Aug. 30, 2004.
4   Gay Talese, *Gay Talese: A Writer's Life* (New York: Alfred A. Knopf, 2006), 47.
5   Quoted in Judy Mandell (ed.), *Magazine Editors Talk to Writers* (New York: John Wiley & Sons, 1996), 184.
6   Lori K. Baker, "What Your Magazine Fact-Checker Wishes You Knew," *The Writer*, July 2008, 28.
7   Joseph Gibaldi, *MLA Handbook for Writers of Research Papers*, 6th ed. (New York: Modern Language Association, 2003), 68.
8   Gibaldi, *MLA Handbook*, 68.
9   Justice Sandra Day O'Connor, *Feist Publications, Inc. v. Rural Telephone Service Co.*, 499 U.S. Code 340, 349 (1991).

5

TALKING POINTERS

HOW TO CONDUCT GREAT INTERVIEWS

KEY POINTS

- How to prepare
- A checklist for successful interviews
- Insights vs. information
- Identifying experts and actors
- Attributions with an attitude

Learning to interview is like learning to drive because it seems easy; overly easy. Once you've done a few interviews, you may think there's nothing more to learn. Then you suffer a major failure and realize how much you don't know. Seasoned journalists, like experienced drivers, approach with some trepidation each new "journey" into unfamiliar territory. They know that steering a conversation in the wrong direction at the wrong time can cause an interview to veer off course or, worse yet, come to a screeching halt.

Creating a list of questions to ask is important but not the most important aspect of an interview. That's the mechanical part: if you do enough research, you can figure out original questions. But great interviews originate with trust. The more that you can convey your trustworthiness and honorable intent, the more likely that your sources will tell you things they have never told anyone else.

Feature and Magazine Writing: Action, Angle and Anecdotes, Third Edition.
David E. Sumner and Holly G. Miller.
© 2013 David E. Sumner and Holly G. Miller. Published 2013 by John Wiley & Sons, Inc.

Trustworthiness is the most important quality you can bring to an interview because it determines how much interviewees are willing to open up. Trust originates from your character, your professionalism and your concern for the truth and for people. If you can convey in tangible and intangible ways that you care about the truth and "getting it right," then people may disclose parts of their lives they've never publicly discussed.

Celebrities and public figures often complain about the way reporters and writers treat them. They fear that journalists come with personal agendas; that reporters will take words out of context or inaccurately quote them. They know writers can make a person look foolish or ignorant by quoting only one sentence and ignoring everything else. Just as you, the writer, size up the interviewee and make assumptions based on first impressions, so does the interviewee come to quick conclusions about you. If he decides that you are a beginner, that you are unprepared or that you seem likely to misconstrue his thoughts, he may give terse and predictable answers to your questions.

Here are 10 ways you can turn off the person you are trying to interview:

1 Arriving late without a valid reason
2 Not dressing professionally (if in doubt, dress "up" and not "down")
3 Boring the subject with questions he or she has answered dozens of times
4 Asking for biographical details (i.e., "Where were you born?" "Do you have a family?") that you could have obtained earlier with more preparation
5 Assuming you are buddies with this person whom you've never met before
6 Talking too much (the interview is never about you; your job is to listen)
7 Failing to bring a tape or digital recorder and, therefore, frequently having to repeat questions and slow the interview while you try to write down the comments
8 Failing to make eye contact or show interest through your body language
9 Failing to use proper English, using clichés or frequently using expressions such as "I was like . . ." or "you know . . ."

10 Asking random questions without a clear focus or angle; in other words, not preparing for the interview

FIRST, YOU PREPARE

Ask professional writers to share their secrets to successful interviews and among their responses you're likely to hear the word "preparation." Obvious advice? Yes, and equally obvious are the follow-up tips. Among them: Writers should do extensive research on the people they interview (throughout this book we mention ways to find these people and immerse yourself in their areas of expertise); writers should compile a list of thought-provoking questions based on library and Internet research; writers should phrase questions in such a way that interviewees can't possibly respond with simple yes/no answers; writers should. . . . And the suggestions go on and on. We include a checklist of interview tips in Sidebar 5.2.

Preparation means defining a clear purpose for the interview. What kind of information do you hope to obtain? Is your purpose learning about your subject's personal life or obtaining information based on his or her professional expertise? Just as every article needs a clearly defined angle, so does each interview. All of the questions you ask should be focused around that purpose.

For all the preparation that you will do as an interviewer and writer, you will never master the art of interviewing. The reason is simple: The writer controls only half of an interview. The interviewee controls the other half, and the writer can never be certain what the interviewee will do or say. Although the advice on our checklist is valid, be aware of another, less predictable secret to a successful interview. You should be willing to move past your preparations and beyond your script if, in the course of the interview, an unexpected but equally interesting story angle surfaces. In short, writers should enter an interview situation with a meticulously detailed roadmap that, when followed, will lead them to the information they need. But they should also be flexible enough to investigate surprise twists and turns that pop up in the course of the interview and take writers into uncharted territory that other writers haven't explored.

Interview with an Interviewer[1]

Veteran National Public Radio journalist Diane Rehm has been conducting insightful two-hour interviews five days a week for more than 30 years. Her list of interviewees includes U.S. presidents, famous athletes and best-selling authors, as well as lesser-known guests. *The Diane Rehm Show* is distributed internationally and is available online. Following are her answers to questions posed by Holly G. Miller.

Q: How do you keep up to date on everything from sports to politics to entertainment? What media do you consume to stay current so you can ask timely questions?

A: As I'm getting ready for work in the morning I listen to NPR's *Morning Edition*; then I come to the office, where *The Wall Street Journal*, *The New York Times* and *The Washington Post* are waiting for me. I read everything that my producers give me. When I get home at 6 p.m., I turn on the first half hour of the *News Hour* [PBS]; then I switch to ABC news at 6:30; at 7 p.m., I watch NBC news with Brian Williams, and then I go back for the last half hour of news on PBS.

Q: How do you feel about conducting an interview on the telephone?

A: I really hate doing interviews on the phone. I want to see the body language; I want to look into a person's eyes; I want to watch what someone is doing with his hands.

Q: What is your strategy when an interviewee rambles and doesn't answer your question?

A: Sometimes I'll interrupt, or I'll take a breath, or I'll use my hand as a gesture to indicate to the person across the table that I want to say something. People who watch me do an interview tell me I look like an orchestra conductor because I'm waving my hands all over the place.

Q: Do you have any stock questions that you rely on if an interview starts to lag?

A: Sure; I ask "how?" or "why?" Also, if I don't understand something, I admit, "I don't get it." I think people appreciate that because, if I don't understand something, chances are an awful lot of other people don't understand it either.

Q: Many of your interviews deal with very hot issues. How do you stay objective when you might have a very strong point of view?

A: I always have a strong and passionate point of view, but I am not here to give people my opinions. I'm here to elicit various points of view so listeners can make up their own minds. That has been my charge right from the start. I do not wish to become the person who tells others what to do.

Q: What do you do when interviewees lay down ground rules on what they will or will not talk about?

A: We're not interested in interviewing them. The only person who got away with that was [former Secretary of Defense] Robert McNamara, who called the night before an interview and said he would not take on-air calls from listeners. The next day, when he came to the studio and the microphones were on, I asked my first question: "Mr. McNamara, you refuse to take questions from our listeners. Why is that?" It was the question to ask.

Checklist for Successful Interviews

1 When setting up an interview, give your interviewee the nature of the topic that you are researching but don't reveal your exact questions. You can say "I'd like to have some time to discuss _____ with you" instead of "Could I have an interview?"

2 Request a specific amount of time for the interview—an hour is usually sufficient—and limit the interview to that timeframe. With busy people, the shorter amount of time you request, the more likely you are to get the interview.

3 Do extensive background research about your topic and your interviewee before you meet. Biographical information for many people is available on the company or organization they work for, or on Linkedin.com or Wikipedia.org. Learn everything you can about the interviewee's expertise, the work he or she does or the subject matter you plan to ask about.

4 For an hour-long interview, prepare at least 20 questions based on your research—more than you think you will need. While you may not get to all of them, it's better to go into the interview with a "road map" than without one.

SIDEBAR 5.2

5 Phrase your questions in a way that encourages the interviewee to offer opinions and feelings and examples.

6 Don't feel uncomfortable with silence or a long pause. If you ask a good question and the interviewee needs time to frame an answer, don't jump in and provide one.

7 Include several questions that will elicit anecdotes from your interviewee, such as "Could you give me an example of when that happened?" or "Tell me that story."

8 Cluster your questions into categories and create smooth transitions: questions about early years; family; career moves; future projects.

9 Use an electronic recorder unless you are pressed for time and won't be able to transcribe the interview session.

10 Listen to each answer that your interviewee gives and prepare to ask follow-up questions that might not be on your list. Follow up an answer with simple phrases such as "Oh?" or "I didn't know that" to encourage deeper answers with more details.

11 Take notes on your interviewee's body language: are they nervous, calm, enthusiastic . . . ?

12 If you plan to ask questions that might anger or alienate your interviewee, save them until you have established a rapport.

Should You Take Notes or Record Your Interviews?

We recommend taking notes and recording interviews with a digital recorder. These cost between $35 and $100 and hold up to 144 hours of conversations. Here are some other advantages:

1 You have an accurate and legal record of precisely what the interviewee said.

2 Digital recorders easily fit in a shirt pocket or purse.

3 You can copy interviews to your computer and listen to them while you transcribe them.

4 Audio files can be e-mailed to editors or fact-checkers.

5 You can fast-forward or rewind interviews more quickly than on a cassette recorder.

6 You can keep permanent archives of all of your interviews on your computer.

SIDEBAR 5.3

The main advantage of recorded interviews is accuracy. No one can write as fast as people talk since most people speak about 170 words per minute. Therefore, writers end up filling in the blanks of their notes with recreated quotes of what they think their subjects probably said. Here are some disadvantages of relying solely on note-taking:

1 You probably miss writing some key words or colorful phrases.
2 You slow down the interview by asking your interviewee to pause or repeat statements.
3 You can't think about follow-up questions because you are busy writing.
4 You can't look the interviewee in the eye and pay attention to body language.

You can record cell-phone conversations with a "wireless phone recording controller," which you can purchase for about $20. Similar units are available for land-line telephones.

INSIGHTS VS. INFORMATION

An interview is a conversation with a purpose. It is not a casual visit that meanders from one topic to another without an obvious direction. But what direction should it take? As an interviewer, you hope to leave an interview with enough insights and information to turn out a good feature story. If you plan to write a profile of a person, you want to tune into the person's character and personality. You want his opinions and feelings. If you are gathering material for an article about a timely issue, you're looking for statistics, facts and explanations. You are also hoping to gather an interviewee's unique perspective on the issue.

Well-known interviewers such as CNN's former talk show host Larry King know the importance of keeping the focus on the person answering the questions and not on the person asking the questions. The word "interview" is misleading because "inter" means "between" and "view" means "thoughts" or "ideas." The word therefore suggests an exchange of thoughts and ideas between two people. But that definition doesn't work in feature writing because readers aren't interested in a writer's thoughts and ideas. Readers care about the interviewee. In his book *Anything Goes*, King writes that "The show has never been about what I think and feel; it's about how the major players in an issue think and feel. That's why it works."[2]

Whether you're a beginning writer or a veteran, the steps you will take in preparing for and conducting a successful interview will likely be the same. In addition to considering the tips offered earlier, you must decide on the "voices" that deserve a place in your story. You also must think on your feet as you implement your plan for your question-and-answer session.

IDENTIFYING EXPERTS AND ACTORS

If your assignment is to produce a profile, your central interview will be the person you are profiling. That "voice" will dominate. Secondary interviews, sometimes called support interviews, will come from sources who can offer different perspectives—a best friend, spouse, employer, coworker, roommate or parent (see Chapter 12). If your goal is an article that probes an issue or tracks a trend, your list of likely interviewees will include at least one voice of authority, plus other knowledgeable persons who have differing opinions on the issue, and one or two persons who are caught up in the trend (see Chapter 16).

Topical features on issues and trends generally have two types of sources: the expert and the participant (sometimes called the expert and the actor). The expert is the voice of authority who has career or educational credentials in the subject you are investigating. The participant or actor is someone who has first-hand experience in the subject you are writing about. The questions that you put to the participants will be more open-ended than those you direct to your authority sources. Participants will often add colorful anecdotes and quotes to your story while the experts give it the voices of authority and enhance credibility.

The expert is a good interview to schedule first. This person commands respect and can offer credible insights and information because of experience, education, position or title. For example, if you are researching obesity in children, your expert may be a pediatrician or a nutritionist and your participant will be a child or parent of a child who has successfully overcome obesity. Similarly, if your assignment is to investigate alcohol abuse among college students, your expert might be a psychologist or addictions counselor and your participant will be a college student who is willing to talk about his or her experience with alcohol abuse. You might ask the addictions counselor, "What are five or six indicators of substance abuse?" You might ask the student, "Describe for me the moment when you realized that you had crossed the line between social drinker and problem drinker."

The more impressive your source's credentials, the more credible your article will be. A hierarchy exists. A doctor has more clout than a nurse; a professor's comments pack more punch than an instructor's observations; the president of a company gets more attention than a department manager. Readers often are skeptical, so you need to provide information from sources with impact.

In addition to the voice of authority, other interviewees will help explore the issue from a variety of angles. For the article about obesity in children, you'll want to hear from teenagers who are teased by peers because of their appearance. For the alcohol-abuse story, you'll want to hear from students who have observed excessive drinking and can provide anecdotes that move the story beyond statistics, advice and warnings.

GET READY, GET SET

A danger of interviewing sources with impressive credentials is that you may feel intimidated when you sit down and begin the question-and-answer process. Control is everything. As an interviewer you control the direction the interview takes and the information the interview produces; you also need the confidence to cut off responses that ramble, and you should doggedly restate questions that the interviewee wants to avoid. The best way to show who's in charge is by exhibiting professionalism the moment you pick up the telephone and request an appointment. Identify yourself, explain your writing project, tell your source how he or she fits into your research and estimate the amount of time you need. Usually an hour is enough for an in-depth interview; a half hour works well for a secondary interview. Instead of asking, "Would you be willing to talk with me?" ask, "When would be convenient for us to meet?"

As you prepare for the session, make use of every available resource. Do a crash course in the topic that you plan to cover and the people you plan to interview. In addition to doing online research, remember that every hospital, university and business of any size has a public relations staff whose job is to deal with media requests. These people operate under different names. In the entertainment industry they're called publicists; in the military they're public-affairs officers; in the business world they're corporate-communications specialists. Whatever the job description, a PR person often is a writer's best friend. One of America's most gifted interviewers, *The Washington Post*'s Bob Woodward, once rated PR people as "generally excellent" when it comes to getting writers the information they need to write a story. They're also valuable in setting up interviews and providing background on the person you are interviewing.

OFF TO A STRONG START

Just as the lead sentence in a story either grabs a reader's attention or causes him to yawn, so does the first question in an interview either capture the interviewee's interest or prompt him to nod off. You want to appear friendly but not casual, confident but not cocky, assertive but not pushy. Your opening question needs to be original and stimulating. It should show that you've done your homework and you're not going to waste time with questions that you could have answered with a little research.

Example: A local homemaker has announced plans to run for the state legislature. Thinking she would make an interesting subject for a story about the changing face of American politics, you set up an interview with her. Which of these questions is most likely to send the message that, as an interviewer, you know what you're doing?

- Have you ever run for office before?
- Almost 52 percent of the voters in our state are female, yet only 14 of the 100 members of the House of Representatives are women. In your opinion, what are the reasons for the imbalance?

The first question is weak in three ways. First, the interviewee can answer it with a yes/no response. Second, you could have found out the information by reading her campaign brochure. Third, her reply isn't likely to yield an interesting or insightful comment. The second question shows that you've taken time to log onto your state's website and have done a gender count. As a reward, you will probably get a thoughtful reply that you can work into your feature and, simultaneously, you will earn the respect of the candidate. She knows she can't shift into automatic pilot and merely repeat the facts from her official biography. She's going to have to frame her comments carefully because her words may influence the way voters feel about her.

As important as it is to avoid an opening question that lulls your interviewee to sleep, so should you avoid making him feel annoyed or angered. Save the sensitive questions until the final few minutes, after you've established a rapport. Even then, be careful not to phrase the questions in such a way that he feels you've turned against him. A good way to distance yourself from a delicate question is to precede it with a phrase such as "Some of your critics say . . ." or "Some people say . . ." and end with "How do you respond to that criticism?" Example: If you are interviewing an athlete who has just signed a multimillion-dollar contract, don't ask "Why do you think you're worth this much money when teachers, police officers and firefighters can barely scrape by on their salaries?" Instead say: "Some critics say that professional athletes are overpaid. How do you respond to that kind of comment?"

BUT WHAT IF . . . ?

As an interviewer, you have to anticipate and successfully react to unexpected events. Although no one can prepare you for all the interesting (and sometimes bizarre) situations you may experience before, during or after an interview, some are predictable. Listed below are a dozen scenarios that you are likely to encounter in your writing career. Put yourself in the situations, consider your options and decide how you would handle them.

1 You're assigned to interview a busy executive. His assistant agrees to arrange the meeting but says that her boss prefers that you fax your questions in advance. It will save time, she says, and he'll have the opportunity to pull together information from his files that might help you write the story.

What are the pros and cons of such an arrangement? Should you say yes?

2 You've called a local attorney and requested an interview to discuss a legal issue that you plan to cover in a Sunday feature. Before he schedules an appointment, he asks how much he'll be paid for the interview. Time is money, he says, and he typically makes several hundred dollars an hour.

What's your response? Should you ever pay someone for an interview Why or why not?

3 Five minutes into an interview, your interviewee is called out of the room. You depress the "pause" button on your digital recorder and proceed to review your notes. She comes back and the interview continues. She gives you great information, and just as the session winds down you notice that you never released the pause button. You have about 10 minutes before your time is up.

How should you use those remaining minutes? Should you admit your mistake and start over?

4 You're interviewing someone who obviously is nervous about being quoted in print. When you set your recorder in front of her, she freezes.

What can you say to help her relax so she will give you the information that you need?

5 You are set to interview a person who has been well coached by his public relations staff. You know that he has a list of talking points that he will keep dredging up regardless of the questions that you ask.

How can you cause him to leave his script and answer your questions with spontaneity?

6 You're set to interview a person who has been at the center of some controversy at some point in his life. You've jotted down a long list of questions, and you know some of them are very sensitive and personal.

How do you handle the interview so he doesn't walk out?

7 Your editor wants a profile article of about 2,500 words. The problem is that circumstances require you to conduct the interview on the telephone, and the person gives you short, clipped answers. You don't have the benefit of describing his body language or the setting. You only have words . . . and not enough of them.

What kind of additional research can you do to salvage the story?

8 You've identified a key source to interview for a feature story you're researching. You call her, she agrees and then asks two quick questions:

Where shall we meet and how much time will you need? The success of your story might hinge on your responses.

What do you say?

9 You're having a great conversation with a source who is giving you colorful quotes and strong anecdotes. The trouble is, your interviewee keeps saying "By the way, that was off the record." The material that is on the record is predictable and boring.

What do you do?

10 At the end of a very successful interview, your interviewee thanks you and says "When will I be able to read this before you turn it in to your editor?"

How do you respond?

11 You've just had a great question-and-answer session with a very quotable source. You want to stay on his good side because you might want to feature him in future articles.

What are some things you can do to build a strong professional relationship?

12 Three days have passed since you conducted a very candid interview. You get a call from the interviewee, who has had second thoughts about a couple of the comments she made. She asks you to please not include them since they could cause her a great deal of trouble. You haven't written the story yet, so it's not as if she's asking you to edit something that is part of your story.

What do you do?

TIME TO SWITCH ROLES

Interviewing is only part of a feature writer's job—the part that casts you in the role of researcher and reporter. Now you have to switch roles and become the writer. This means that you need to figure out what you're going to do with the material you've gathered during your interviews. You're certainly not going to use every comment uttered by every source. Which quotations are strong enough to warrant inclusion in your article? Are you going to use partial quotations? Are you going to use indirect quotations? Are you going to paraphrase some of the comments that you've collected? Are you going to tighten or "clean up" any of your interviewee's answers? If the person you've interviewed occasionally makes a grammatical error, should you fix it? If the person has the habit of saying "you know" too often, can you delete that phrase?

Here's what we suggest: After you've completed an interview, go through your notes (or transcript, if you've taped the conversation) and underline or highlight those comments that are likely to spark an emotional reaction from readers. Look for words that might surprise, amuse, anger or shock your readers. Look for ideas, opinions and insights. These highlighted sentences or parts of sentences will probably make the strongest quotations. If you have to cut through a lot of rambling words to get to the core of an interviewee's comment, consider using a partial quotation. Pull out the heart of the statement, put quotation marks around those words, and paraphrase the rest of the sentence. Likewise, if you understand a key point that your interviewee made but he didn't articulate it very well, consider paraphrasing it.

Some editors believe the best way to write the first draft is without using any of your notes. This forces you to put down on paper only those fresh ideas that are at the top of your memory. Writing from memory helps you see the forest; then you can go back and take care of the trees. It helps you write with a conversational style. If you remember these ideas off the top of your head, they are probably going to be the same comments and ideas that readers find most interesting and compelling. Then you can go back, verify quotes and fill in missing comments from your notes.

Some style and punctuation notes:

- End a direct quote with a comma followed by the quotation mark followed by the attribution verb "said" or other attribution verb. Example: "I always wanted to go to the moon," said the astronaut.
- If you begin with the attribution verb, put a comma after it before you begin the direct quote. Example: He replied, "I knew I'd have to major in engineering if I wanted NASA to hire me."

Aim for a 50–50 balance between direct quotes and paraphrases of what your subject says in your article. Don't try to quote everything or paraphrase everything. The more articulate your subject, the more you can use direct quotes. If your interviewee is less articulate, you will need to use more paraphrasing. In general, too many quotes make it more difficult for the reader to comprehend the information. Do the reader a favor by paraphrasing some of it. The box, below, presents some guidelines about when to quote and when to paraphrase.

Quotations vs. Paraphrases

When to Quote	When to Paraphrase
Use direct quotes when the comments: • give a concise, revealing anecdote • cluster words in a colorful or entertaining manner • establish an emotional connection with the reader • emphasize a significant point or display the subject's expertise • reveal the subject's personality, character or values in a unique way	Paraphrase when the comments: • offer biographical information or pure facts • present numbers or statistical data • are long or redundant quotes you can rewrite using fewer words • give information that is already public knowledge (which you may not include at all) • offer information that is dull but essential to the story

SIDEBAR 5.4

Here are some examples of certain words that should never be encased in quotation marks.

- Empty comments: "It's a pleasure to be here," said the speaker.
- Clichés: The scientist said he likes to think "out of the box."
- Statistical information: "I am married and have two sons," said Smith.
- Obvious observations: "Whichever team has the most points at the end of the game will win," said the coach.

It's not a good idea to include quotations from two different sources in the same paragraph. This confuses readers. Instead, give each source a separate paragraph.

Publications often have policies regarding "cleaning up" quotations. Most editors don't object to a writer deleting an occasional "you know" phrase or correcting a minor slip in grammar. The important point is that a writer should never tamper with the meaning of an interviewee's

He Said, She Said: Words with an Attitude

Before you begin to integrate quotations into a story, you'll need to decide whether you are going to write your attributions in present tense or past tense. Examples: "My first celebrity interview didn't go well," admits the journalist (present tense). "My first celebrity interview didn't go well," admitted the journalist (past tense). Whatever your decision, be consistent throughout the article.

Some words of attribution carry little if any "baggage." They don't influence the reader's perception of the speaker or add any color to the speaker's comment. Among them are:

said	mentioned
commented	added
responded	remarked
stated	observed
explained	noted
clarified	pointed out

Other words have an attitude. They either suggest the emotional state of the speaker or offer clues to the speaker's personality. Some people call these "loaded words" because they are loaded with unspoken meaning. A few examples are:

insisted	swore
argued	proposed
blurted	whispered
stressed	shouted
asserted	whined
revealed	begged
affirmed	cried
confided	grumbled

Note: The only words that a person can legitimately "hiss" are those with a string of "s" sounds. ("Stop sounding so silly," she hissed.) Avoid attributions such as laughed, giggled, gulped, sniffed and smiled. Remember, it's impossible to "smile" words or to sniff and speak at the same time. (Try it!) Wrong: "Let's go out," she giggled. Correct: "Let's go out," she said with a giggle. Above all, don't allow your sources to "share" words. It suggests that your interviewee is dealing out words: one for you, one for me. ("Skiing is my favorite form of exercise," she shared.)

SIDEBAR 5.5

comment. If you are uncertain about the meaning, you should contact your source and ask for clarification.

And this brings up two final suggestions. First, a good next-to-last question to put to an interviewee is this: "Have I missed anything that you feel is important?" Second, the last question before you turn off your recorder or close your notebook should be: "Where can I reach you by phone in the next few days in case I need to clarify or double check your comments?"

IN-CLASS ACTIVITIES

Students: Divide into teams of two. Instructor: Pass around an envelope containing the names of well-known persons currently in the news who represent a variety of fields—politics, entertainment, sports, business or religion. Each team of students should pull a name from the envelope and take 15 minutes to create a list of 10 questions that it would be appropriate to ask the person during an interview. The questions should be arranged in logical order and phrased in a way to elicit thought-provoking answers.

Instructor: Display on a screen a current feature article from a website of a magazine or newspaper. Students: Read the article aloud and compile a list of all persons quoted in the article. Build a class discussion around these questions:

- Why did the author choose to interview each person?
- What did each interviewee contribute to the story?
- Whose "voice" was *not* heard but should have been included?
- Could any interviewee have been omitted without diminishing the value of the article?

ASSIGNMENTS

Students: Create a list of a dozen open-ended question that any interviewer could adapt and use in almost any interview situation.

Students: Identify a person who is newsworthy because he/she is knowledgeable about or involved in a timely issue on campus. Interview the person and write a 500-word article that balances information about the issue with insights from the interviewee.

NOTES

1   Interview with Holly G. Miller, June 11, 2008.
2   Larry King and Pat Piper, *Anything Goes* (New York: Warner Books, 2000), 114.

PART II

TAKING YOUR ARTICLES TO THE FREELANCE MARKET

"Beyond finding and managing their work, 21st-century writers have to step up their game in promoting their writing as well."

Robert Lee Brewer, senior content editor
2012 Writer's Market and WritersMarket.com

Whether you're a mass-communication student vying for an internship or a veteran writer hoping to advance your career, a jam-packed portfolio attracts an editor's attention. Successful freelancers know how to analyze the marketplace, craft an angle and create pitch letters that reflect the interests and needs of a publication's readers.

TO MARKET, TO MARKET

SHOPPING YOUR WORDS AROUND

KEY POINTS

- The importance of building a portfolio
- Discovering available resources
- Collecting writers' guidelines
- Analyzing markets
- Five films that take you inside the publishing industry

A good way for feature writers to build their reputations, expand their portfolios and attract the attention of editors is to accumulate published clips early in their careers. Rather than explain to an editor what you *think* you can do, it's better to show an editor what you've already done. Clips prove your writing ability.

The bulk of this book concentrates on teaching the skills you need to create interesting and informative feature articles. In this chapter and the one that follows, we want to shift the emphasis and discuss how to market the words that you write. Specifically, how do feature writers sell articles to publications on a freelance basis? We feel this is an important question to answer for five reasons.

1 Freelance bylines sometimes lead to full-time jobs. Certainly a benefit of getting published is the ability to tuck a tear sheet into the envelope

Feature and Magazine Writing: Action, Angle and Anecdotes, Third Edition.
David E. Sumner and Holly G. Miller.

that contains your résumé. Clips push you a notch above those who don't have them.

2   If you work in public relations, part of your job may involve writing and placing articles about your client or employer. A media-relations specialist needs to know how to approach editors and convince them that a feature idea is newsworthy.

3   Staff members of local newspapers occasionally write articles that may interest readers beyond their immediate circulation area. The idea of earning a byline in a national publication is appealing, but these writers need help in knowing where to look and how to identify likely markets for their stories.

4   Persons who have worked full-time for media organizations may decide to leave their salaried jobs and try their hands at freelancing. They want to know how to make the transition from one side of the editor's desk to the other.

5   If your dream is to write a book someday, the best way to build credibility and gain visibility among publishers is by earning frequent bylines in national periodicals. Read the biographies of best-selling book authors and you'll see that most of them launched their careers at magazines.

How to "Nationalize" a Local Story

SIDEBAR 6.1

Many writers fail to sell their work to national publications because the articles that they submit are too local in scope. For example, a story about a college basketball team that devotes several hours a week to tutoring underprivileged kids may earn rave reviews from readers of the school's newspaper, but offer the same article to a national magazine and you can expect a rejection. Why? The story is of limited interest because it involves just one campus.

Don't be discouraged. Often a writer can "nationalize" an article by doing a limited amount of additional research. Let's continue with the example of the basketball team and see how nationalization works.

* Determine whether it is a trend. Perhaps what is happening on the local campus is also happening at other schools. Send e-mails

to athletic directors at a sample of universities across the country and ask whether they encourage athletes to do community service. If a sizable number answer "yes," you've documented a national trend. Your story's readership has just expanded.

- Do the math. Based on your e-mail survey, create some statistics that verify the trend. Your assertion that a trend exists will acquire credibility when you write that "Of the 20 schools surveyed, more than half support programs to involve athletes in volunteer activities."
- Look for quotable sources. When you write a local story, you interview local sources. When you write a national story, you solicit comments far beyond your home area. Go back to your survey and identify one or two out-of-state athletic directors whose observations will have clout with national readers. Conduct brief interviews. An additional quote from an official from the National Collegiate Athletic Association will round out your research.
- Piggyback on something in the news. Look for ways to make your story timely. When you pitch your article to an editor, point out that sports pages too often focus on athletes in trouble. Your article offers a refreshing change from these negative headlines.

Transforming a local story into a national story doesn't involve as much work as you might think. In the case of the student athletes, most of the article is going to deal with what's happening at the nearby campus. The difference is that the writer is going to use the local example to illustrate a national trend. Statistics and quotes from national sources will help to create a larger context within which the local story unfolds.

DISCOVERING AVAILABLE RESOURCES

Hundreds of resources are available to freelance writers hoping to break into print. In fact, an entire industry has emerged to serve people who want to sell their words to newspapers, websites and magazines. *Writer's Digest* publishes an annual guide of "101 Best Websites for Writers" based on surveys of their readers. A good place to start is Freelancewriting.com, which publishes writers' guidelines from hundreds of magazines. Other products include reference books that list the names and addresses of publications; monthly and bimonthly writers' magazines that offer tips on how and where to sell freelance articles; critique services that edit manuscripts for a fee; writers' workshops that schedule marketing sessions led by editors; newsletters, blogs and webinars that keep subscribers up to date on changes in the publishing industry; and writing-related websites that sponsor chat rooms where writers swap tips about potential markets.

We can't begin to cover all the places where you can tap into marketing advice. The number of products expands and contracts daily as websites and newsletters come and go. All we can do is to introduce you to a few major print and electronic resources and then let you take it from there. We also want to suggest several ways that you can evaluate a publication to determine whether it is a good place to send your queries, proposals and manuscripts.

A logical launch point for any discussion of marketing is WritersMarket.com, a searchable database that is available by paid subscription and is updated every business day. It includes contact names and information for several thousand market listings. These range from book publishers to consumer magazines, from trade journals to regional publications and more. The roots of this online resource stretch back to 1921 when the first edition of *Writer's Market* hit the bookstores. Still published annually, the 1,000-page *Writer's Market*—like its electronic counterpart—gives you addresses of consumer and trade magazines, a listing of contests, sample query letters and articles about the business side of writing. Both the print and the online products let you know whether a magazine accepts e-mail submissions, how long you are likely to wait for a response from an editor, whether a publication expects photos to accompany the words and what the pay scale is. These resources are especially helpful for writers who want to send their articles to publications that aren't available on the newsstand and may not be on library shelves.

As an example, if you look up *The Georgia Review*, you learn that the publication has been around since 1947 and that 99 percent of its content is supplied by freelancers. That's encouraging. More good news: Editors at the quarterly purchase between 12 and 20 nonfiction articles a year; they welcome submissions from little-known or unpublished writers; they respond to queries within two weeks; they buy first rights only; and they generally publish a manuscript within six months to a year after they accept it.

The value of the electronic version of *Writer's Market,* of course, is its capacity to stay current. From month to month, WritersMarket.com's overseers are likely to make hundreds of changes to their listings. Editors are a mobile bunch; they switch jobs, titles and responsibilities frequently. The editorial needs of publications also shift. It's possible that information gleaned from any printed market guide is out of date by the time you read it. You don't want to pitch an idea to an editor who no longer works at a magazine. Worse yet, you don't want to send a proposal to a magazine that has ceased publication. Electronic resources alert you to magazines that have failed as well as start-up publications that are in the early stages of building their stables of freelancers.

The simplest way to make sure you're pitching the right article to the right editor is by making a telephone call to the magazine. Call the number listed in *Writer's Market* and explain to the receptionist, "I'm writing an article about X topic and would like to know which editor I should send it to." At smaller magazines you may even get to talk to the editor, who can give you advice and suggestions.

The parent company of *Writer's Market*—F + W Media, Inc.—also publishes *Writer's Digest* magazine, one of two major writing magazines. The other is *The Writer,* which has been around since 1887. Both magazines include marketing information in every issue. They usually cluster potential markets by categories. One month they might focus on publications geared to teens; another month they might choose to highlight men's muscle magazines. Each listing gives an editor's name and tells what he or she wants to see. The magazines also publicize (and sometimes sponsor) writing competitions. The annual *Writer's Digest* contest typically draws close to 16,000 entries in 10 categories, one of which is magazine feature articles.

For persons interested in writing for Christian or inspirational publications, the *Christian Writers' Market Guide,* available from Jerry B. Jenkins' Christian Writers Guild in Colorado, is updated and released each January. It contains information on almost 600 print periodicals and more than 200 online publications. The Guild's website (www.christianwritersguild.com) offers other books, contests, blogs and webinars related to writing and selling manuscripts. These resources are particularly helpful because many writers are unaware of the number of inspirational publications that exist. Most of the magazines have small staffs, are not sold on newsstands and are available only by subscription or as giveaways by churches.

COLLECTING WRITERS' GUIDELINES

The writers' guidelines that magazines make available may help more than anything else. These guidelines are free and describe the kinds of materials the editors are interested in seeing, the preferred length of articles and the typical payment that contributors can expect. Some editors go into great detail and offer separate guidelines for different types of submissions— travel article guidelines, fiction guidelines, photography guidelines and so on. Freelancers sometimes can find guidelines posted on the publications' websites, although they are frequently buried in odd places.

A quick way to locate the websites of some 3,500 magazines is to visit Yahoo.com and look for the "news and media" link (http://dir.yahoo.com/News_and_Media). From there, click on the magazine that interests you. Our best advice, after you get to the publication's website, is to scroll to the bottom of the page and look for words such as "contact us," "press center," "media," "submissions" or "write for us." Sometimes the information you find there isn't encouraging. Major publications such as *The New Yorker* flatly state: "We cannot consider unsolicited nonfiction." The market-savvy freelancer doesn't waste time and energy sending material to publications that have policies that clearly discourage submissions.

Search engines such as Yahoo.com and Google.com have become so sophisticated that you can frequently find exactly what you are looking for using search terms such as "writers' guidelines" followed by the specific title or type of the magazine you are looking for. For example, a search using the term "writers' guidelines health magazines" yields guidelines for more than a dozen magazines in this category.

Lesser-known magazines or regional publications often offer helpful tips on breaking into print. As an example, on the website of *Atlanta Magazine* (atlanta.com), the editors include a section called "How to pitch to *Atlanta Magazine*." Besides wanting the obvious—articles related to the Georgia metropolis—the editors state that they rarely run one-source stories; that they advise first-time contributors to pitch short pieces not to exceed 1,500 words; that they expect to receive a list of all sources mentioned in the article (for fact-checking purposes); and that they like stories that are so provocative that a typical reader response is "Wow! I had no idea!" The smart freelancer follows these tips to the letter.

Some publications publish their future editorial calendars online for advertisers and writers smart enough to look for them. As an example,

Men's Journal includes a "media kit" that contains an editorial calendar. The kit also offers key demographic information such as subscribers' ages, education levels and marital statuses and whether or not they have children. Again, sometimes you can use Yahoo.com or Google.com with search terms such as "editorial calendar" followed by the specific title or type of the magazine you are looking for.

Editorial calendars and demographic details serve as tools for a publication's advertising staff. They give potential advertisers an idea of the content of each issue of the magazine and the subscribers who read it. Based in part on that information, an advertiser decides whether or not to buy space. Sometimes the information is very general, which is of little help to writers. However, several magazines offer details that are invaluable. *Road & Travel Magazine* clearly states in its writers' guidelines (www.roadandtravel.com/company/Editorial/writerguide.html) that it is aimed at upscale consumers, with a slant toward women who are in the 29–59 age category. Potential contributors are welcome to contact editors—by e-mail only—with article ideas for either the monthly online publication or the newly launched blog.

ANALYZING MARKETS—ON YOUR OWN

Besides visiting websites, accessing guidelines and tracking down editorial calendars, a writer can learn a lot about a magazine by analyzing back issues. When done carefully, this analysis alerts the writer to the kinds of articles that editors are likely to buy. It also can indicate whether or not the publication welcomes freelance submissions from newcomers. The writer who does not research a publication runs the risk of creating a query letter that is clearly inappropriate. "Familiarize yourself with our magazine before querying—our tone, audience, approach, the types of articles we do and don't do," suggest the editors of *The Writer* magazine in their submission guidelines, published on their website.

Part of a writer's challenge is to figure out the demographics of the publication's readers, pick up on new directions that the editors are pursuing and determine whether the magazine is mostly staff written. As you conduct your analysis, take note of how often a publication revisits a topic and whether it has recently covered the topic you want to propose. All this information, plus the tips you glean from reference books, websites, guidelines and calendars, should help you figure out whether your unsolicited material has a chance of earning a place in a future issue. Good market research can greatly reduce the number of rejection letters that a freelancer receives.

Get to know the readers

Editors, in addition to the advertising staff, know a lot about their readers. They know the gender breakdown, and they know how many subscribers live in each of the 50 states. They know their readers' average age, marital status, household income and education level. They know whether their readers are predominantly conservative or liberal in their politics. They know what kinds of products their readers buy, where they are likely to travel on vacation and whether they prefer to drive or fly to those destinations. (We know a travel editor who is constantly challenged to find fresh articles about Florida—her "mature" readers' favorite vacation spot.)

This demographic information, as we mentioned earlier, is essential when a publication's sales representatives call on potential advertisers. Companies make advertising decisions based on circulation figures, magazine content and demographic data. It's not good enough to know that a magazine has a million readers. Potential advertisers ask, "Of those million readers, how many are likely to purchase our products?" Example: A magazine read by young families is a good place to schedule ads for vans, whereas a magazine read by upscale singles is a likely match for sports car manufacturers. Companies that sell cosmetics are more apt to buy space in magazines read almost entirely by women than in a magazine with an even split between male and female readers. Companies that produce computers want exposure in business publications; companies that make running shoes earmark a chunk of their annual advertising budgets for fitness magazines.

The same demographic information that helps advertisers identify publications with the right audiences for their products helps writers identify publications with the right audiences for their articles. Young couples might welcome an article that offers tips on buying a first home, whereas upscale singles might want guidance on shopping for a condo. Writers can tune into the demographics of a publication by studying its cover, reading its letters to the editor and taking note of its advertising pages.

Here's how it works. Say you have an idea for a feature article and you want to pitch it to a magazine that you often read. Even if you feel you know the publication well, sit down with a recent issue, skim through it and take notes on these elements:

- *Cover.* Look at the face and study the cover lines. What kind of reader would find this celebrity and these articles appealing? Ask yourself whether your article idea would interest that reader. Would the topic of your proposed article make an appropriate cover line for this publication?
- *Letters to the editor.* People typically don't sit down and dash off notes or tap out e-mails unless they feel strongly about a topic. Do the letters alert you to topics that anger, offend, please or rally the publication's readers? Ask yourself whether your article idea would spark a similar favorable or unfavorable emotion.
- *Advertising pages.* Try to discern and describe the consumer who is the target for the advertisements. Full-page ads in popular consumer magazines with more than a million readers frequently cost $150,000 or more. Advertisers willing to pay this much money want access to the readers most likely to buy their products. Remember that certain ad pages—the back cover for one—can cost even more. Ask yourself whether your article idea would appeal to that targeted consumer.

Take note of the editor's notes

Somewhere toward the front of a magazine you're likely to find a standing column written by the publication's editor. These columns usually occupy a single page or less and have accurate but often unimaginative names such as "Editor's Letter" (*WSJ Magazine*), "Editor's Note" (*Money*) or "Letter from the Editor" (*Vogue*). They are easy to overlook because they're usually wedged between major advertising pages or placed near the more interesting table of contents. But don't be tempted to turn the page and move on. Writers trying to tune into a publication's editorial needs should view these standing columns as required reading. They contain all sorts of clues. They explain new directions the publication is taking, announce staff changes and offer hints about the magazine's point of view and its position on issues.

As an example, in the March 2012 issue of *Money*, the managing editor told readers that the magazine was preparing to celebrate its 40th anniversary. Across 10 issues leading up to the milestone, the magazine would honor 40 people with great accomplishments in their communities (related to the area of personal finance). The interesting point came at the end of the note: "We'd love your help on this project," wrote the editor. "If there's an individual or group you think deserves a shout-out, write us."[1]

Staff changes mentioned in editors' notes are important for a couple of reasons. First, they give you the names of the editors to whom you should address your query letters and article proposals. Second, they might tip you off to changes ahead for the publication. Often publishers expect their newly appointed editors to shake up the content and bring freshness to the magazine. When the editor-in-chief of *Runner's World* used his column to introduce a new contributing editor, he commented that the new writer would "build a bridge between the elite [runner] and the everyman—a key part of RW's mission."[2] Smart freelancers translate that to mean that the editors are interested in articles that reach out to runners who don't fit into the "elite" category.

Of course, sometimes the editor's column communicates bad news for potential writers. This was the case when *The Magazine Antiques*, a high-quality monthly publication, announced in its editor's letter in 2010 that it would reduce its frequency by combining issues in January/February, June/July and November/December. The reason: "We bow to the necessity of the times," wrote the editor.[3]

As you read the editor's note in a publication, pay attention to the tone of the writing. Is it conversational or formal? Breezy? Precise? Any attempt at humor? To what kind of reader does it seem directed? Is your style of writing compatible with the editor's style?

Pick up on masthead clues

You can pick up on valuable clues by reading the fine print of a publication's masthead. Contrary to popular belief, the masthead is the inside box (or Web page) that lists the names and titles of staff members, not the title logo on the cover. First, determine the size of the staff. A small staff might mean that the magazine depends on freelance writers for much of its content. That's a good sign. It also might mean that the editors are very busy and may be slow in responding to your query letters. Bad sign.

Look at the titles of the various editors listed on the masthead. Sometimes a magazine with a large staff is very exact in its areas of responsibility. Rather than assigning all nonfiction material to an articles editor, it might break down this general category and divide submissions according to specialties. Depending on the topic of your manuscript, your submission might find its way to the desk of a lifestyle editor, beauty editor, new products editor, legal affairs editor, special projects editor and so on. Addressing your material to the right person in the first place will cut down on response time and display professionalism on your part.

Some publications won't consider submissions from writers they don't know. Instead, they rely on a group of regular contributors for their content. These writers often are listed on the masthead as "contributing editors." By comparing the masthead with the table of contents, you can figure out whether the publication welcomes submissions from newcomers. If the bylines on published articles are the same as the names on the masthead, this is not a good market for an unknown writer.

One more item to check before you move on: Often somewhere on the masthead you will find a sentence or two relating to unsolicited freelance submissions. Typically this information is at the bottom of the masthead and takes the form of a disclaimer. It states that the publication assumes no responsibility for unsolicited articles and photos. That doesn't necessarily mean that the editors aren't willing to look at material from new writers; it merely protects them from financial claims if the material is lost.

Study the table of contents

You'll want to survey several issues of the magazine to identify recurring features or departments. Publications frequently ease new writers into their circle of contributors by first buying short items that fit into standing departments. We will talk more about these foot-in-the-door opportunities in Chapter 11.

Most magazines have predictable content. They follow an editorial formula that they know their readers like. For example, each issue might contain two personality profiles, one major and one minor travel piece, three diet and fitness stories, a roundup of film and book reviews, a couple of advice columns and several how-to articles. Because this lineup varies little from month to month, you can almost predict what submissions the editors will likely consider.

Read sample articles

As part of your analysis, read and critique several articles from different sections of the magazine. Ten questions to answer as you read each feature are:

1   What is the length of the article?
2   What kind of lead does the author use?
3   Does the story have any accompanying sidebars?
4   Is the topic aimed at readers of a certain age group, gender or background?
5   Which one of these words best describes the writer's tone— conversational, formal, sassy, breezy, condescending, authoritative, preachy?
6   Does the author write in the first person (I, me, my, our), second person (you, your) or third person (he, she, they, their)?
7   How many sources are quoted?
8   Are there any anecdotes?
9   Does the article fit into a particular category—how-to, calendar-related, profile, roundup or personal essay?
10   Is the vocabulary easy or difficult?

After you've read a variety of articles, look for characteristics that are present in all the stories. These probably reflect the preferences of the editors and the readers. Ask yourself: Are the articles about the same length? If not, what is the range? Do the articles contain a lot of quotations from expert sources? Do most of the articles have sidebars? Is there a prevailing tone to the writing?

Much like a person, a well-edited magazine has a distinct personality, a unique voice, an established point of view and a certain style. These traits usually resemble the personality, voice, point of view and style of the publication's readers. Even magazines in the same genre—fashion, health, home décor, travel—differ from each other. The challenge for the freelance writer is to identify the characteristics the magazine and its audience share and to offer material that is compatible. We often say successful writers are like chameleons: they have the ability to produce articles that blend perfectly into the magazines that publish their work.

Finally, as you analyze the content of a magazine, notice changes in its appearance. A new design can signal a new direction. As an example, late in 2003, *Prevention* designed a new look and introduced new features aimed squarely at its fastest-growing segment of readers—females under 50. The magazine's circulation has skyrocketed in recent years, a fact that its editor links to Americans' fascination with healthy living. Knowing *Prevention* makes an effort to reach out to women by offering articles about nutrition and fitness trends should help the freelancer who is trying to break into that market. A check of the magazine's demographic profile adds more clues: the readership is 86 percent female, with a median age of 56.[4]

NEW KIDS ON THE BLOCK

Sometimes it's impossible to read and evaluate content and design because the magazine's editors haven't released their first issue yet. Each year brings the introduction of many new publications to the marketplace. The average number of new magazines launched in the U.S. has ranged between 500 and 1,000 for the past 10 years. "A total of 71 titles appeared on the nation's newsstands for the first time in March of 2012," according to Prof. Samir Husni, a magazine journalism expert at the University of Mississippi (www.mrmagazine.com). Not all survive. Because start-up staffs often are small, these new magazines are excellent places to send query letters. Getting in on the ground floor has its benefits. But how can a writer get a handle on content without first seeing and reading an issue or two?

The answer is in the mail. To generate excitement for a new publication, its promotional staff usually initiates a mass mailing to describe the product and offer a reduced rate for "charter subscribers." A detailed letter often outlines exactly what the magazine will contain. Sometimes a slimmed-down sample of the magazine—a "premiere issue"—follows. Upon receipt of the promotional letter or sample issue, a freelance writer should try to read between the lines and surmise the editor's vision for future issues. Often the pay scale is modest, but writers who help "grow" a magazine from its launch to economic stability will be rewarded with coveted assignments and better compensation.

From Documentary to Docudrama

Although magazines haven't provided the backdrop for as many motion pictures as newspapers, a few standout films exist. Here are five examples—from documentary to docudrama to sheer fiction—that offer insights into the culture that exists at certain magazines. All are available on DVD.

Annie Leibovitz: Life through a Lens gives viewers a behind-the-camera peek at what went into creating some of the greatest *Vanity Fair* and *Rolling Stone* covers. The 2008 documentary (83 minutes) tracks the life of iconic photographer Annie Leibovitz and features interviews with the artist and many of her celebrity subjects.

The September Issue is a fascinating documentary, released in 2008, that shows the work involved in producing *Vogue* magazine's biggest issue in its long history. The camera tracks famed editor-in-chief Anna Wintour as she oversees the content of the September 2007 magazine. The 90-minute film offers insights into the staff hierarchy at a major publication.

Shattered Glass is a fact-based film about a staff writer at *The New Republic* magazine who fabricated several of his explosive articles and eventually was exposed and disgraced. The 2003 film is fairly short (94 minutes) and delivers a strong message in a somber but entertaining package.

Almost Famous is based on writer-director Cameron Crowe's experiences as a teenager who manages to get an assignment from *Rolling Stone* to cover an "almost famous" band. Although the 2000 film (122 minutes) didn't do well at the box office, it was critically acclaimed and earned an Oscar for Crowe. If nothing else, it shows the power of a great query letter.

The Devil Wears Prada was a best-selling novel before it was made into a film in 2006. The fictitious story tracks the career of a small-town girl who takes a job as assistant to a powerful editor at a New York-based fashion magazine. The comedy-drama (109 minutes) is fun to watch and depicts the cutthroat side of haute couture journalism.

PERSISTENCE PAYS

Even with all the available marketing aids, freelance writers receive many more letters of rejection than letters of assignment. Having the right idea and pitching it to the right publication at the right time requires skill, hard work and a bit of good luck. Too many writers, new to the profession, try their hands at freelancing then give up after one or two rejections. A wiser strategy is to remember that writing is a business, and like all businesses it has its share of setbacks. Each publication—and there are thousands out there—represents an opportunity. For the writer in search of a market, persistence pays. Never give up.

IN-CLASS ACTIVITIES

Instructor: Create a list of lesser-known national magazines. Ask each student to choose a publication from the list, research it outside class and prepare a brief (5-to-10-minute) "market report" to present to the class. Students: As part of your research, visit the publication's website, study its writers' guidelines and find its listing in one of the market guides mentioned in this chapter. When you deliver your market report to your classmates, emphasize the editorial formula of the magazine and evaluate the freelance opportunities.

Students: Based on each market report, brainstorm as a group and come up with two or three article ideas that might be appropriate for the publication.

ASSIGNMENTS

Students: Research and write a 750-word article about a trend that is evident on your campus. Some ideas: entrepreneurial students who start businesses while in school; older students who return to school in hopes of making career switches; a renewed interest in foreign languages among students who anticipate careers in a global economy; guys preparing for professions once dominated by women (nursing, elementary education); faculty members who practice what they teach (a political science professor who is a state legislator or a drama instructor who is active on the stage).

Students: Reread Sidebar 6.1. Create a plan for turning your local trend article into a story with widespread appeal that you could pitch to a national magazine. How much research would you need to do? Whom would you need to interview to broaden the scope? Which magazines might be interested in your article?

Students and instructor: Watch one of the films listed in Sidebar 6.2. What lessons did the film impart? Did it portray magazine journalism in a positive or negative way?

NOTES

1   Craig Matters, "It's Still the Economy—Only More So," *Money*, March 2012, 9.
2   David Willey, "An Elite Education," *Runner's World*, April 2012, 20.
3   Elizabeth Pochoda, "Editor's Letter," *The Magazine Antiques*, Jan.–Feb. 2010, 6.
4   Peter Johnson, "Prevention Is Healthy," *USA Today*, Dec. 4, 2003, 4D.

7

PITCH-PERFECT QUERY LETTERS

KEY POINTS

- The two goals of a query letter
- How to format a pitch letter
- The essential components of a query
- All rights vs. first rights
- Sample query letters

Entire books are published to explain what a query letter is and what it's supposed to do. We can summarize both topics in two sentences. Definition? A query is a one-page, single-spaced pitch letter (or e-mail) that a freelance writer sends to an editor. Purpose? It pitches an article idea and provides tangible proof of the writer's journalistic skills. In short, a letter of inquiry—which is where the word "query" comes from—asks the editor two questions: How do you like this idea? Do you think I have the talent to pull it off?

For example, guidelines for *Mother Jones* (available at www.motherjones.com/about/writer-guidelines) say:

> Best bet is to query us by mail, regular or e[-mail]. Tell us in no more than a few paragraphs what you plan to cover, why it's important and interesting, and how you will report it. The query should convey your approach, tone, and style, and should answer the following: What are your specific qualifications for writing on this topic?

The stakes are high. If the letter doesn't capture the editor's interest and calm all doubts about the writer's ability, the result is no assignment, no

Feature and Magazine Writing: Action, Angle and Anecdotes, Third Edition.
David E. Sumner and Holly G. Miller.
© 2013 David E. Sumner and Holly G. Miller. Published 2013 by John Wiley & Sons, Inc.

byline and no article. For that reason, queries fall into two categories—winners and losers. There is no middle ground. A "winner" means that the editor says "yes" and invites the writer to submit the article. A query that is a "loser" results in a rejection letter, most often a form letter straight from the office photocopy machine. Occasionally the rejection includes a short list of labeled boxes that the editor can check to indicate why the staff rejected the query. These responses are usually generic—"this manuscript does not meet our current needs"—and offer little guidance for the writer trying to tune into a magazine's needs.

If a publication's editors like the query but aren't familiar with the writer, they may ask the writer to submit the article on speculation. Translation: The editors have no obligation to buy the article if it isn't as good as the query letter indicates. Beginning writers should be willing to work "on spec" until they have established their credentials in the marketplace.

If the editors like the query and have worked previously with the writer, they often will send the writer a contract that specifies a deadline, the number of words needed and the amount of money they will pay for the finished article. Unlike working on speculation, the writer is assured of payment. That doesn't mean the writer is assured of publication, however. If the resulting article fails to meet the editors' expectations, the writer may need to revise the submission. Occasionally editors decide not to use an article at all and, according to the contract, are obligated to pay the writer a "kill fee." Translation: The writer will earn at least a portion of the amount originally specified in the contract. This typically ranges from 20 to 100 percent of the total fee agreed.

IN PURSUIT OF PERFECTION

Queries cannot be marginal, passable or even pretty good. They have to be flawless in presentation and terrific in content. Most are not, which explains why the majority are rejected. Occasionally editors will reject a query letter without reading a single sentence. One of our favorite stories tells of a writer who used tiny manicure scissors to clip words from various publications to fashion a query letter that resembled a ransom note. The freelancer must have spent hours finding the right words and then snipping and pasting them onto a piece of stationery. By contrast, the editor, a friend of ours, needed only a moment to reject the gimmicky submission. In another case, an editor rejected a query letter from a medical writer without even opening the envelope. The letter was addressed to Ms. Patricia Johnson. The editor's name: Mr. Patrick Johnson. The editor wasn't unduly sensitive about his name; he rejected the query because he doubted the writer's attention to detail. If the author couldn't get gender right, could the magazine trust him to get the facts straight in a medical story?

Many editors never meet their contributing writers face to face. The only way they judge competency is, first, by the appearance of the writer's correspondence and, second, by the content of the correspondence. Let's take a closer look at each of these key elements.

First impressions are important

Flawless presentation means attractive stationery and single-spaced text that is formatted in flush-left and ragged-right paragraphs. Publications vary in whether they accept e-mail or "snail mail" query letters only. Check their guidelines. If you're sending your query by snail mail, the paper and envelope should match; the type font should be simple and professional; and the letterhead should not be cluttered with silly graphics—quill pens, inkpots, computer monitors—or quotations from famous authors. Some writers try to underscore their previous article sales by including lists of publications in small print on the left-hand side of the query letter. Be careful; there's a fine line between looking professional and appearing pretentious.

The computer gives the writer the ability to design appealing packages that are extensions of the sender's personality. It also tempts writers to experiment with fonts that are difficult to read and graphics that distract from the content. There is no excuse for a less-than-perfect-looking query. Queries should be businesslike in appearance and creative in content. They also should be addressed to specific editors. Beginning a query with an anonymous "Dear Editor" means that no one is likely to respond. Do whatever you must to learn the name of the editor who evaluates query letters. This usually is as easy as checking the magazine's website or masthead or making a quick telephone call.

What's the big idea?

Assuming a query passes the appearance test, the editor will begin to evaluate the creativity of the idea and the skills of the writer. Knowing whether an idea is right for a magazine is the easy part. Editors understand their readers and can gauge reader interest in any given topic. Editors also know how recently their publication has featured a topic, and they typically won't revisit the subject for about three years. The exception is the occasional "update" when a major change occurs or a new angle surfaces. Also, certain evergreen topics are of sufficient interest to warrant regular exposure in some magazines. These include fitness, fashion and health tips in women's magazines, money-management advice in business publications and stories about high-profile personalities in entertainment weeklies.

As an editor evaluates the idea, he's also looking for clues to the writer's ability. A typo or misspelled word raises questions of accuracy. A writer who includes clichés in a query is likely to include more clichés in an article. If run-on sentences, endlessly long paragraphs and difficult vocabulary fill a query, they will more likely weaken an article. The query serves as a preview of things to come—good and bad.

"As an editor, I like to envision writers with their sweatshirt sleeves rolled to the elbow as they write their letters with the kids asleep, the dog snoring

SIDEBAR 7.1

Formatting a Query Letter

Most business letters, query letters and even cover letters for jobs and internships should be written in a block format. That means:

- Put your return address and contact information and the date in the upper-right-hand corner of the letter.
- Write the editor's name and address and then leave two blank lines.
- Write the salutation followed by a colon (e.g., "Dear Mr. Smith:").
- Leave two blank lines after the salutation and before the first paragraph.
- Do not indent the first line of the paragraph.
- Single-space your paragraphs and leave a blank line between each paragraph.
- End the letter with the closure "Sincerely" or "Yours truly" followed by a comma.
- Leave four blank lines for your hand-written signature and then type your name.

and all lights out next door," says Hank Nuwer, former magazine editor and author of *How to Write Like an Expert About Anything.* "Good letters encourage a sense of a writer at work. Letters that are too formal, banal and cliché-ridden make me think of grad students sweating blood to write dissertation proposals. Which would I rather read? Hey, what do you think?"[1]

ESSENTIAL COMPONENTS OF A QUERY

Most successful queries contain five components, strategically arranged for maximum impact. Unfortunately, many beginning writers confuse the order, put the least important element first and are disappointed when their letters fail to yield favorable responses. Here are the components that we recommend, listed according to their correct placement within the query:

1 Compelling lead paragraph
2 Summary of the topic
3 Statement of timeliness
4 Nuts and bolts information
5 Writer's credentials

Crafting the lead paragraph

Just as the lead paragraph of an article has to grab the reader's attention, so does the introductory paragraph in a query letter have to spark an editor's interest. For this reason, many successful queries begin with anecdotes—true stories, not hypothetical ones—that plunge readers into the topics that the writers are proposing. As an example, a query that pitched an article about identity theft might begin with this anecdote:

> Shon Bolden of Hillsboro, Ore., is a 23-year-old tire store worker who attends college part time. About four years ago, he tried to change his bank account to another bank, but the new bank refused the transaction. When he asked why, the bank said it had run his Social Security number through a credit bureau and found 14 people were using his Social Security number. Later he started receiving bills for items he had never purchased. Shon discovered that his financial identity had been stolen. Identity thieves had opened accounts in his name at about a dozen retail stores and had run up big bills.

Besides engaging the editor's attention, this opening paragraph hints at the tone of the future article. The editor can assume that the author will deliver a manuscript written in the same conversational tone as the query letter that proposed it. Whether the opening paragraph of a pitch letter is an anecdote, a provocative statement, an insightful quotation or a question, it frequently re-emerges as the article's opening paragraph.

Summarizing a timely topic

Assuming that the first paragraph of the query succeeds in hooking the editor's attention, the second paragraph should summarize the article's topic and underscore its timeliness. It often resembles the "nutgraf" or billboard paragraph we will describe in Chapter 8. Continuing with the example of the identity theft article, the billboard paragraph might state: "Shon is one of half a million Americans each year who are victims of identity theft—the country's fastest-growing crime. He is one of several persons who testified before the House Banking and Financial Services Committee last October."

In addition to explaining what the article is about, this billboard paragraph provides the third essential element in our list. It establishes the timeliness of the story by alerting readers to the fact that they could be at risk *right now* because identity theft is the country's fastest-growing crime. Suddenly the issue becomes personal; the author moves past the description of a single crime victim and makes the point that what happened to that victim could happen to anyone.

The same 1–2–3 formula—compelling lead, topic summary and statement of timeliness—that works for a hard-hitting article about identity theft is equally successful in a query that pitches a less serious subject. For example, suppose you decide to propose an article for a women's magazine about couples who choose to take separate vacations. You identify a publication that might be interested in such a story and you begin your query letter with this introductory paragraph: "Bob and Lynne Gray recently celebrated their 10th wedding anniversary by taking the vacation of their dreams. He headed for a camping trip in Michigan's remote Upper Peninsula; she opted for a week at a spa in Southern California."

Because the topic that you are proposing is much bigger than a profile of an otherwise compatible couple who choose to go their separate ways, the second paragraph places the anecdote in a larger context. It summarizes the topic and establishes its timeliness. "The Grays aren't alone. In the past three years nearly a quarter of all U.S. travelers have taken solo vacations. Although 53 percent are men, women are rapidly playing catch-up. To capitalize on this travel trend, websites, magazines and tour companies are designing trips and creating products that cater to the destination whims of female adventurers."

Nuts and bolts information

After crafting the necessary paragraphs that build interest, summarize the topic and establish timeliness, the writer next must outline the nuts and bolts of the proposal. This involves answering several pertinent questions: How many words will the article contain? Will it include any sidebars? What kinds of photos are available? When will a draft be ready? Who are the sources of information? Whom do you plan to interview and quote? At this point you are not displaying your creativity; instead, you're merely imparting vital information.

Writer's credentials

What most effective query letters have in common is that the word "I"— referring to the writer—does not appear until the end of the correspondence. A query should never begin with a statement about the writer. That information is the least important element of the letter. The writer should place his credentials toward the end, and, if he runs out of space, he can omit them entirely. By the time an editor has read the body of a pitch letter, he will know whether the proposed idea suits the magazine's audience and whether the letter's author has the skills to deliver the goods.

Among the most appropriate credentials to include are those that link the author to the topic. For example, if you are pitching the article about identity theft and you were once victimized, that fact is worth mentioning. If you and your mate typically head in opposite directions for your vacations, you are a likely candidate for the solo travel assignment. Recapping your academic degrees will have little impact. Explaining that you once had a poem published in your high-school newspaper will impress no one.

Remember that a query letter is a sales letter. As such, you should feel comfortable including anything that will enhance your chances of making a sale. A clipping of a recently published article—not your high-school poetry—is a good way to establish credibility. If you are a writer who also takes photographs, you might want to include a sample of your work or direct the editor to a website where your work is posted.

A business card attached to the query could lead to a future assignment. Editors sometimes reject a query because the idea isn't right for their publication but like the writer's style. They file the business card with a notation on the back. The next time they need an article by an author from a certain geographic area, they flip through their cache of business cards.

WHAT NOT TO INCLUDE IN A QUERY

Your academic degrees aren't the only thing to omit from a query. Although some writers always state in a pitch letter the kind of rights they are willing to sell, we think that discussion is better delayed until after the editor expresses interest in the article. Most publications are willing to negotiate rights at the point when the editor offers a contract to the author. Introducing the topic into the conversation at the query level seems as inappropriate as typing your Social Security number on a submission in anticipation of payment. Save it for later.

When the time is right, you will need a basic understanding of copyright law beyond the plagiarism issues we discussed in Chapter 4. Selling an article to a publisher means relinquishing partial rights in exchange for payment. Generally speaking, the more you are paid, the more rights you give up. Beginning feature writers deal with three kinds of rights—first rights, reprint rights and all rights (see Sidebar 7.2 for an explanation).

Another pet peeve of many editors is a paragraph of gushy praise for the magazine. Avoid sentences such as "I just love your publication and read it from cover to cover as soon as it arrives each month." The editor will know that you read the magazine "from cover to cover" if your query letter proposes an article exactly right for the publication's readers. By contrast, few things frustrate editors more than proposals that indicate the writers never took time to review the publication. A favorite war story of Ohio writer Bob Hostetler dates back to his three years as editor of *The Young Soldier*, a Salvation Army publication geared toward youth. "In the Salvation Army, adult members are called 'soldiers,' and children are called 'junior soldiers,'" explains Hostetler, now a freelance author of more than a dozen books. He continues:

> Anyone familiar with the Salvation Army or with the magazine would know this. Still, every so often I would receive a query letter proposing an article for *The Young Soldier* about how to disassemble and assemble an M-16 rifle or about the newest developments in tank warfare. Obviously those writers had no idea what I did from 8:30 to 4:30 every day.[2]

Whereas freelance writers should never exaggerate their credentials in a query letter, neither should they tell negative tales on themselves. Lines that a writer should not include in a query are: "I don't know anything about this topic but thought it might be fun to learn," "I've never published an article before" and "I just retired from my real job and have decided to become a writer."

Selling Your Rights

Most magazines are registered with the U.S. Copyright Office as single collective entities. The articles that appear in the magazine are not copyrighted individually in the authors' names. Magazines typically purchase partial rights to each article from freelance writers. Before your work appears in print and before you cash the magazine's check, you should have a clear understanding of the rights you are selling. Keep all correspondence that states whether the publication has purchased first rights, reprint rights, electronic rights or all rights.

First rights

Publications most typically purchase "first rights" or "first serial rights" from freelance writers. "Serial" is a librarians' term for any periodical published as part of a series, on a regular timetable, such as daily, weekly or monthly. By selling first serial rights, you give the magazine the first opportunity to publish the article. After the article is published, you retain the right to sell reprint rights to other publishers as many times as you want.

SIDEBAR 7.2

Reprint rights

While the formal term is "second serial rights," this arrangement is usually called reprint rights and means exactly what it says. Many print and online publications purchase reprint rights if the original publication's readership doesn't overlap with their own. Only the highest-circulation periodicals insist on buying editorial material that has never appeared elsewhere. Usually payment for reprint rights varies from 10 to 50 percent of the magazine's payment schedule for first rights.

All rights

If you sell all rights, you give the publisher full copyright ownership for reproduction and distribution. You should avoid selling all rights unless the publisher insists and the payment is sufficiently high. All rights means the publisher can publish the article in its magazine, put it on its website or publish portions in another magazine it owns or in a subsequent book or CD-ROM with a collection of articles. Unfortunately for writers, an increasing number of large publishers want to purchase all rights because it gives them the freedom to use the material in a variety of print and electronic formats.

WHEN TO QUERY

As we've mentioned previously, some beginning writers go to all the trouble of researching and writing their articles before they submit query letters to see whether any editor is interested in the topics. This makes little sense. The writer-editor relationship often involves a dialogue as an article takes shape. The dialogue begins but doesn't end with the query letter. Frequently an editor will say "yes" to a proposal and then will offer suggestions as to length and angle. The editor may request that the submission take the form of a how-to article or a profile with a sidebar. The writer who has completed the project has to start over.

Most veteran writers submit their query letters at one of two points in the writing process:

1 They have an idea and have decided on a slant. *Query.*
2 They have an idea, have chosen the slant and have conducted their interviews. *Query.*

The advantage of sending a query at the first point in the process is that you have invested little time and energy. If no editor expresses interest in the idea, you've lost nothing. You file the idea for the future and move on to another project.

The advantage of sending a query at the second point, after you've done your interviews, is that the query will have more substance. You can include a comment from one of your sources. You can create an anecdote based on your research. If your spadework has caused your enthusiasm to surge, that excitement will spill over into the query and may be contagious enough to affect the editor. You'll have a good idea of how long the article should be, and you can pitch any ideas that you have regarding sidebar possibilities. The only disadvantage to querying at this point is that you have invested several hours in doing research. If no editor asks to see the finished article, that time is lost. However, if the topic isn't time-dated, you may be able to revisit it in the future.

SNAIL MAIL VS. E-MAIL QUERIES

Should you or shouldn't you? Only editors can answer the question of whether a writer should fax a query, send it by e-mail or let the post office do the honors. As we indicated in Chapter 6, the writers' guidelines of a publication usually state whether electronic submissions are acceptable. E-mail queries work well in three instances: if the idea you are proposing is time-dated and you need an immediate reply from an editor; if you and the editor have a long-standing professional relationship; or if the magazine has stated that its editors prefer e-mail rather than other types of correspondence. Throughout the publishing industry, e-mail correspondence has gained widespread acceptance. Some magazines even have a place on their websites where writers can pitch story ideas.

An e-mail query has the same two jobs to perform as a traditional query. It has to propose a great idea and convince the editor that the writer can deliver an equally great manuscript. The query is often shorter, but the author should include enough details to help the editor make the right decision.

Here's a sample of a query that pitches an article to an editor of a national general-interest magazine. Sending it by e-mail is permissible because the writer needs to find a buyer for the idea before the topic loses its timeliness. Also, she has written previous articles for the editor, is on a first-name basis with him and doesn't have to convince him of her skills. The major challenge is to ignite his enthusiasm for the topic she is proposing.

Dear Ted:

The city is magnificent in spite of itself. With scaffolds encasing its monuments and clean-up crews scaling its spires, St. Petersburg, Russia, is withstanding another siege—this one a massive makeover in preparation for the city's 300th anniversary celebration. The party will peak on May 27.

The perception persists that what's left of the old Soviet Union surely must be gloomy if not dangerous. A few assurances: Russia is safe, and Big Brother won't hassle anyone who aims a point-and-shoot camera at a government building. English is widely understood, and most places accept U.S. dollars as readily as rubles. American money goes far here, but shoppers aren't tempted to part with much of it. Antique stores offer icons and other remnants of the monarchy, but the buzz is that buyers have to relinquish all treasures at the border. The safest purchases are the most predictable—fake fur hats, T-shirts and an endless supply of nesting dolls. Among the most bizarre sets of dolls are those that depict Russian leaders and include Gorbachev with his signature head splotch, a woozy Yeltsin and a nondescript Putin. A favorite T-shirt reveals a profile of Lenin and the word "McLenin's" superimposed over the familiar Golden Arches of McDonald's. The back of the shirt carries the old communist symbol, the red star, and the message "The Party Is Over."

But residents of St. Petersburg hope the party is just beginning as they roll out the red carpet for tourists who want to celebrate the upcoming anniversary. What these visitors are likely to see is the subject of an article I'd like to write for the spring issue of your magazine. May I send you a draft on speculation? Great photos accompany the 2,000-word story that I have in mind.

Whether or not the editor agrees to consider an article about St. Petersburg won't depend on the writer's ability to deliver a good story. He is familiar with her work and her e-mail confirms her skill. However, that doesn't mean that he will say "yes" to her proposal. Editors reject article proposals for reasons that go beyond the ability of the writer or the value of the idea. Here are the top four reasons for rejection:

1 The magazine has a backlog of articles to publish before its editors buy new material.
2 Another writer is under assignment to produce an article on the same topic.
3 The article isn't right for the magazine's readers.
4 The magazine published a similar article a few months ago.

P.S. TRY AGAIN

Writers who bypass the query and send their completed articles to publications often experience a long wait. Unsolicited submissions typically end up in the slush pile, where they might spend several months before anyone looks at them. Editors evaluate query letters but they forward the slush to a first reader, who is likely to open each envelope and, simultaneously, reach for a printed rejection slip. Professional writers submit queries; beginners send manuscripts.

There are exceptions. In a few instances, even the professionals send completed articles. This is the case when a writer is dealing with a newspaper or magazine that states in its guidelines that it prefers manuscripts to queries. Editors of daily publications in particular often don't have time to engage in back-and-forth correspondence with freelance writers. They want to see the finished product. Magazine editors who usually prefer queries to manuscripts will make an exception for articles that are very short—two or three pages—or those that fall into the category of humor. Since it is difficult to describe what is funny, they like to judge for themselves.

Although rejection letters are part of every writer's life, some such letters are easier to take than others. Occasionally an editor will scrawl a postscript on the bottom of the dreaded rejection note. A personal comment—"great idea, but not right for us"—is meant to encourage the writer to keep trying. The unwritten message is: "Don't give up."

SAMPLE QUERY LETTERS

The following letters achieve the two goals of every query. They propose ideas that are timely and linked to trends unfolding right now. What's more, the authors leave no doubt that they are skilled writers who can handle the assignments—even though both are college students just beginning their writing careers. Notice the tone: conversational and almost breezy. The letters are short but show evidence of some research. Neither letter mentions the author's qualifications; the letters *show* that the students write well.

Sample query 1

Dear _____:

It's been three hours since you last logged in. You quickly enter your e-mail address and password expecting to find the usual details of your classmate's complicated relationship status or tagged photos from your best friend's luau. Five new notifications await you. One is from Alex: a comment on your wall from your new friend across the street. Another is from Alexis inviting you to next weekend's Thirsty Thursday party. Your heart drops as you look to see the last three are from none other than your own *mother*. Suddenly you realize your tainted innocence—the pictures, the status updates, a world you have worked so hard to keep secret—has been opened to the one person you never wanted to show. Mom, welcome to Facebook.

Whether students like it or not, individuals 35–55 years of age are the fastest growing population in social media. This sobering fact leaves many young adults in unknown territory. Do these students throw caution to the wind and continue to use their Facebook pages and Twitter feeds as means of escape, or do they choose to respond by hiding aspects of their relationships and life choices for fear of prying eyes?

With your permission I'd like to send you on speculation a round-up article featuring students' perspectives of parents in social media and stories of how they have responded. This story is timely because the term "helicopter parent" was recently included in the Merriam-Webster dictionary and because the 35-year-old age demographic now represents over 30 percent of the entire Facebook user base. Both students and parents will enjoy the insights from the various perspectives on this issue.

Sincerely,

Charlie Holcomb[3]

Sample query 2

Dear _____:

Beep. Beep. Item after item passes the checkout scanner. Beep. Hundreds of dollars worth of groceries are unloaded from the cart. Beep. Dozens of plastic bags are stuffed with assorted foods and supplies. Beep. The cashier scans the final item. Beep. At the end of her transaction, extreme couponer Chrissy Larkin leaves the store with a cart full of groceries and a check from Walmart for $37.

Larkin is a professional couponer who teaches seminars titled "Coupon Shopping 101" throughout her home state. She prides herself on teaching people to "save money or shop for free."

I recently have had the privilege of sitting down with Larkin to discuss the secrets to her money-saving success. She spoke about several surprising strategies that can turn anyone into an extreme couponer.

With your permission I would like to send you on speculation a how-to article teaching readers the key components of extreme couponing. This story is timely due to the current economy. In an economic recession, readers are searching for ways to save money. This story is also timely because of the TLC hit television series *Extreme Couponing*.

Sincerely,

Kelly Gualdoni[4]

IN-CLASS ACTIVITIES

Students: Prepare a one-page query letter outside class that pitches a timely article idea to a specific editor at a specific publication. Bring the letter to class in a form that allows everyone to view it simultaneously (either project it on a screen or distribute hard copies). The class will assume the role of a magazine's staff. After each student has presented his/her query, the magazine staff should offer feedback and render a decision: accept the proposed idea on speculation or reject it. The magazine staff may also suggest revisions to the query.

Students: This chapter contains three complete query letters—the first pitches a travel article about St. Petersburg, Russia; the second offers a witty overview of older Americans who are using social media and how their college-age children are reacting; the third proposes to teach readers how to save money by using coupons. Reread the letters in class and discuss:

- How does each author convey his/her knowledge of the topic?
- How does each author convey his/her competence as a writer without sounding boastful?
- How does each author grab the editor's attention in the first paragraph?

ASSIGNMENTS

Students: Write a few sentences that could be used as the closing paragraph for all your query letters. In it, explain in honest but positive language your qualifications as a writer. Keep it on file for frequent use.

Students: Choose an article that you have already completed. Write a query letter that uses the first paragraph of your article as the opening paragraph of your query. Write subsequent paragraphs that summarize the story and identify your sources. Add the closing paragraph that explains your qualifications.

NOTES

1   Hank Nuwer, *How to Write Like an Expert About Anything* (Cincinnati, Ohio: Writer's Digest Books, 1995).
2   Workshop lecture, May 21, 2004.
3   Used by permission.
4   Used by permission.

PART III

ADDING ACTION AND ANECDOTES

Editing a magazine is very much like throwing a party—and, as we all know, the best parties are about getting the right mix of people together.

Stefano Tonchi, editor in chief
W

Magazine writers know how to achieve a nice balance of facts, anecdotes, background and quotations from the right mix of people. With the skills of a news reporter and the gifts of a storyteller, the writer produces copy that often achieves a certain level of literary quality. Because magazine deadlines are more leisurely than those of daily journalism, their readers have higher expectations.

8

WHERE TO BEGIN

THE FIRST 100 WORDS

KEY POINTS

- Four tasks of a feature lead
- Nutgrafs and billboard paragraphs
- Leads that succeed
- Leads to avoid
- Establishing "bookends"

If the opening paragraphs of a feature story don't grab readers' interest, the content of the article—regardless of its importance—may remain forever unread. An article's introduction has four jobs to accomplish: attract attention, introduce the topic, set the tone and establish the point of view. To add to the writer's challenge, the best leads occupy limited space. The opening sentence of a newspaper feature may contain as few as 12 to 15 words; the opening sentence of a magazine feature lead may double or even triple that word count, depending on the audience.

Here are two examples from very different publications that are geared to highly specialized audiences. As you read them, ask yourself whether they accomplish the four tasks of effective leads.

- Of the 600 or so students enrolled each year at New York Theological Seminary (NYTS), only 15 are residential—but they are *extremely* residential. Each year 15 men from prisons throughout the state of New York are selected for the seminary's master of professional studies class

Feature and Magazine Writing: Action, Angle and Anecdotes, Third Edition.
David E. Sumner and Holly G. Miller.
© 2013 David E. Sumner and Holly G. Miller. Published 2013 by John Wiley & Sons, Inc.

that meets inside the walls of Sing Sing Correctional Facility in the town of Ossining.[1]

- "Ten years ago, Steve Jobs was alive, Bob Hope was alive, Johnny Cash was alive. Now we're outta jobs, outta hope and outta cash." I heard that from a TSA agent in New York the other day, as he eyed me for explosives. We laughed, but there was a poignant edge.[2]

Both lead paragraphs introduce serious topics. The first is about educating prisoners; the second is a commentary about the stalled economy. Both writers use a humorous tone to lighten their heavy topics. Both quickly establish the point of view—story one uses the third person; story two uses the first person. Both opening sentences contain fewer than 25 words. Neither writer has to "dumb down" her vocabulary because both publications serve readers who are well educated and knowledgeable about the topics at hand. The first example, taken from *In Trust* magazine, is aimed at governing boards of seminaries. The second example, published on the opinion page of *The Wall Street Journal*, is aimed at a readership that is savvy on economic and political issues. Although college students might not find either lead particularly engaging, both examples work well for their intended audiences.

COMING TO TERMS WITH LEADS

Organizing a feature story is a lot like solving a complex jigsaw puzzle. By the time you sit down in front of your computer screen, you've gathered an assortment of bits and pieces of information, many of them disjointed, that you now must assemble into a seamless "picture" for your readers. Where do you begin? Which note or quote do you pull from your stash of research and use to create that all-important paragraph that will lead into the content? Which piece do you set aside to serve as the perfect wrap-up to your article?

Many journalists agree that the most difficult part of writing articles is creating attractive leads and satisfying endings. One of our colleagues underscores the importance of strong beginnings and appropriate conclusions with this comparison. He says that feature articles, like airplanes, are most vulnerable to crash during takeoff and landing. His point: An article can contain great information, but, if the opening paragraph (the "takeoff") doesn't grab and hold readers' interest, they may turn the page and move on. The ending of an article, like the landing of an airplane, should be smooth rather than abrupt, fast-paced rather than prolonged. Like pilots who know their destinations before taking off, writers should identify their endings before beginning their articles. Otherwise they risk getting lost, taking detours or wandering in circles as they try to decide how and when to stop.

Writers use three terms—often interchangeably—to describe the opening paragraphs of feature articles. Each term has an appropriate meaning. "Lead" is a fitting description because an effective first paragraph *leads* readers into the story. "Hook" is an accurate term because a strong opening paragraph *hooks* readers' attention and nudges them to continue. "Introduction" is a logical label because writers use the initial paragraphs to *introduce* their topics and establish the tone and point of view of their articles. If a writer is going to tell a story from his own point of view, as in a personal essay, the word "I" is likely to appear somewhere in the lead. If the tone of the article is going to be conversational rather than academic, that attitude is going to be evident from the first sentence.

Writers often labor for hours over their introductory paragraphs. They fine-tune, add, delete and exchange words until they are satisfied. They scrutinize their notes in search of effective hooks. They experiment with anecdotes, provocative quotations and surprising facts that may have surfaced during the research phase. Some writers tell us that they can't move forward with their articles until they have the leads precisely as they want them. Other writers prefer to forge ahead, complete their rough drafts and then return to their opening paragraphs to do the fine-tuning—the adding, deleting and exchanging of words. Whichever process works best for you is the process you should follow.

Taken together, leads and endings serve as the bookends of articles. They hold everything in place. Once you have created the lead paragraph and the closing paragraph, you have established your boundaries. The next challenge is to arrange the remaining content in logical order. This is not easy, of course, but the lead paragraph should give you a direction and the closing paragraph should give you a destination.

BEYOND THE SUMMARY LEAD

Unlike reporters who cover breaking news events and get to the point quickly, feature writers have the luxury of setting up their articles with well-crafted and engaging opening paragraphs. This doesn't mean that they never use the familiar, no-frills summary lead that answers basic questions—who, what, where, when, why and how. It simply means that they have the flexibility to experiment with more engaging approaches.

Summary leads have taken a lot of criticism in recent years. They were the predictable way of getting into a story for so long that a backlash was inevitable. "Boring!" claim their critics. Maybe so, but what summary leads lack in creativity they make up for in information. Here are two examples of summary leads that appeared in articles related to the skyrocketing price of gasoline during the summer of 2008 and the spring of 2012.

The first lead introduced a news story published in *Rolling Stone*: "Four-dollar-a-gallon gas prices are eating away at the summer-concert business, with top festivals and tours taking unexpected box-office hits over the past few months."[3] This 29-word opening sentence contains, in a nutshell, the essence of the article. It answers the six basic questions. Who? Gasoline. What? Is eating into profits. Where? On the concert circuit. When? This summer. How? By reducing attendance. Why? Because prices have soared to $4 per gallon. Depending on their level of interest, readers could stop reading after the lead sentence or could continue to learn the details of those rock artists who played to capacity crowds and those performers who canceled their bookings.

A similar summary lead, published four years later, worked equally well to introduce a news feature also linked to rising fuel costs. *USA Today* tied escalating fuel costs with the calendar in this way: "Don't expect relief from high gasoline prices by flying to your spring break vacation. Airfares already are up this year, and every sign is they'll remain high for summer vacation, too."[4] Like the *Rolling Stone* lead, this one is aimed squarely at the publication's audience (*USA Today* is popular reading material for airline passengers). It answers many of the basic questions. Who? You (understood). What? Shouldn't expect relief from high gas prices. Where? On flights. When? Spring break. Why? Prices are soaring (again). The lead succeeds because it summarizes in two sentences the gist of the article. Subsequent paragraphs flesh out the story's premise with statistics, quotations from experts and anecdotes about people frustrated or angry about the high cost of airline tickets. Readers who are not interested in the supporting information can turn the page after the lead paragraph.

Some feature writers, bogged down by writer's block, create summary leads as a way to get a few words on their computer screens and achieve some momentum. After their articles have begun to take shape, they often go back to their summary statements and top them off with more creative leads. However, they don't delete the summary paragraphs. Instead, they keep them as their second or third paragraphs, often called billboard paragraphs or "nutgrafs." Such paragraphs, which we refer to throughout this book, tell readers what the story is about, in a nutshell. Many editors expect every article to contain a nutgraf or billboard paragraph. The logical placement is immediately after the lead.

LEADS THAT SUCCEED

In our opinion, few rules are unbendable when it comes to feature writing. A gifted writer can make almost anything work. For that reason, we encourage students to experiment with a variety of lead paragraphs and then decide which ones they like best. Factors to consider include:

- *The publication.* Many newspapers and magazines prefer short articles limited to a page that don't require much time to read. In these cases the editors are likely to depend on the old workhorse, the summary lead.
- *The topic.* How-to articles usually get to the point quickly because readers are anxious to access the advice and care little about creative introductions. Often profiles and articles that probe complex issues lend themselves to more leisurely treatment.
- *The audience.* Demographic data such as age, profession and education levels sometimes influence readers' preferences regarding writing styles. Persons who read for entertainment may enjoy descriptive opening paragraphs; persons who read for information may prefer a straightforward approach.

Every journalism textbook has its own vocabulary for classifying and describing leads. Except for the well-recognized anecdote lead, there are no universally recognized "types" of leads. We conducted an informal survey of about 60 articles in a dozen popular consumer magazines. About 80 percent of them mentioned a person in the lead—via either an anecdote, quote, narrative or scenario of some kind. In his book *Magazine Writing That Sells*, Don McKinney explained these four basic ways to begin a story:

- Start by telling a story.
- Start by letting someone else talk.
- Start by thrusting us into the action.
- Start by telling us what you're going to tell us.[5]

From the many options available, we've chosen to describe six leads that work well regardless of the publication, topic or audience. We accompany each description with one or two examples to serve as models.

Anecdote lead

Anecdotes are little stories about people that occurred in a specific place at a specific time. Often called the "chocolate chips of feature writing," they are perhaps the most frequently used leads in feature and magazine stories. Readers love these little stories that illustrate rather than dictate the important facts of a feature. In an article titled "Why China's Weight-Loss Industry Is Gaining," note the specific details in the opening anecdote that illustrate the larger theme of China's weight-loss industry:

> As an only child growing up in Shanghai, Simon Wang was plied with dumplings, ice cream and Kentucky Fried Chicken by his parents and grandparents. After tipping the scales at 220 pounds, the 26-year-old decided to join Weight Watchers last month.
> "I will get a heart attack more easily than a normal person," says Wang, who is 5 feet 9 inches tall and wants to shed 55 pounds. "When I get older I will have lots of problems, maybe high blood pressure and a lot of other illnesses."[6]

In writing about the desegregation of a Southern high school, journalist Josh Peter captured the story's essence with an insightful opening anecdote. The series of articles, published in *The Times-Picayune* (New Orleans), was a finalist in the "diversity" category of the annual "Best Newspaper Writing" competition sponsored by the American Society of Newspaper Editors. Notice how the opening three sentence fragments set the scene for the action that unfolds in the locker room.

> Friday night. Homecoming. An hour before kickoff.
> In the darkened locker room, hushed but for the sound of cleats scraping the concrete floor, one voice pierced the quiet.

"Juicy!"

Jarid Caesar called over teammate Anthony "Juicy" Trosclair, captain of the Riverside Academy football team, to hear the song he listens to before each game.

There they sat, side by side on a wooden locker-room bench: Trosclair, the white defensive lineman, and Caesar, the black running back, each pressing a headphone against one ear and nodding to the beat.

It was a moment once unthinkable at this small private school in Reserve.[7]

Scenario lead

By accurately recreating a place, the scenario lead allows readers to "see" the backdrop against which the story unfolds. The key to creating a successful scenario lead is to avoid too much description. Don't include every detail; be selective; use a light hand in sketching the environment. Let the reader's imagination take over from there and fill in the gaps.

In the following *Vogue* lead, the author invites her readers to join her—or at least to eavesdrop—as she and her guest enjoy a leisurely chat over a glass of wine. The guest is actress Meryl Streep; the project is a profile article that will occupy eight pages (plus cover) in the magazine; the newspeg is the release of *The Iron Lady*, the film about former British prime minister Margaret Thatcher. (Streep went on to win the Academy Award for her performance.) Before the author gets into the heart of the interview, she creates a sense of place. Notice her sparse but precise use of details. The conversation doesn't merely occur in the afternoon, but at 4:20; the site isn't just a restaurant, but the restaurant located on the mezzanine of Union Station. The use of present tense gives a feeling of immediacy.

> "Oooh, they have oysters," says Meryl Streep, perusing the menu with intent. "Would you like to get some oysters? Wouldn't oysters be great to eat right now?" It's 4:20 in the afternoon. We are the only people in the restaurant on the mezzanine at Union Station, Washington, D.C. I pass, but Streep says, "I think I'll have some oysters. And a glass of Chardonnay."[8]

Shock lead

Lead paragraphs that contain a shock element are likely to grab and hold readers' attention at least for a little while. They succeed if, in the course of doing research, the writer uncovers a truly surprising bit of information. Chances are the information that surprised the writer also will surprise the readers. Sometimes, as in the case of this first example, the lead sentence is relatively short. The humorous tone, established at the outset, continued throughout the article, as the author gave an overview of new electronic gadgets available to consumers. "Shortly before Valentine's Day, a study was released claiming that 47 percent of men in Britain would give up sex in return for a big-screen plasma television. As with all matters relating to technology, numbers are key: precisely how long were these men prepared to go without sex? And how large a screen?"[9]

Sometimes a writer combines categories of leads, as Wendy Brenner did for her introduction to a feature article for *The Oxford American*. The story was a finalist in a National Magazine Awards competition. Part shock and part anecdote, the opening paragraph is humorous and memorable. Notice the understated, casual tone.

> One day in 1971 in Wilmington, N.C., 14-year-old Dean Ripa was at home performing surgery on a cottonmouth snake, and it bit him. This was unfortunate for a couple of reasons. He knew enough about snakes to know he would probably not die, but he did need a ride to the hospital, which meant his parents were going to find out about the 50 snakes he was keeping in their spare room: rattlesnakes, the water moccasins he'd caught in local swamps, even several cobras he had purchased via mail-order—he had a king cobra years before he had his driver's license.[10]

Blind lead

A blind lead raises readers' curiosity by omitting a key piece of information. The omission causes readers to continue reading until they satisfy their curiosity. The lead is "blind" because it doesn't immediately identify by name the person or persons who are the subjects of the article. That important fact remains a mystery until a later sentence or paragraph clarifies it. In the following example, from a feature article about a former rock musician who dramatically changed his lifestyle and traded careers, readers don't learn the identity of the interviewee until the third sentence.

> Business majors can party. They can get wasted, wake up the next morning, hit 18 holes, and still make afternoon classes. But few have the expertise of

Duff McKagan, bassist for Guns N' Roses and Velvet Revolver, and student at the Albers School of Business and Economics at Seattle University.[11]

Direct or indirect quote lead

A quotation can serve as an effective lead if a speaker has said something noteworthy that sums up the article's main idea. A variation on the quotation lead is the indirect quotation lead. This works well if you want to capture the essence of what someone said but you don't want to use the speaker's exact words. Here are examples of both options. First, a direct quote from a fitness expert succeeds because his comment would likely surprise readers who hold different opinions. Thus it combines the shock/ surprise and direct quote categories. "'Unless you're training for a marathon, bike race, or triathlon,' says Rodolpho Reyes, 'Cardio is an inefficient waste of a guy's time.'"[12]

For a profile article about one of the world's best-selling romance novelists, a magazine writer opened with an indirect quotation and ended the paragraph with a direct quote. This lead contains elements of the scenario, indirect quote and direct quote leads.

> The trouble with writing at home, says author Janette Oke over the din of her dishwasher, is the ever-present lure of housework. It's always there, tugging her away from her computer, beckoning her from her research and causing her to leave her characters fending for themselves, mid-plot, somewhere out on the Canadian prairie. "Once a housewife, always a housewife," she adds with a shrug that lets you know she wouldn't have it any other way, thank you.[13]

Direct-address lead

The direct-address lead invites the reader to participate in the story. How? The writer speaks directly to the reader by using the word "you" in the opening paragraph. The resulting lead is much like a conversation between writer and reader. Often the narrator is offering friendly advice to the reader. The weakness of direct address leads is that the writer can appear condescending and fail to respect the intelligence of most readers. Another weakness is that the writer can assume that the described scenario is common or familiar to readers when it is not. That's why it's so important to know the characteristics of the readers for whom you are writing.

In the following example, the article's author first describes a common scam and then offers 10 suggestions on how not to become a victim.

> You think you're logging into the coffee shop's Wi-Fi network to check your e-mail. But you may actually be connecting to a crook. Scammers have gone public, invading libraries, airports, hotel lobbies, coffee shops and other spaces that offer public Wi-Fi network connections to the Internet.[14]

MISTAKES TO AVOID

The same characteristics that can cause introductory paragraphs to succeed also can cause them to fail. For example, including details is commendable, up to a point. But too much data can bog down a lead paragraph and turn it into a catchall. Some editors call this a "luggage lead" because the writer tosses in all sorts of random items. Rambling on and on, it may contain dates, ages and other specifics that the author would be wise to save and weave in later. Example: "Linda Brown, 45-year-old wife of John Brown and mother of Sue, 8, Jay, 6, and Bill, 2, launched a campaign in December to clean up the three-mile stretch of beach that edges her family's property on Long Island that is littered with trash from weekend campers who failed to observe the 'no trespassing' signs that Linda posted in July." (Huh?)

Touches of humor are always welcome, but sometimes writers try too hard to be cute and elicit groans instead of chuckles from readers. A profile article about cartoonist Jim Davis, creator of Garfield, is a case in point. Example: "Forget the nine-lives theory. Garfield, the fat cat in the orange and black glad wags, the one with the droopy lids, the thoughts that bite and the paws that refresh, is within a whisker of turning nine."[15] (Ugh!)

Giving human characteristics to inanimate objects can create funny pictures in readers' minds and distract readers from the article's content. Example: "If walls could talk, these would speak of five generations of a farm family trying to survive the tantrums of Mother Nature." The problem here is that readers know that walls can't talk and, although Mother Nature is capable of some wild weather, she doesn't throw tantrums.

Beginning an article with a question can engage readers, but asking a barrage of questions usually wilts them. Example: "Do you have a teenager who is approaching dating age? Are you worried by all the stories you've heard about kids making bad choices when they're out with friends? Are you wondering what you might do about it? Are you willing to carve out some quality time to address the issue?" (As a reader, are you tempted to turn the page?)

Many beginning writers, assigned to cover events, rely on chronological lead paragraphs that make their stories resemble the minutes of a meeting. Example:

> The concert began at 8:10 p.m., after the arena's maintenance crew fixed a problem with the sound system. The audience applauded the four back-up musicians when the band members came on stage, warmed up and then played a medley from their recent CD. The cheers grew louder as the lead singer of the group took her place in front of the microphone at 8:45 p.m. She cleared her throat and nodded to the drummer. He gave the countdown to the first song.

Perhaps the most objectionable introduction of all is the hypothetical lead that is the product of the writer's imagination rather than the result of his research skills. Feature writing, like news writing, is based on truth. A hypothetical lead is fiction and has no place in the media. Don't resort to concocting scenarios or creating imaginary or composite people. Say you are assigned to write an article about university students who spend a lot of time and money on campus but never complete their education. Hypothetical lead: "A college student, undecided about his career goal, might change majors five times before leaving school without a degree." Instead, you find a real person who faced the dilemma that your article explores. Lead based on research: "Joe Smith, a sophomore at UCLA, changed majors five times before leaving campus last June without a degree." (See the difference?)

ENDINGS THAT SATISFY READERS

Bringing an article in for a smooth "landing" is more of a challenge for the feature writer than for the news reporter. The traditional inverted pyramid organization is still acceptable for a news story. The reporter clusters the most important facts of a story in the opening paragraph. Subsequent paragraphs flesh out details in descending order of importance. The rationale for this kind of organization is that a reader can stop reading at any point and still know the highlights of the story. Or, an editor, pressed for space, can cut the article from the bottom without fear of discarding important information.

The feature article requires more thought and planning. A good article can "crash" in its closing paragraph if the author makes one of these mistakes:

- repeating information in an effort to re-emphasize a previously stated point
- supplying conclusions that the writer wants the reader to draw from the article
- leaving key questions unanswered
- allowing the story to dribble off or fade away without a sense of closure

Often the best way to identify an ending for an article is to revisit the lead paragraph. Many writers bring their stories full circle by returning to a question they raised in the lead, by quoting the person who was quoted in the introduction or by supplying the ending to an anecdote that served as the article's hook. For example, we know a writer who researched a story about how microchips embedded in animal collars have greatly reduced the frequency of pets being lost. The story began with an anecdote about a dog owner whose German shepherd went missing. The owner ran a lost-and-found ad in the newspaper for two weeks before someone spotted the pet and alerted its owner. The anecdote served as an introduction to the article that then explored the development, availability and effectiveness of microchips. The last paragraph of the story circled back to the pet owner for a wrap-up comment that articulated his intention to purchase one of the chips for his dog's collar.

IDENTIFYING THE BOOKENDS

If three writers were to tackle identical assignments and interview the same sources, they would likely come up with three different articles with three different leads and endings. There is no single "right" way to start a story, organize its major points and bring it to a conclusion.

As you scan your notes and transcripts, try to identify several possible leads and potential endings. Don't stop with just one lead or one ending; give yourself a range of choices. From these choices, select the lead that you like best and type it onto your computer screen. Next, select the ending that seems most appropriate and type that paragraph onto your screen. With your "bookends" in place, you can return to your notes and determine how best to arrange the material between the bookends.

If getting started is a struggle for you, try constructing a basic summary lead. You can always go back and improve on it. Creative writers recognize that they have several options and they allow themselves plenty of time to experiment before completing their final drafts.

IN-CLASS ACTIVITIES

Instructor: Invite a guest speaker to class (preferably a feature writer or lifestyle editor from a local newspaper or magazine). Students: Conduct an in-class interview that focuses on the person's career. After the interview, divide into teams, with each team creating two possible lead paragraphs. The first lead should be a simple summary sentence; the second should be an anecdote, a scenario or an indirect quotation.

Students: Review your notes from the in-class interview and identify a strong quote that would serve as an appropriate ending for the article. With the lead and ending in place, discuss how you would organize the rest of the article.

ASSIGNMENTS

Instructor: Assign students to read a specific feature article in a current magazine or in the lifestyle section of a large newspaper. Students: After reading the assigned article, create at least three alternative leads. Which do you prefer?

Students: Survey the opening paragraphs of several feature articles in major online and print magazines. Try to categorize them. Does a particular category of lead seem to dominate?

NOTES

1 Emilie Babcox, "Maximum-Security Seminary," *In Trust*, Autumn 2011, 5.

2 Peggy Noonan, "This Is No Time for Moderation," *The Wall Street Journal*, Oct. 15–16, 2011, A15.

3 Steve Knopper, "Gas Prices, Economy Shake Sales for Summer Tours," *Rolling Stone*, July 10–24, 2008, 18.

4 Bart Jansen, "High Fuel Costs Raise Price of Flying, Too," *USA Today*, March 14, 2012, B1.

5 Don McKinney, *Magazine Writing That Sells* (Cincinnati, Ohio: Writer's Digest Books, 1994).

6 Frederik Balfour, "Why China's Weight Loss Industry Is Gaining," *Bloomberg Business Week*, July 10, 2010. www.businessweek.com/magazine/content/10_24/b4182013742927.htm.

7 Josh Peter, "About Face, Part One, in *2005 Best Newspaper Writing* (Washington, D.C.: The Poynter Institute for Media Studies and CQ Press, 2006), 187.

8 Vicki Woods, "Force of Nature," *Vogue*, Jan. 2012, 106.

9 Patricia Marx, "Tech Stuff," *The New Yorker*, March 10, 2008, 82.

10 Wendy Brenner, "Love and Death in the Cape Fear Serpentarium," in *The Best American Magazine Writing* (New York: Columbia University Press, 2006), 267. (This article was originally published in *The Oxford American* and was later, as a finalist in the National Magazine Awards competition, included in *The Best American Magazine Writing 2006* anthology.)

11 Joel Stein, "Guns N' Capital," *Bloomberg Businessweek*, Oct. 3–9, 2011, 114.

12 Grant Davis, "Cardio Is Back," *Men's Journal*, Aug. 2008, 73–76.

13 Holly G. Miller, "Janette Oke: The Prairie's Own Companion," *Ink*, Dec.–Jan. 1994/1995, 20.

14 Sid Kirchheimer, "Hot Spot Hacker," *AARP Bulletin*, Sept. 2011, 24.

15 Holly G. Miller, "Jim Davis: He's Got the World by the Tail," *The Saturday Evening Post*, Nov. 1984, 52.

9

ACTION, BREVITY AND STYLE

KEY POINTS

- Create action using people
- Use action verbs
- Write in active voice
- Avoid dead constructions
- Include the details
- Write concisely
- Choose your viewpoint

In the early 1970s, audience research by *Time* magazine discovered that its "People" section had achieved the most readers of any department. This section contained brief news items about entertainers, sports celebrities, politicians and other public figures—news about their marriages, divorces, disputes, legal troubles, lawsuits and other such tidbits. *Time*'s discovery led to the company's launch of *People* magazine in 1974, which grew to become the United States' most profitable magazine 20 years later.

The moral of the story? People like to read about people's actions. For example, a travel story about the city of Luang Prabang, Laos, in *Condé Nast Traveler* began with this narrative about the daily routine of a Buddhist monk.

Feature and Magazine Writing: Action, Angle and Anecdotes, Third Edition.
David E. Sumner and Holly G. Miller.
© 2013 David E. Sumner and Holly G. Miller. Published 2013 by John Wiley & Sons, Inc.

Every morning at four o'clock, a thirty-one-year-old Buddhist monk named Say Phetchaleun gets up to pray. He wraps himself in one of his two papaya-colored robes, crosses the courtyard of his temple, and falls to his knees for an hour of meditation on the 227 rules by which he has vowed to live . . . . A former auto mechanic with a love for Lao pop music, Say has begun every day like this for the past four years. He hopes to spend the rest of his life doing the same.[1]

While the *Condé Nast Traveler* story went on to explore scenic sites in this city of 100,000 people, it began with an example of one person (a Buddhist monk) who illustrated the character and culture of the city.

People are behind every controversy, product, lifestyle trend and political issue. Writers use people to tell these stories because people invent products, create controversy, introduce laws, buy and sell stocks, discover cures and popularize new fads or hit songs. The informative and entertaining story must bring those people into the spotlight because readers are more interested in reading about what people do than in abstract concepts or ideas.

In 2008 *The New Yorker* published a story, "Up and Then Down: The Lives of Elevators," about the worldwide growth of the elevator industry. Filled with facts, statistics, trends and the history of elevators, the story could have been boring. The author, Nick Paumgarten, enlivened it, however, by telling about Nicholas White, a 34-year-old man trapped for 41 hours inside a stalled New York City elevator.[2]

Readers enjoy anecdotes like this for three reasons. First, anecdotes illustrate a general topic with a specific example and make it understandable. They create a real-life illustration of an abstract concept. Second, anecdotes show people doing things so readers can "see" them, feel their emotions and imagine themselves in the same situation. And third, anecdotes not only make articles more intriguing but also add credibility and believability. Readers more readily believe ideas or arguments when they see them occurring in a specific setting with real-life people.

All writing uses one of four basic building blocks: *narrative, dialogue, description* and *exposition*. Narrative involves "people doing things" and dialogue involves "people saying things." Exposition involves "explaining things" and description involves "describing things." Would you rather read about people or things? While that's an oversimplification, it explains why narrative and dialogue are crucial.

Narrative moves the story from point A to point B and finally to point Z. Dialogue makes people come alive through their conversations with each other. Consider these excerpts from *The New Yorker* story, "Up and Then Down: The Lives of Elevators," which illustrate these building blocks.

First, *narrative* describes action; it tells a story while moving through that story's points. The more narrative you include in your writing, the more it will hold readers because it creates movement and propels the action. For example:

> The longest smoke break of Nicholas White's life began at around eleven o'clock on a Friday night . . . . White, a thirty-four-year-old production manager at *Businessweek*, working late on a special supplement, had just watched the Braves beat the Mets on a television in the office pantry. Now he wanted a cigarette. He told a colleague he'd be right back and, leaving behind his jacket, headed downstairs [on the elevator].

Second, *dialogue* recreates conversation, which introduces human emotion and feelings. For example:

> The time passed in a kind of degraded fever dream. On the videotape, he lies motionless for hours at a time, face down on the floor.
> A voice woke him up: "Is there someone in there?"
> "Yes."
> "What are you doing in there?"
> White tried to explain; the voice in the intercom seemed to assume that he was an intruder. "Get me . . . out of here!" White shrieked. Duly persuaded, the guard asked him if he wanted anything. White . . . asked for a beer.

Third, *description* paints a word picture. The best stories create an experience of the senses. The reader doesn't only learn something from a good feature story; he feels, sees and hears it. While description can enhance some scenes, it's best to keep it brief because too much can bore the reader. The elevator story contained few examples of "description" because the story was mostly narrative, dialogue and exposition. But this paragraph describes the way that passengers typically arrange themselves in an elevator:

> "Passengers seem to know instinctively how to arrange themselves in an elevator. Two strangers will gravitate to the back corners, a third will stand

by the door . . . until a fourth comes in, at which point passengers three and four will spread toward the front corners, making room in the center for a fifth."

Fourth, *exposition* explains the background and context in which a narrative occurs. It introduces facts, statistics and concepts. Like description, keep exposition paragraphs brief and weave them throughout the story. For example:

In New York City, home to 55,000 elevators, there are 11 billion elevator trips a year—30 million every day—and yet hardly more than two dozen passengers get banged up enough to seek medical attention. The Otis Elevator Company, the world's oldest and biggest elevator manufacturer, claims that its products carry the equivalent of the world's population every five days.[3]

Exposition is the style of writing in which most textbooks are written (and we've tried to use as little exposition as possible). Most features in popular consumer publications are heavy with narrative, dialogue and quotes. They contain only enough description and exposition necessary to provide context for the story.

USE ACTION VERBS

The movie *Indiana Jones and the Kingdom of the Crystal Skull* began in the American Southwest during the height of the Cold War between the United States and the former Soviet Union. In it, Indiana Jones and his sidekick, Mac, just barely escape a clash with Soviet intelligence agents on a remote airfield. After Prof. Jones returns home to his job at Marshall College, the dean tells him that his controversial activities have made him suspicious and that the government has pressured the university to fire him. Soon after that, Jones meets an archaeologist who seeks his help in making what is possibly the most spectacular archaeological find in history—the Crystal Skull of Akator. So Jones decides to leave the college and travel with the archaeologist to the remote mountains of Peru to search for the treasure. But they quickly realize that Soviet agents are following, trying to beat them to the hidden site of the Crystal Skull.

This plot summary of the latest *Indiana Jones* movie illustrates the similarities between action-filled movies and action-filled writing. Compare it with this lead paragraph from an article about Peru in the *American Anthropologist*:

> Much has been written about the maritime foundations of Andean coastal civilization. One topic archeologists have focused on is the role of marine resources in early Peruvian prehistory. This debate involves questions about the extent to which marine resources were utilized relative to terrestrial animals and/or plants and whether marine resources could support sedentary Preceramic Period coastal populations. Early sites are found associated with the shoreline, river valleys and vegetative communities known as *lomas* . . . . Eventually more permanent settlements were possible in lomas, in part because marine resources were now exploited in addition to lomas ones.[4]

Which example do you prefer to read? Most people prefer the adventures of *Indiana Jones*. This comparison doesn't demean the importance of academic research and scholarly writing. But it does show that the styles of writing differ dramatically.

How many times have you started watching a movie that couldn't sustain your interest? The pace seemed slow and the plot ambiguous. You wondered whether you'd missed something. However, don't underestimate your viewing sophistication. The movie was probably boring.

Action-filled movies and action-filled writing display similarities. Action scenes and strong characters propel a movie and hold viewers' attention until the end. Every viewer knows how boring a talking head or purely scenic movie can be; it's the action that makes it interesting. Likewise, action scenes and strong characters propel good writing and hold readers' attention until the end.

The best feature writing uses action verbs in every sentence, avoiding verbs such as "is," "are," "was" and "be" as much as possible. To practice what we preach, this chapter uses few forms of the verb "to be" except for examples explaining why to avoid them. Using action verbs generates reader involvement more than any other writing technique. For example, Laura Hillenbrand's book *Unbroken* tells the story of Louie Zamperino, whose plane crashed in the Pacific during World War II and who survived on a raft for more than a month before Japanese soldiers captured him and took him to a prisoner-of-war camp. The book was named the "Best Nonfiction Book of the Year" in 2010 by *Time* and remained on the *New York Times* best-seller list for two years. This paragraph illustrates the heart of the action as the plane hit the ocean and sank:

As the plane disintegrated around him, Louie felt himself pulled deep underwater. Then, abruptly, the downward motion stopped and Louie was flung upward. The force of the plane's plunge had spent itself, and the fuselage, momentarily buoyed by the air trapped inside, leapt to the surface. Louie opened his mouth and gasped. The air hissed from the plane, and the water rushed up over Louie again. The plane slipped under and sank toward the ocean floor.[5]

Notice the action verbs: disintegrated, pulled, stopped, flung, spent, buoyed, trapped, leapt, opened, gasped, hissed, rushed, slipped and sank. Note these action verbs in the Indiana Jones example: begin, escape, return, tell, make, pressure, fire, meet, seek, decide, leave, travel, search, follow, beat.

Avoid the boring verbs is, are, was, were and be because they don't describe anybody doing anything. Here are some examples of weak verb phrases with revisions containing an action verb:

- the ideas *are* different / the ideas *differ*
- my decision *is* to quit smoking / I *decided* to quit smoking
- the teacher's conclusion *was* / the teacher *concluded*
- she *was* in a hurry / she *hurried*
- his belief *is* / he *believes*

SIDEBAR 9.1

Twenty-Six Action Verbs

accelerate	nudge
bargain	organize
convert	persuade
decide	quote
eat	reject
forecast	simplify
greet	translate
hurry	upgrade
invest	verify
join	win
kick	x-ray
laugh	yell
manage	zip

WRITE IN ACTIVE VOICE

Most students fail to recognize the difference between tense and voice. What's the difference? The verb's tense describes *when* the action occurs. The verb's voice describes whether the subject of the sentence *acts* (active voice) or the subject *is acted upon* (passive voice). You can write active or passive voice verbs in all six tenses: present, past, future, present perfect, past perfect, future perfect. The examples in Sidebar 9.2 use the subject "artist" and verb "design."

Active Voice vs. Passive Voice

Tense	Active Voice	Passive Voice
Present tense	the artist designs	is designed by the artist
Present perfect tense	the artist has designed	has been designed by the artist
Past tense	the artist designed	was designed by the artist
Past perfect tense	the artist had designed	had been designed by the artist
Future tense	the artist will design	will be designed by the artist
Future perfect tense	the artist will have designed	will have been designed by the artist

SIDEBAR 9.2

"Use active voice and not passive voice." You will hear this rule over and over again from teachers and editors for the rest of your career. Active voice creates better writing than passive voice for three reasons:

1 Active-voice sentences emphasize *who* performs the action.
2 Active-voice sentences always use *fewer words* than passive sentences.
3 Active-voice sentences *clarify* the "who did what to whom" relationship.

AVOID DEAD CONSTRUCTIONS

Dead constructions quickly bore the reader. One writer calls them expletives. Whatever you call them, these are phrases such as "there is," "there are," "there was," "there will be," "it is," "it was" and "it will be." These constructions display no life and convey no action. The pronouns "there" and "it" are on life support—used only because the author can't find a more colorful noun. The linking verbs—various forms of "to be"—lead your writing to the graveyard and the reader to the next page.

This rule has no exceptions: You can always improve a sentence beginning with a "dead construction" or "expletive" by eliminating the dead construction and replacing it with a noun and verb. Sidebar 9.3 displays some examples of dead constructions followed by recast sentences with an improved action-verb structure.

An article in *The Writer* by David Galef advises writers: "Go back to your old manuscripts and delete all those expletives. You'll be amazed how much it can tighten the prose. When should you do it? There's no time like the present. No, scratch that expletive. Do it now."[6]

SIDEBAR 9.3

How to Replace Dead Constructions with Action Verbs

Poor	There's a large animal in the professor's house.
Improved	A large animal roams the professor's house
Poor	There are flaws in his personality.
Improved	His personality is flawed.
Poor	It is time for the commissioners to do something about the water problem.
Improved	The commissioners need to fix the water problem.
Poor	There were tears in her eyes as she accepted the "Outstanding Editor" award.
Improved	Tears came to her eyes when she accepted the "Outstanding Editor" award.
Poor	It was a loud noise that shocked the dog.
Improved	A loud noise shocked the dog.

The following 100-word example from an academic business journal exhibits frequent use of passive voice and "is," "are" and "were" verbs.

> As a result of healthy market growth in recent years, the competition level within the Australian computer hardware market is assessed as moderate. Personal computers are becoming more of a necessity than leisure equipment due to the increasing importance of online communication, and large amount of information being processed on a daily basis. Buyers are generally price sensitive and more interested in the quality and specifications of products and customer' loyalty is rather low; brand awareness, when it exists, it is more towards manufacturers than retailers, reducing the power of the latter to some extent. The main suppliers are computer hardware manufacturers, often large sized, with operations established in many international markets.[7]

The revised example that follows contains half the number of words; no passive voice; no "is" "are" or "were" verbs; and no dead constructions. It uses these seven action verbs in its five sentences: grow, experience, consider, buy, examine, display and purchase.

> The Australian computer hardware market has grown in recent years and currently experiences moderate competition. Australian buyers consider personal computers a business necessity and not a leisure pastime. Before buying, they examine product quality, specifications and price. Buyers display more brand awareness and loyalty to manufacturers than to retailers. They purchase computers mostly from large international manufacturers.

INCLUDE THE DETAILS

If a dog comes snarling up to the screen door, give the reader the name and breed of the dog; for example, "Spike the pit bull came snarling up to the door." Instead of saying "This person graduated from college," say "The engineer graduated from the University of Hawaii." Here are more examples of making abstract words more detailed

Abstract: music
Detailed: rhythm and blues, heavy metal, hip-hop

Abstract: bad weather
Detailed: thunderstorm, rain and sleet, overcast

Abstract: flower
Detailed: lily, sunflower, zinnia

And here are some examples of replacing an abstract sentence with a concrete sentence:

Abstract: The audience enjoyed the concert.
Detailed: The audience gave the performer two standing ovations.

Abstract: He earned a fortune from concert performances last year.
Detailed: He earned $16 million from concert performances last year.

Abstract: The musician had a lousy day, and everything went wrong.
Detailed: The musician had a flat tire and lost her purse today.

Learn to fill your articles with colorful, specific details, and editors will love you. Give readers visual, auditory, olfactory, gustatory and tactile descriptions that will captivate their imaginations.

WRITE CONCISELY

"Since brevity is the soul of wit, and tediousness the limbs and outward flourishes, I will be brief," said Polonius in Shakespeare's *Hamlet*. This oft-repeated phrase, "Brevity is the soul of wit," means that articulate, intelligent speech and writing should use few, but wisely chosen, words.

While Carey Winfrey was editor of *Smithsonian* magazine, an independent research company named the magazine "most interesting" based on a survey of the readers of the digital editions of 170 magazines. In a tribute to Winfrey, a colleague wrote,

> His foremost concerns were clarity and brevity. The magazine's text editors all felt the sting of his "huh?" or "un-understand" penned in blue ink in a galley proof's margin. Clarity, of course, is the key to brevity, and he was forever urging writers and editors to get with it. "Right about here is where I'd be reaching for the remote," he would say of a too-long passage.[8]

Winfrey's comments indicate why every writer and editor values conciseness. Most lawyers and historians write reasonably well, but few of them master brevity and clarity. Why is brevity important for writers? Following are seven good answers. Wordy, redundant writing

- makes readers work harder to understand it
- takes more time to read
- bores and tunes out readers
- reveals a lack of appreciation for the reader's time
- reveals laziness on the part of the writer
- has a high unemployment rate with many words not having a real job
- shows a lack of vocabulary for the most accurate word

Wordy writing makes readers feel as if they are following a slow-poke driver on a no-passing highway. It annoys and frustrates them. Good writers know how to choose words that express precisely what they intend to say and no more. Good writers respect their readers. Here are some tips:

- Leave your opinions and observations out. Just the facts, please.
- Use lots of nouns and verbs. Ditch the adverbs and flowery language.
- Avoid "helping verbs" such as is, was, had, should, been, and so on. Stick to simple action verbs in present or past tense.
- Avoid beginning a sentence with dead constructions or "expletives."
- Make sure every word has a job—a job it shares with no other word.
- Create brevity by eliminating one word at a time. You don't have to delete whole paragraphs.
- Think like an editor and ask, "What does the reader need to know?" "Will the reader miss anything if I delete this sentence?"
- Make every sentence a zinger and not a slow-poke.

CHOOSE YOUR VIEWPOINT

First person? Second person? Third person? Most feature and magazine stories use the third-person viewpoint. The writer is the narrator. The writer tells a story about other people and reports an objective set of facts and circumstances. The words "I" and "you" occur infrequently. For many reasons, the third-person viewpoint is also the safest route for beginning writers.

If you don't have a clear reason to write in first person, then don't. Beginning writers want to use first person because it seems easy. They think it requires less research and reporting. But it's actually the most difficult kind of writing to do without boring or turning off readers.

"The number one mistake that most beginning writers make is to write in the first person automatically just because it feels comfortable, when the fact is that the reader doesn't know you and doesn't care about you," wrote Art Spikol, a *Writer's Digest* columnist.[9] It creates the impression that the writer thinks himself more important and influential than he is. Readers are not interested in the personal experiences of unknown writers.

On the other hand, the first-person viewpoint can enhance a few types of writing. First, you can write about yourself when you have a dramatic story to tell. Writing about true, life-and-death experiences clearly lends itself to a first-person narrative. *Guideposts* magazine, for example, publishes dramatic, inspirational stories written from the first-person viewpoint. These stories convey a tone of warmth and familiarity. Readers are interested in hearing the inspirational stories of people who have achieved success or overcome dramatic setbacks.

Second, when the article explains a news topic of wide public interest, the writer can share on-the-scene insights not possible in the third person. When the first-person viewpoint appears in feature stories in magazines such as *The New Yorker* or *Atlantic Monthly*, the writer's personal experiences are not the main point. The point is that the experiences add credibility because writers describe situations or incidents that they personally witnessed. The purpose of sharing these insights is not to draw attention to the writer's views but to bring insight to the news topic that he or she is discussing. When used judiciously, a first-person approach lends credibility to on-the-spot reporting and creates more rapport between the reader and the writer.

Another example of the first person is service journalism or how-to articles whose purpose is to give readers practical information. Writers can use the first person when they are experts or have significant experience with the topic they are exploring. Used this way, it can enhance both credibility and rapport with readers. However, the writer's credibility as an expert must be obvious to the reader. You have to introduce yourself as an expert with either formal credentials or experiences that qualify you to write authoritatively on the topic.

The fourth use of the first person is in personal essays, opinion pieces and blogs. Many magazines publish a personal essay page that invites contributions from readers. Newspapers publish syndicated columns and guest op-eds that frequently use first-person writing. Columnists and bloggers use the first person to establish a personal relationship with their readers. Most users of Facebook and Twitter write their messages in the first person.

In all cases, use the first-person viewpoint sparingly.

Great writers are invisible to their readers. Readers become so captivated by the material they are reading that they never think about who's writing it. Most readers don't care about writers' thoughts or experiences. Writing is like holding up a mirror and pointing it outward to reflect the sunlight. Your job is to reflect light on your subject.

Second-person writing using the "you" voice can create a personal relationship between the writer and the reader. It enables the writer to speak to the reader as one friend speaks to another friend. Second-person viewpoint is also effective in service journalism and "how-to" material; for example, this book. It can be combined with the first-person viewpoint when the writer is an expert on the topic.

The second-person viewpoint has two limitations, however. First, it can annoy readers when the writer uses it to create a false familiarity with the reader that doesn't exist. It's like strangers and clerks who call you by your first name the first time they meet you. Don't assume you "know" the reader; don't assume you know exactly what readers like or dislike, or what they have experienced. A second limitation is that it creates the risk of "talking down" or appearing condescending to the reader. The second person works best when it comes across as one friend talking to another— not as an expert telling a beginner how to do something. If the writer conveys any hint of arrogance, then readers will detect it.

The third person is the most common viewpoint in magazine and feature writing. While it depends on the tone and voice of the magazine, probably 90 percent of all magazine features are written in the third person. They follow the typical "he," "she" and "it" approach to reporting on the subjects, never mentioning "you," "I" or "we." The third person also the best approach for beginning writers. If you do excellent research and reporting, then all you have to do is tell the reader what you discovered. Good, solid factual reporting can—and will—speak for itself.

IN-CLASS ACTIVITIES

Instructor: Give students copies of a feature story you have chosen or use one of the Pulitzer Prize-winning feature stories available at Pulitzer.org. Students: Underline all verbs in active voice (in any tense) and circle all verbs or verb constructions in passive voice (in any tense). Discuss the passive-voice verbs and possible reasons why they were used.

Instructor: Send students an article you have selected in a Word document and ask them to use Word's grammar and spelling check to determine its readability statistics, including: (a) average number of words per sentence; (b) average number of characters per word; and (c) percentage of sentences in passive voice. Then ask them to determine the readability statistics for one of their own stories and compare the two.

ASSIGNMENTS

Students: Browse the stacks of academic journals in your school's library. Pick out a paragraph from an academic journal from any discipline and rewrite it more concisely using only active voice and action verbs, and no dead constructions.

Students: Revise the following five sentences (or others assigned by the instructor) to add action verbs and eliminate dead constructions: "there is," "there are," "there was," "it is" and "it was."

- There were 10 women competing for the title of homecoming queen.
- There are dozens of websites that offer advice and tips on preparing a résumé.
- It was thrilling to watch the team win its final game.
- It will be a mistake if your cover letter and résumé are not completely truthful.
- It is important to remember that success yields to hard work.

Students: Take a notebook on a 45-minute walk around a neighborhood or campus. List the 10 most vivid impressions made on you using your senses of sight, hearing, taste and smell. Use action verbs to describe your impressions.

NOTES

1 David Ebershoff, "Loving Luang Praband," *Condé Nast Traveler*, Aug. 2011. www.cntraveler.com/features/2011/08/Loving-Luang-Prabang (accessed July 9, 2012).

2 Nick Paumgarten, "Up and Then Down: The Lives of Elevators," *The New Yorker*, April 21, 2008, 106–115.

3 Paumgarten, "*Up and Then Down*," 106–115.

4 Elizabeth J. Reitz, "Faunal Remains From Paloma, an Archaic Site in Peru," *American Anthropologist*, New Series, 90, 2 (June 1988), 310–322.

5 Laura Hillenbrand, *Unbroken: A World War II Story of Survival, Resilience, and Redemption* (New York: Random House, 2010), 119.

6 David Galef, "Expletives Deleted," *The Writer*, Jan.–Feb. 2012, 27.

7 "Computer Hardware Industry Profile: Australia," *Marketline Industry Profile: Computer Hardware Industry Profile: Australia* (London, Feb. 2012), 1–24.

8 Terence Monmaney, "Most Interesting; Winfrey Steps Aside After a Decade," *Smithsonian*, Dec. 2011, 5.

9 Art Spikol, *Magazine Writing: The Inside Angle* (Cincinnati, Ohio: Writer's Digest Books, 1979), 109.

10

ANECDOTES

MINING FOR GOLD

KEY POINTS

- Definition: little stories that illustrate big ideas
- The power of anecdotes
- Six characteristics of anecdotes
- Where to find great anecdotes

> In the spring of 1962, Timmie Jean Lindsey was a 30-year-old Texan with a past. She had six kids, a deadbeat ex-husband, and an ex-boyfriend who had talked her into tattooing his name on her chest. She wanted to rid herself of the garish tattoo, but at Houston's Jefferson Davis hospital, she met a doctor who had an even more daring idea: After having felt a warm silicone bag of blood and thinking it felt awfully nice, he and a colleague had recently invented a new breast implant—and needed a human guinea pig.

An article about a surgical procedure that originated five decades ago could be clinical and boring or—as the above lead paragraph illustrates—clever and funny. It also could qualify as a "calendar-related" feature story (see Chapter 15), as in the case of this article, which marked the golden anniversary of a now-common elective operation. In 2012, the author, Florence Williams, caught up with Timmie Jean Lindsey, who underscored the calendar connection with the following comment: "'That's how it all started,' says the 80-year-old Lindsey, on the 50th anniversary of the first silicone implantation."[1]

Feature and Magazine Writing: Action, Angle and Anecdotes, Third Edition.
David E. Sumner and Holly G. Miller.
© 2013 David E. Sumner and Holly G. Miller. Published 2013 by John Wiley & Sons, Inc.

In a one-page article in the high-style magazine *W*, Williams managed to include the history of breast implantation, up-to-date statistics and a prediction about what's next for patients eager to embellish nature's gifts. Over time, readers might forget the facts and stats in the article, but they likely will recall the "human guinea pig" who was the first to go under the knife 50 years ago.

People remember anecdotes—little stories that illustrate big ideas. For that reason, feature writers use them as leads and endings; they also scatter them throughout their articles to clarify and humanize data. Some of the best anecdotes surface during the interview process when the interviewer presses his interviewee for specific details about a key moment or event. Another good source for memorable anecdotes is a writer's personal experience. This was proven more than two decades ago by a couple of entrepreneurs with a creative book idea that almost never made it to print.

The story goes this way: Two pals, Jack Canfield and Mark Victor Hansen, assembled a manuscript of more than 100 heartwarming anecdotes that they felt certain would lift the spirits of readers. They offered their collection to 140 publishers, none of whom shared their enthusiasm for the project. Undaunted, the authors visited a booksellers' convention in California and convinced an editor from a small Florida press to read a few pages on his flight home. The editor opened the package in an airport lounge and soon had tears streaming down his cheeks. The result? Hansen and Canfield had a deal, *Chicken Soup for the Soul* had a publisher and America had a best-seller. With more than 112 million copies of their books now in print (200 titles, 40 languages), the authors have ladled chicken soup for the woman's soul, the baseball fan's soul, the bride's soul, the Canadian's soul, the writer's soul—the list goes on and on.

We retell this familiar success story for two reasons. First, the phenomenal sales of the *Chicken Soup* series prove that readers love little stories, especially those that are dramatic, inspiring or humorous. (The books hold the world record for having the most titles on *The New York Times* best-seller list at one time.) Second, the story about Canfield and Hansen is an example of an anecdote. It's an anecdote about anecdotes.

CREATING A SCENE

Most editors will tell you that the best feature articles connect with readers' emotions, and this makes a feature story memorable. "Editors see tons of 'sermonic' articles," says Mary Ann O'Roark, a former editor at *Seventeen*, *McCall's* and *Guideposts*. "In those articles, the writer says, 'Here's my wisdom, and I impart it to you.'" The result is a "stuffy lineup of information," explains O'Roark. Instead, "editors want good stories prepared in ways that engage readers. An article must entertain before it can educate and enlighten."[2]

One way that a writer can create engaging and entertaining articles is by learning to identify, write and place anecdotes. These tightly composed mini-stories are as much at home in speeches, sermons, comedy monologues and books as in feature stories. They create attention-getting leads, satisfying wrap-ups and colorful illustrations throughout a manuscript. They humanize dry data. Example: An article about a major medical breakthrough may contain all sorts of important information, but the article becomes memorable when the author inserts an anecdote about a patient whose life has changed because of the medical breakthrough.

People want to read about other people. Long after readers forget the key points of a story, they remember the colorful anecdotes that showed rather than told the significance of the key points.

THE POWER OF THE ANECDOTE

Fiction writers are skilled at creating memorable anecdotes. They know the techniques of building drama, painting word pictures and describing characters so realistically that readers understand and care what happens to the characters. For this reason, book publishers occasionally hire novelists to serve as writers or ghostwriters for nonfiction books. The publishers want their nonfiction books to have the same color, impact and readability as a good novel. That doesn't mean they want the writer to fudge on facts or embellish the truth. Absolutely not. Accuracy is the top concern of all writers of nonfiction, even novelists recruited for nonfiction projects.

What fiction writers bring to nonfiction assignments is something that goes beyond the essential ABCs—accuracy, brevity and clarity—of good journalism. They have mastered the art of storytelling. They have the ability to describe real people and actual events in compelling ways. They recognize when a piece of writing is starting to lose momentum, and they understand how to pick up the pace by inserting a poignant or humorous true story or scene. They have the skill to add dabs of color to what might have been a black-and-white documentary.

CHARACTERISTICS OF ANECDOTES

You don't have to be a fiction writer to craft memorable anecdotes. Successful feature writers follow six pieces of advice.

Keep them short

Anecdotes should never overshadow the points they support or the topics they illustrate. They should not be so long or so strong that they pull readers' attention away from the main subject of the article. This means that writers, after creating anecdotes on their computer screens, read and reread the sentences aloud, zapping words and deleting punctuation as they go. They notice adverbs and adjectives and remove those whose presence they can't defend. After they have reduced the story to its bare bones, they edit the remains.

This search-and-destroy mission is a familiar process that skilled writers have followed for centuries. As an example: The Irish poet and playwright Oscar Wilde once arrived at a party complaining of exhaustion. His host asked why he was so tired. "All day I worked on one of my poems," explained Wilde. "In the morning I took a comma out, and in the afternoon I put it back in."

Make them relevant

This 51-word anecdote about Oscar Wilde illustrates the point that the paragraph previous to it makes—that good writers constantly tinker with their copy, even spending time debating the need for a comma. The Wilde story was relevant to the topic. We included the longer anecdote about *Chicken Soup for the Soul* earlier in this chapter because it continued the discussion of anecdotes in general and underscored the idea that little stories are popular with readers. Again, it was relevant to the topic.

An anecdote must have a purpose; otherwise, it only adds clutter to an article. As we said in Chapter 8, anecdotes often make effective lead paragraphs. Used as a lead, an anecdote can fulfill three important purposes:

- It can provide a colorful introduction to the topic of the article by piquing readers' interest and luring them into the article.
- It can create an emotional bond with readers by describing a familiar situation. This prompts the reader to respond, "I've been there; I've felt that same way."
- It can establish the tone of the article. If it's light and breezy, it signals that an article will be entertaining and fun to read.

Some anecdotal leads serve all three purposes. They introduce a topic, build a bond with readers and create a tone that will carry throughout the text. As an example, students trying to decide where to enroll in college might identify with the co-ed featured in this anecdotal lead in a *Wall Street Journal* feature:

> As a high-school senior from Connecticut, Diva Malinowski took a coast-to-coast tour of 10 public universities, bearing acceptance letters from each.
>   She fell in love with Fargo.
>   "The minute I stepped onto campus, I knew that North Dakota State was for me," says Ms. Malinowski, a 21-year-old senior who matriculated from Miss Porter's School, a private academy for girls in Farmington, Conn.
>   Ms. Malinowski is evidence of an unlikely trend: the growing allure of higher education in North Dakota.[3]

The last sentence—"the growing allure of higher education in North Dakota"—serves as a bridge to the article's main point. The feature isn't about Diva Malinowski; instead, it explores the surprising trend of students from more sophisticated (and warmer) home states opting to head west to spend four years in a state that ranks 48th in the United States at attracting tourists.

Keep them real

A strategy that often strengthens the bond between writer and reader is including the word "you" in the lead anecdote. In Chapter 8, on hooks and leads, we called this the direct-address lead. By using "you," a writer reaches out as if to say, "Hey, reader, pay attention! I'm talking to *you!*" In the following example, the common bond between writer and reader works only if the reader is old enough to relate to the situation that the lead describes.

> You're downsizing. After so many years at the same address, you've decided to make your move. Florida, maybe. Or perhaps a smaller, more manageable place close to home with less lawn to mow and driveway to plow. Your friends recommend the laid-back life of a condo community. Sounds inviting. Whatever the choice, only one thing stands between you and your new digs. The attic.[4]

This lead introduced a how-to article that helped readers to separate trash from treasure as they cleaned out attics and basements and prepared to relocate. Obviously geared to older readers, the one-paragraph lead contains 64 words. Six of those words are a form of "you." Taken together, the sentences describe a problem that "you" (the reader) faced—getting rid of a life's accumulation of stuff. Subsequent paragraphs resolve the problem and provide the end of the anecdote. To qualify as an anecdote, readers need to know the solution that "you" discovered.

The problem with the direct-address approach—and the reason we recommend it with caution—is that it often results in a hypothetical anecdote that the writer invents rather than a situation that he reports. A similar lead, based on *real* people facing a *real* dilemma, can establish the same kind of bond:

> Susan and Don Shaw are downsizing. After so many years at the same address, they're making their move. Florida maybe. Or perhaps a smaller, more manageable place close to their Minneapolis home with less lawn to mow and driveway to plow. Their friends recommend the laid-back life of a condo community. That sounds inviting, they admit. Whatever the choice, only one thing stands between them and their new digs. The attic.

Stress the specific

A powerful anecdote gives readers a tightly focused example that illustrates a general idea. It has one or two specific people doing specific things at a specific time and place. The more specific you are, the more impact the anecdote has. As an example, which of the following sentences do you prefer as the lead paragraph to an article about teen runaways?

- A Texas teenager ran away from home last winter because she was tired of her parents' arguments. She's still missing.
- Three days after Christmas, Meg Jones, 13, stuffed a pair of jeans and a T-shirt into her backpack and ran away from her parents' split level in a posh suburb of Houston. She couldn't tolerate their bickering any longer. They still haven't found her.

Whenever you add specific information to a story, you also add words. This means you must make a decision: Should you be brief or should you be specific? The answer is that writers should be brief *and* specific. Most writers include a range of anecdotes in their articles. They want variety. One anecdote might be of the bare-bones variety and contain only two or three sentences. Another may be more fully fleshed out and offer several details. The writer decides the degree of development that each anecdote deserves. If an article runs long, the writer looks for anecdotes to trim or delete. A good test to give a manuscript is to remove an anecdote and then read the manuscript from beginning to end. If the article flows well and is interesting, the anecdote was unnecessary.

Give them a beginning, middle and end

If an anecdote lacks these elements, it doesn't qualify as a little story. As we indicated in Chapter 8, writers often create scenarios that serve as backdrops to their stories. These scenarios are colorful but they don't tell a complete story. Instead, they set the scene for a story. Here's an example of a scenario:

> Long before the borrowed white limo delivered its very important passenger to the entrance of the Bowling Green, Ky., Holidome, word went forth to expect someone special. The clue was Room 168. Flowers had arrived at 11; a fruit basket followed at noon. By 12:30, green punch, wheat crackers and a cheese ball under plastic were arranged smorgasbord-style on the boguswood credenza.[5]

This opening paragraph gives readers a sense of how people in a small town prepared to welcome a celebrity guest, in this case Miss America Sharlene Wells. It describes a place, complete with flowers and fruit. However, until something happens to someone, it's not an anecdote. Later in the same article, the writer offers readers an anecdote:

> A few days after winning the Miss America title in Atlantic City, Wells was interviewed and photographed by a words-and-pictures duo from *People* magazine. She had the sniffles, her eyes were bleary and, besides that, her feet hurt. The photographer assured her that the picture he wanted was the heads-and-shoulders variety—she had no reason to put on her shoes. She acquiesced, secured the crown to her blonde hair, arranged the folds of her reptile-patterned dress and assumed a regal pose.
>
> Imagine her shock the next week when the picture was published full frame—her stockinged feet revealing a full complement of Dr. Scholl's medicated disks. Ouch. The California designer Mr. Blackwell promptly named her to his infamous worst-dressed list and said she looked like an armadillo in corn pads. "Wasn't that cute?" she asks. "I learned never to trust a photographer."[6]

These paragraphs do more than create a scenario. They tell a cause-and-effect story. Something happened to Miss America and that "something" qualifies it as an anecdote. A photographer duped her into posing for a picture (cause). She was embarrassed after she saw the picture in print (effect). At the end of the anecdote she is a slightly different person because she has learned something from the experience.

In the case of a split anecdote, the beginning of the anecdote serves as the article's lead, and the end of the anecdote, many paragraphs later, concludes the article. Readers have to complete the entire article to find out what happened to the person introduced in the opening paragraph. Example: Suppose you are writing an article about the dangers of not wearing a seatbelt. You interview someone who was almost killed in an automobile accident, and you decide to use half of the story as your lead. It might sound like this:

> Bill Ryan never thought it would happen to him, but last Valentine's Day the unthinkable occurred. He hadn't snapped his seatbelt in place because he was only driving a few blocks to pick up his son after swim practice. He saw the van approach, clearly out of control. He heard the screech of brakes, felt himself lifted from the driver's seat and catapulted forward. Then everything went blank.

You stop short of telling readers the rest of Bill Ryan's story. Instead, you continue the article. You offer statistics about seatbelt usage and include comments and advice from various experts whom you interviewed. Not until the last paragraph of your article do you return to Bill Ryan and answer the questions that your lead raised.

> Ryan was one of the lucky ones. He limped out of the hospital—pins in both legs—four weeks after his car's head-on collision with the van. The doctors who patched him up say that with six months of physical therapy he'll be as good as new. He claims he'll be better than new because "Now I know how fragile life is, and I'll never put mine on the line again."

Place them strategically

You can overdo a good thing. If you have uncovered two great anecdotes that support the same point, don't use both. That's like assigning two people to do one person's job. Select the story you like the best and file the second for possible use in some future writing project. An overabundance of anecdotes can turn an article into a disjointed collection of random stories.

Deciding where to drop in an anecdote is a skill that all feature writers should cultivate. Too many writers, aware of the power of a good story, grab readers' attention with colorful anecdotal leads but then consider their jobs done. They follow the anecdotes with paragraph after paragraph of dry facts, which risks lulling readers to sleep. Strategically placed throughout an article, anecdotes can give readers a "time out" from information overload. A colorful illustration can offer a welcome pause in an article's narrative, insert the human element and underscore a point.

As an example, midway through an article about body language—"How to Read Between the Lines"—a magazine writer feared her article contained too much advice and was beginning to sound sermonic. She tucked in an anecdote to give readers a break and to illustrate the effectiveness of strong body language. The little story added humor and color as it described a meek secretary's confrontation with a gruff executive. To lead into the anecdote, the writer quickly explained the background of the story: A secretary had been asked by her boss to pull together a report. On the day it was due, her boss wasn't around and she needed someone to approve what she had written before she mailed it. This led to a face-to-face standoff with a man several rungs above her on the corporate ladder. The article's author let the secretary tell the story in her own words.

"The executive looked at me and growled, 'What do you want?' I explained I was on a tight deadline and politely asked him to read my report to make sure it was correct. The man bellowed, 'I don't have time!' I marched across his office, planted my feet firmly in his carpet, and folded my arms as if to say, 'I'm here to stay.' He put his head down, shuffled his papers and tried to ignore me. But I never stopped staring at him. After a few minutes he looked up, grumbled, and reached for the article." Not until she had left his office with the wad of approved pages tucked under her arm did she begin to shake. "I couldn't believe my boldness," she said.[7]

The vivid scene, complete with "he-said-she-said" dialogue, makes a point and creates a bond with readers who identify with the secretary. The article's writer could have made the same point by simply stating "strong body language has the capacity to empower a powerless person." Instead, the writer chose to use an anecdote to illustrate the fact and to add some zest to the article.

SEARCHING FOR ANECDOTES

The best anecdotes are those that you discover in the course of your interviews. This ensures that the colorful little stories that you include in your articles haven't appeared in dozens of other articles. Use these questions frequently when you interview people: "Could you give me an example of that?" "Can you tell me about a time when it happened to you?" "That" or "it" in these questions could refer to any statement or point your interviewee has made. In a pinch, you can always find memorable anecdotes in published collections or on websites. These anecdotes typically deal with historical events and famous people. However, they may lack freshness. The anecdotes about Oscar Wilde and the *Chicken Soup* books, told earlier in this chapter, are examples of often-repeated stories.

Hal Karp, a contributing editor who writes frequently on auto safety for *Reader's Digest*, says that finding good anecdotes is difficult but essential. "I often spend two or three days or even a whole week trying to find one anecdote," he admits. Where does he look? He makes telephone calls to "points of contact" related to the type of anecdote he's seeking.

For example, if I'm looking for accident victims, I ask, "Where are all the points of contact for an accident victim?" Victims come in contact with paramedics, police and emergency room doctors. So I start going down the list. I call fire departments, paramedics and law enforcement officers.[8]

The way you phrase your questions during interviews can determine your success in drawing out new and memorable anecdotes. Let's review four of the anecdotes included in this chapter and try to guess the questions that brought forth the stories.

Questions for the North Dakota State student:

1 As a high-school student in Connecticut, how did you hear about North Dakota State?
2 Describe your first impression of Fargo when you stepped off the plane.
3 As you weighed the pros and cons of the campuses that you visited, what gave N.D. State the edge?

Questions for Miss America Sharlene Wells:

1 What was the first mistake you made after winning the pageant?
2 Describe the interview that led to the embarrassing picture in *People* magazine.
3 Recreate the moment when you first saw the published photograph. How did you react?

Questions for accident victim Bill Ryan:

1 Beginning with the time you got into your car, recount the drive that led up to the accident.
2 What went through your mind as you saw the van coming toward you?
3 Describe the scene when you first regained consciousness in the hospital emergency room.

Questions for the secretary who confronted her supervisor:

1 What circumstances led to your standoff with the corporate executive?
2 Recreate those few moments when you were at an impasse in his office.

3 What went through your mind as you stood your ground and waited for his response?

Most people speak in generalities. They gloss over major moments with simple statements such as "I was angry," "I was embarrassed" or "I was scared." Beginning interviewers accept the generalities and move on to their next questions. Sharp writers recognize the potential drama behind such statements, zero in for details and don't stop asking questions until they have the whole story, told in living color.

IN-CLASS ACTIVITIES

Students: One of the anecdotes in this chapter—the *Chicken Soup for the Soul* story—contains about 150 words. Edit the story to fewer than 100 words. Read out loud.

Instructor: Bring to class three or four published feature articles that have anecdotal leads. Read the opening paragraphs to the class and see whether the students can discern the topics of the articles. Discuss whether or not the anecdotes serve as smooth and colorful introductions to the subjects that the articles examine.

ASSIGNMENTS

Students: Ask a friend to describe a specific moment of victory or defeat. Through follow-up questions, try to pull out as many colorful details as you can. After you have collected the information, shape it into an anecdote of three sentences. Review the material and flesh out the story to a paragraph of about 150 words. Split the anecdote in half in such a way that the first half might serve as the lead of a feature article and the second half might serve as the ending of the article.

Students: Visit the website of the *Chicken Soup* book series (Chickensoup.com). Follow the "Submit a Story" menu, which includes guidelines for submission. Create a possible entry that complies with the guidelines.

NOTES

1   Florence Williams, "Golden Globes," *W*, May 2012, 84.
2   Lecture, July 29, 2004.
3   Kevin Helliker, "Frigid North Dakota Is a Hot Draw for Out-of-State College Students," *The Wall Street Journal*, July 16–17, 2011, 1.
4   Holly G. Miller, "Treasures in the Attic," *Columns*, Spring 2004, 7.
5   Holly G. Miller, "On the Road with Miss America," *The Saturday Evening Post*, May–June 1985, 42.
6   Miller, "On the Road," 43.
7   Holly G. Miller, "How to Read Between the Lines," *Today's Christian Woman*, Oct.–Nov. 1991, 76–78.
8   Interview with David E. Sumner, Nov. 15, 2003.

PART IV

DIFFERENT FORMATS, DIFFERENT RESULTS

"If someone knows me and likes my work, they're more likely to allow me to tell their story. But it also cuts the other way."

Anderson Cooper, television journalist

At the heart of all feature stories is the interview. After they've gathered information from background resources and one-on-one conversations, writers have the option of shaping the material into a variety of forms such as profiles, trend stories, how-to articles and briefs.

11

BRIEFS

SHORTCUTS TO PUBLICATION

KEY POINTS

- Offering a local angle
- Briefs vs. fillers
- Shopping for shorts and briefs
- Flexible list articles
- Pulling from personal experience

Magazines that have interactive websites—and most of them do these days—give editors up-to-the-minute reports on the topics and issues that interest their readers. Staff members can monitor which articles in the online versions of the publications attract the most "clicks" or "hits." Editors value this information as they plan future content. Frequently the most popular features are not the in-depth cover stories that occupy much of the magazine's pages but the colorful blurbs, briefs and brighteners that pepper the pages throughout the issue. These quick-read items can take the form of a flexible list, a stand-alone anecdote that prompts a laugh or makes a point, a timely piece of advice, a mini-profile that explores a single aspect of its subject, or a sidebar to a long feature. Briefs often help new writers to get their foot in the door of national publications.

The length and range of fillers, shorts and one-pagers vary; briefs include everything from 50 words for a quip or quote to 750 words for a mini-profile or personal essay. Readers like "shorts" because they are quick to

Feature and Magazine Writing: Action, Angle and Anecdotes, Third Edition.
David E. Sumner and Holly G. Miller.
© 2013 David E. Sumner and Holly G. Miller. Published 2013 by John Wiley & Sons, Inc.

absorb and less intimidating; they offer variety, can be clipped and saved, and play to the current preference for skip-and-skim media. Art directors and layout editors welcome short items because they add color and energy to a page. They can be clustered, boxed, set at an angle or dropped as an attention-getter onto an otherwise gray page. Editors value short items because they ensure flexibility. If a major feature article runs long, an editor can remove a short to accommodate the need for extra inches. If an advertiser decides at the last minute to cancel an ad, the editor can retrieve a self-contained short from a file and plug it into the open page without disrupting the rest of the publication.

OFFERING A LOCAL ANGLE

Unfortunately, many new writers overlook the opportunity to break into print with short, and often local, items. We know of an aspiring young travel journalist, bound for Europe on his first trip, who mailed a flurry of query letters to newspaper and magazine editors offering lengthy articles about every stop on his itinerary. Using a bulleted format sometimes called a gang query because it includes multiple story ideas, he tossed out three possible titles:

- "Barging Through Burgundy"
- "Jack the Ripper's London"
- "Prague's Incredible Flea Markets"

The ideas were creative, yet all but one editor responded with a standard thanks-but-no-thanks rejection note. The lone encourager was a staff member at one of the giant New York-based travel magazines who scrawled across the bottom of the query: "Sorry, foreign assignments only go to our senior contributors." Then the editor added as an afterthought, "But I notice you're from Ohio. Anything going on out there?"

The beginner didn't realize that some national publications—not just travel magazines like this one—produce as many as four or five regional editions. The cover story and most main features in an issue don't vary, but a certain number of pages are dedicated to editorial material about people and places within a specific region. For example, magazines shipped to the West Coast might contain a one-page story about a small family winery in

California's Anderson Valley; readers in the Southwest won't see the winery story but they'll be alerted to a new bed-and-breakfast inn near Santa Fe. Midwest subscribers won't have access to either the wine or the inn stories but might read about the growing popularity of the annual Heartland Film Festival in Indianapolis.

Regional editions make sense for a couple of reasons. First, readers are eager to learn about people close to home and about things they can do and see on a tank of gasoline. The publication that offers a steady stream of ideas for regional attractions is likely to build readership and retain subscribers in those locations. Second, advertisers are more apt to buy space in publications that contain stories linked to their service areas. A small airline that schedules daily flights in and out of Key West, Fla., might be interested in placing an advertisement in a publication that features "The Cuban Cuisine of Key West."

Editors who operate from offices in New York City, Los Angeles or Chicago need to know what is new and interesting in out-of-the-way places around Key West, Fla.; Santa Fe, N.M.; and, yes, Indianapolis, Ind. They're interested in bright and brief articles that offer readers a variety of content choices. The editor who asked the Ohio freelancer "Anything going on out there?" was dead serious. The smart writer should have taken the hint, forgotten about the barge in Burgundy and checked out the riverboat docked near Cincinnati or the fabulous rose festival each June in Columbus.

THE WIDE, WIDE WORLD OF SHORTS

Short articles seldom require a query letter (we explained queries in Chapter 7) and they serve as foot-in-the-door features that can eventually lead to major assignments, internships or—best of all—permanent jobs. The student journalist who feeds a New York editor a constant stream of brief but bright items from Ohio, Oregon or North Carolina may earn a place in the publication's stable of trusted contributors. The editor lets the writer know about major stories slated for future publication and the writer responds with related shorts that help expand the articles into editorial packages.

Example: An editor plans a feature about a new crop of young entrepreneurs—recent college grads who take risks and start their own companies rather than join established corporations. A writer from Michigan hears about the project and offers a 500-word mini-profile of two sorority sisters who have launched a successful catering service out of a Detroit storefront. The article, "Tea for 200," adds an element of humor as well as geographic and gender diversity to the 3,000-word package, which is dominated by males who have built businesses around their high-tech skills.

Before long, the back-and-forth communication between editor and writer results in a professional relationship that benefits both parties. The editor's network of writers grows, and the publication takes on a national flavor, thanks to fresh voices reporting stories from rural and suburban areas of the country. Who knows, the writer may even earn a place on the publication's masthead as a contributing editor or a regional correspondent. This may not translate into a salary (a token honorarium is sometimes the best a contributing editor can hope for), but it ensures that any story idea that the writer submits is seriously considered. It also means that, when an editor has an important assignment to make, he will look first to his list of contributing editors. Before long that Ohio writer may get a firm assignment to barge through Burgundy, shadow Jack the Ripper around London or scout bargains at Prague's flea markets.

BRIEFS VS. FILLERS

By definition, shorts are interesting, informative and relevant nonfiction items of various lengths. Don't confuse them with fillers, a term that suggests items that have little purpose other than to take up space. (Out of habit, some editors use the terms interchangeably, but they know the difference.) Years ago, newspapers and some magazines often kept on hand a supply of random fillers to dust off and drop into a story that didn't quite fill the allotted space. It was possible for a reader to finish a profile article about a Washington politician or a Hollywood celebrity and then be informed that "The capital of Nevada is Carson City" or "The average person uses 123 gallons of water a day."

Fortunately, the old-fashioned variety of fillers is rare these days. Editors no longer fear white space; in fact, they welcome "air" because it allows a story to "breathe." Also, technology now permits an editor to eliminate small amounts of unwanted air by slightly adjusting the space between lines and words.

Unlike fillers, shorts are a planned, not a random, part of a publication's content. They might take the form of humorous anecdotes of under 100 words, such as you see in *Reader's Digest*, or recipes, appropriate for a magazine such as *Woman's Day*. They might be brief inspirational stories that fit perfectly into the pages of *Guideposts*. They can be 300-word how-to articles—"Five Steps to a Great Mid-Career Résumé"—for an issue of a business magazine or the business pages of a daily newspaper. Or they might offer a quick compilation of shower gift ideas for the bride-to-be for the front page of almost any newspaper's feature section in June. They might occupy a box, a column or an entire page. All are tightly focused and self-contained, and they never include the line "continued on page. . . ."

SHOPPING FOR SHORTS AND BRIEFS

The amount of research necessary to produce a marketable short varies. For the story about shower gifts for the bride-to-be, the writer might browse the specialty shops of a mall and visit the websites of high-end boutiques. As she "shops," she is taking notes on unusual items that a young couple would be unlikely to purchase for themselves. Two or three brief interviews with retail buyers about what's hot this season will provide insider tips from experts who have a handle on trendy merchandise.

Sometimes a single interview with an expert source provides enough information for two or three shorts. For example, a college journalist might research a profile article for the campus newspaper about a literature professor and come away with three ideas to pitch to larger publications. The professor mentions during the interview that many teenagers lose interest in recreational reading during their middle-school years. The journalist picks up on the comment and asks the professor to expand on it. The writer then poses several follow-up questions, such as:

- What should parents look for when they buy books for their kids?
- How do contemporary books such as the Harry Potter series or the *Hunger Games* trilogy compare with the "classics" that adults remember, such as the revived Nancy Drew mysteries or the Narnia books?

- How can you tell whether a child is ready for a book that deals with serious themes?
- Are comic books bad for kids?

From this conversation come these three shorts:

- "How to Keep Your Kids Reading This Summer"
- "The Five Best Kids' Books of the Year"
- "When Harry (Potter) Met Nancy (Drew)"

The same three story ideas also might spring from a report, issued by experts and reported in the media, saying that the reading skills of American teenagers are rapidly diminishing. The sharp writer, always looking for breakthrough studies conducted by reputable researchers, clips the news story and contacts a credible expert—that same literature professor—for comments. The resulting interview doesn't have to be long because it is tightly focused on ways that parents can reverse a disturbing trend. Depending on the angle that the writer chooses to take, the shorts may be appropriate for publications aimed at parents, grandparents, librarians or educators.

FLEXIBLE LIST ARTICLES

One of the article possibilities mentioned above—"The Five Best Kids' Books of the Year"—could be packaged as a list article. Editors at many newspapers and magazines welcome list articles because these features can be expanded or reduced as space allows. More important, list articles make great cover lines that motivate readers to buy magazines. "When we put lists on the cover, our newsstand sales go up," said *Men's Health* editor David Zinczenko in a televised interview about the power of lists. In his blog, Zinczenko offers lists that inform readers on timely topics: the six worst foods to eat at the movies, the eight ultimate flat-belly summer foods, the five best hot sauces for any meal and the six things your dad wants for Father's Day. "Lists are perfect for guys with short attention spans," jokes Zinczenko.[1]

As an example of an evergreen (always-in-season) article, prolific freelance writer Dennis Hensley once created a list of tasks that an airline traveler can accomplish when stranded by an unplanned layover in an airport. He got the idea, as you might guess, when he was delayed for several hours by a canceled flight. The article—which we include in Sidebar 11.1—resulted in multiple sales because it appealed to a broad audience. By changing examples within the article, Hensley could aim it at men or women, college students, business travelers or family vacationers. Because the topic has long shelf life, the article could be tweaked, updated, shortened or lengthened for ongoing marketability. Hensley told us that one publication that wasn't pressed for space printed "10 tasks that a traveler can accomplish during a layover." Another editor, with less available space, pruned the list to seven tasks.

The Hensley article contains a numbered list of "tasks." Some authors dispense with the numbers and give each item a name. Sidebar 11.2 offers an example of a calendar-related list article that was first published on a website called KeepKidsHealthy.com and has since appeared in several other publications. The author, John Riddle, recognized that it would have perennial value and he retained the rights to the article. (See Chapter 7 for a review of "reprint rights.")

List articles usually follow a two-part formula. First, you need an introductory paragraph that sets up the article by explaining the purpose of the list. Since these articles are straightforward, the introduction should be brief and to the point. Second, the list is presented in either a bulleted or a numbered format. Examples of timely list articles—with the magazines that published them—include:

- "Five Easy Stretching Exercises You Can Do in 10 Minutes" (*Healthy Living Made Simple*)
- "31 Ways to Get Smarter in 2012" (*Newsweek*)
- "100+ Ways to Get Rich" (*Ebony*)
- "10 Home Remedies That Work" (*AARP Bulletin*)
- "50 Ways to Make Money Online" (*Small Business Opportunities*)

Although list articles seem simple to write, most of them require research. If you want to write about "12 Foods That Sharpen Your Memory," you will need to do a great deal of background reading and then interview a medical doctor or nutritionist who has impressive credentials related to the topic. Your reward for the time that you invest in such an article is the likelihood that you will sell it many times to many publications. The wise writer who recognizes that an article might be marketable more than once takes care to sell only first rights or one-time rights to a publication.

Seven* Ways to Overcome "Terminal" Problems[2]
(* Or As Many Ways as Space Allows)

You're stuck on a two-hour layover between Dallas and Denver. What do you do when there's little time to do anything? You'd be surprised.

I travel a lot. I also wait a lot. I love the former, loathe the latter. But if I go any distance by plane or train these days, I find myself a victim of the one-to-four-hour layover.

Recently, for example, on a flight from Chicago to Fort Myers, Fla., I spent two and a half hours airborne and three and a half hours waiting in Atlanta for a connecting flight. Absurd, right? Nevertheless, it's a reality.

For someone like me, who takes the phrase "time is money" as his life's motto, wasting time sitting in terminals is akin to setting fire to five-dollar bills. No doubt you feel the same way. No matter what business we are in, travel cannot be avoided. Out-of-state conventions, visits to the company's home office, conferences, seminars, business meetings and customer relations seem to keep us in the air or on the tracks more and more each year. With travel costs soaring, many of us find it necessary to seek out the discount rates; usually, these bargain fares only compound the number of layovers, stops and "dead hours."

I have come to grips with the problem by game-planning ahead of time ways in which I can use layover hours to my best advantage. Let me share with you several activities that you can do while waiting for your next flight departure.

1. Go shopping. As long as the terminal is overrun with kiosks and vendors anyway, you may as well make use of them to take care of several necessary tasks. Sure, you might pay a little more for the convenience, but the time you will save for yourself will justify the added expense. So, go ahead and buy presents to take home for the kids; get that haircut you need; have your shoes shined; and order ahead the rental car you'll need in your next town.

2. Put together a fail-safe kit. Even if you travel as little as five or six times a year, you still are a potential victim of misrouted luggage. As a guard against this, you should put together a small all-purpose kit, made up of functional items that you can purchase at any terminal's gift shop or newsstand. These items can be

stashed in your carry-on bag or in your briefcase. I recommend such things as a tin of aspirin, toothbrush and toothpaste, comb, snacks and a razor. Even if your luggage arrives late, you can still freshen up in the terminal restroom or in your hotel room before that first meeting.

3. Do your homework. It's wrong to think the only kind of book you can read in a noisy terminal is a novel, since "light reading" doesn't demand strong attention. In truth, a professional magazine, a training manual or other work-related documents are easier to read. Why? Because they are the kinds of printed materials that you read with a highlighter in hand. You frequently stop to underline important points, make notes in the margins or circle key terms. It's sporadic reading and is perfect for a distracting environment. Save the novel for the quiet of your flight.

4. Draft a business letter on your laptop. We all have sticky problems we must deal with—an irate client who needs to be soothed, an associate in another office who needs to be queried, or a hard-to-reach prospect you desperately want to contact. The layover in the terminal gives you a chance to write such a letter carefully. Send it as an attachment via e-mail or save it until you're back at the office and can print it out for snail-mail delivery.

5. Call clients. Make use of all those minutes you have accumulated with your cell phone carrier to catch up on calls. A couple of cautions: Find a quiet corner so your conversation won't be interrupted by other passengers making calls; don't skim through your phone list and place unnecessary calls merely to kill time.

6. Clean out your purse or wallet. Here, at last, you've got time to rid your purse or billfold of outdated credit cards, slips of paper, a stash of pens that don't work and a collection of business cards from people you never call. After you've completed your chores, consider balancing your checkbook.

7. Play "what if" mind games. While seated in the terminal, use the time to challenge yourself with problems that may arise in the coming months. Strategize on possible solutions. If a job opens up in another department, should you apply? If you have the opportunity to relocate, should you do it? You need a new car; so what are the pros and cons of leasing rather than buying?

Preventing Holiday Stress[3]

The holiday season is here, and if you listen carefully you'll hear more than just the sounds of "Silent Night" playing in the background at your local mall. Those other sounds you hear are the cries of stressed out shoppers, parents, sales clerks and children, who are overdosing on sweets and other holiday goodies.

But things don't have to be that way in your house. You can nip the stress beast in the bud and prevent it from attacking you and your loved ones. It takes a little common sense followed by a large dose of patience. Follow these four tips to help prevent holiday stress from ruining the most wonderful time of the year for you and your family:

The Right Attitude—Face it, with the wrong attitude, a trip to the mall or to cut down the Christmas tree can be disastrous. Everyone needs to have an attitude check at this time of year because with the right attitude, people are cooperative and respectful of each other. Parents should set a good example for their children by having the right attitude throughout the holiday season (and it wouldn't hurt to continue that tradition throughout the rest of the year either).

Flexibility—The most common reason people become stressed around the holidays is because their expectations are not met. They didn't think the holiday meal with all the relatives would end up with people arguing. Or they thought that their children would behave and stay happy while being dragged to marathon shopping trips to the malls and outlet stores. Flexibility is the key. When you are flexible, you realize that not everything will turn out the way you hoped it would. When you are flexible, you realize that if things turn out differently, it's not the end of the world.

Menu Control—The average weight gain between Thanksgiving and New Year's Day is six to 12 pounds. At this time of year people eat more because they go out more. Try and limit the number of calories you consume at a party or holiday meal. Have plenty of lower-fat, lower calorie choices available. Offer fruit along with other desserts. Plan at least one healthy meal as a family every day.

Order in the House—If you have young children, you know how their routines are frequently disrupted during the holidays. When a child's routine is changed—perhaps you've canceled the afternoon nap to take him to see Santa—he may become cranky, uncooperative and ruin the adventure for everyone. Do your best to keep some order in the house by adhering to familiar schedules.

PERSONAL-EXPERIENCE SHORTS

Some editors solicit short items pulled from a writer's personal experience. These anecdotes may be humorous or inspirational but not complex enough to support a full-length feature. They have maximum impact on readers when the author distills the "message" rather than dilutes it with a lot of description and background information.

Good examples of inspirational shorts are the little stories contained in a standing column in *Guideposts* called "Mysterious Ways." (Examples of these are posted on the magazine's website and range in length up to 750 words.) Each anecdote comes from the writer's personal experience, recounts an incident that cannot be explained by logic and has the capacity to raise gooseflesh on readers. At the center of each story is an unforeseen turn of events that skeptics would call "luck" and religious believers would call a "God thing." For example, an unpredicted shower drenches a burning house where young children are sleeping unattended. No one else in the neighborhood experiences the rain, and the pavement around the house remains perfectly dry.

As popular as "Mysterious Ways" is with readers, the column almost didn't get off the ground. Editors at *Guideposts* kept rejecting "miracle stories" because they didn't fit into the magazine's mission to equip readers with practical tools to help them face and overcome life's inevitable obstacles. After all, a reader who struggles with a problem similar to the one recapped in the magazine cannot expect a duplicate miracle to provide a happy ending. Only after these "miracle" submissions continued to pour into their offices did the editors decide to group them under the common label of "Mysterious Ways" and offer them as unexplainable stories of faith. That was years ago. Since then, the column has evolved into a mainstay and typically tops the list of subscribers' favorite features.[4] Its popularity supports the notion that people like "short reads" that stir emotions. (Visit www.guideposts.org/tell-us-your-story to submit an entire manuscript to the editors.)

RECYCLING ANECDOTES

A great place to look for shorts is within articles you've already written. Most stories contain anecdotes, and many anecdotes can stand on their own merit. The editors at *Reader's Digest* survey scores of magazines in search of stories within stories that meet the *Digest's* high publication standards. For example, a 2,000-word profile of Garfield creator Jim Davis published in *The Saturday Evening Post* yielded a 100-word nugget about how Davis grew up on a farm and often was confined to his home because of asthma. His mother encouraged him to pass the time by sitting at a window and sketching the family's "outdoor" cats. The anecdote may have caught the eye of the *Digest* editors because it showed how a negative situation (asthma) could result in a positive outcome (fame as a cartoonist). Also, the little story would appeal to the *Digest's* middle-aged readers who have been reading Garfield strips since the cat debuted on America's comic pages in 1978. The lesson here is that demographics are important, even when combing your copy for small, salable blurbs.

To enjoy a second life as a "short," an anecdote doesn't have to deal with celebrities. Some publications compile stories about noncelebrities under a title that clearly identifies the common element that unifies the content. *Reader's Digest* compartmentalizes 100-word stories into columns with labels such as "Off Base," which are anecdotes related to military life; "@ Work," which are career-related stories; "As Kids See It"; "Campus Comedy"; "Life's Like That"; and "School Days." The *Digest* encourages contributors to submit their anecdotes to the editors by typing them directly onto the magazine's submission form on its website.

Magazines typically solicit submissions about people who reflect their readers. A publication geared to runners will welcome blurbs about interesting people who share that passion. A magazine for career women may look for anecdotes that fit into a monthly feature called "Timeout" that offers ideas on how to reduce job stress. A magazine for teachers may solicit brief stories about educators who have developed creative ways to deal with universal classroom challenges.

BEYOND THE BLURB

The longest short is the one-page story, which usually contains no more than 500 to 750 words. The one-pager is a challenge to write because the author has to prune every unnecessary word from the text. This means that the article that emerges can have only one focus. If it's a profile, it zeros in on a lone aspect of the person's life; if it's an essay, it centers on a single key point. A one-page travel article would never try to embrace the entire city of Nashville but might transport readers to a historic pub in Music City where wannabe singers take turns at an open microphone.

Regardless of whether you want to submit 50-word jokes or 600-word articles to a publication, the steps that lead to success are the same.

- *Do your homework.* Survey several publications and determine whether they use short items. Pay particular attention to the table of contents, where you'll find a listing of departments and standing features. For example, *Home & Away* publishes a back-of-the-book feature called "Back Home" that invites writers to submit short travel-related stories. If you have a good story, you just might earn a byline. Tip: Check the magazine's website, where previously published articles are frequently archived.
- *Analyze several short items.* What seems to be the preferred length? Are they clustered under a common title? Do they carry bylines? If so, do the bylines belong to regular contributors or members of the staff? In other words, does a newcomer have a chance of breaking into print?
- *Keep up on trends.* The best shorts are timely items. Often editors cluster nuggets linked to trends, new research, innovations and recently released statistics.
- *Keep your eye on the calendar.* Editors love to drop in seasonal shorts: "Three Causes of Holiday Depression" (December); "Quiz: How Compatible Are You?" (February/Valentine's Day); "A Checklist for Winterizing Your Garden" (September). We talk more about seasonal features in Chapter 15.
- *Be patient.* Remember that short items with a long shelf life are always in demand. The problem is that editors aren't always sure when they will have just the right place for them. If an editor tells you he wants to hold your short for possible use in the future, be willing to wait.
- *Be resilient.* This is a competitive business. As an example, *Guideposts* welcomes submissions but admits on its website that it receives thousands of submissions every month. Those odds aren't good. To help potential contributors, some magazines offer a variety of tips, including topics that the editors are most interested in seeing addressed.

IN-CLASS ACTIVITIES

Students: Working in teams of two, come up with an idea for a list article appropriate for each of these audiences: young parents; single female professionals; retirees who like to travel; college grads looking for their first jobs.

Students: Reread one of the list articles in this chapter. Discuss how the author might explore the same topic for a different audience. If you choose "Seven Ways to Overcome 'Terminal' Problems," redirect the content to a family traveling with young children. If you choose "Preventing Holiday Stress," tweak the content to make it appropriate for young, single males.

ASSIGNMENTS

Students: Pull from your files a recent article that you have written. Rewrite it, cutting its length by at least half. Working with the long version of the article, isolate an anecdote that might stand alone as a "short." Pare it down to as few words as possible without forfeiting any of its impact.

Students: Visit the library and survey several national magazines, taking note of those that publish regional editions. On a map, draw a 50-mile circle around the location of your home. Identify five points of interest within that radius. Select the one that is most appealing and write a 300-word story. Submit it to a magazine or a large-city newspaper that publishes a regional edition that includes your location.

NOTES

1 Interview on CBS *Sunday Morning*, June 8, 2008.
2 Copyright Dennis E. Hensley (used by permission).
3 Copyright John Riddle, contributing author (used by permission).
4 Van Varner, *His Mysterious Ways* (New York: Ballantine Books, 1988), xi.

PROFILES
SLICES OF LIFE

KEY POINTS

- The difference between "portrait" and "photo" profiles
- Criteria to determine a subject's newsworthiness
- Twelve sample open-ended questions
- Packaging options: the roundup and Q & A

In *Almost Famous*, a semi-autobiographical film by journalist-turned-screenwriter Cameron Crowe, a teenager attaches himself to a rock group to write a profile for *Rolling Stone* magazine. In the course of the story, 15-year-old "William" (played by actor Patrick Fugit) comes of age as a person and as a writer. The first draft of his article is shallow and full of hyperbole, and reads like a news release generated by an overly enthusiastic publicist. The editors at *Rolling Stone* promptly reject it. His next attempt, an honest portrayal based on personal observations, several days of shadowing and a variety of interviews, earns praise and launches Cameron/William on a successful career. The published article acknowledges the band members' shortcomings but also captures their strengths. The musicians emerge as very real and likeable characters. William scores a byline and earns a sale. (For his efforts, Crowe won an Academy Award for the year's best original screenplay.)

The difference between the first and final drafts of William's profile is similar to the difference between a portrait and a black-and-white

Feature and Magazine Writing: Action, Angle and Anecdotes, Third Edition.
David E. Sumner and Holly G. Miller.
© 2013 David E. Sumner and Holly G. Miller. Published 2013 by John Wiley & Sons, Inc.

photograph of a person. Most successful feature writers avoid the first and pursue the second.

AVOIDING PROFILES THAT GUSH

If you've ever visited an art gallery, you've probably seen formal portraits of famous people—presidents, world leaders, members of royalty and high society—who smile (or glower) down at you from gilded frames. You recognize some of them, but barely. The portraits are likenesses of people on their very best days. Gone are the wrinkles, blemishes and other imperfections. The artist has thickened the hair, whitened the teeth, bobbed the noses, flattened the ears and trimmed the tummy. Misty colors and soft brushstrokes have embellished the gifts of nature and eliminated the ravages of time. If the subject of the portrait had a flaw, the artist has either ignored or downplayed it.

You ask: Were these people *really* as attractive in life as they appear on canvas? Answer: probably not. Wealthy folk throughout history have spent hundreds of thousands of dollars to have artists portray them as they *wished* they had looked in their prime.

What do these overly complimentary portraits have to do with you as a writer? Just this: Some feature editors are satisfied with profile articles that are written versions of see-no-evil portraits. Such articles are usually based on single interviews and superficial questions. The result is a shallow, overly complimentary likeness of the interviewee that contains no insights into the struggles or shortcomings that helped to shape him. If a profiled person is a celebrity who has had a well-publicized problem that the publication must acknowledge or risk losing credibility, the writer downplays the problem with carefully chosen euphemisms. Inappropriate behavior becomes "playfulness," run-ins with the law shrink to "skirmish" status, multiple marriages emerge as "broken relationships" and periods of substance abuse are downgraded to times of "unwise lifestyle choices." If these esteemed icons smoked marijuana in their college days, they certainly didn't inhale.

Authors who write these profiles and editors who publish them don't intend to be dishonest or misleading. They merely subscribe to the old advice: If you can't say something nice about a person, don't say anything at all. They aren't in the business of probing beyond the superficial. The

What Makes a Person Newsworthy?

- *Prominence*: For a national magazine, the prominent person is likely a celebrity or a well-known politician, author or business executive. For a campus publication the prominent subject could be a professor, athlete or student government officer.
- *Perseverance*: Readers love stories about persons who have overcome great odds to live out a dream or persevere in the face of adversity. Examples: A blind student graduates from law school with honors; a single mom juggles four jobs to complete her degree.
- *Oddity*: Ideas might include the first female to play on the boys' soccer team or the student who earned a perfect score on the SAT and entered college at age 12. Example: The *Chronicle of Higher Education* once published a profile about a man who had earned 11 degrees.
- *Achievement*: Success stories are everywhere, and the reading public never tires of them. Examples: The local singer who earns a recording contract; the business major who launches a company from his dorm room; the athlete who breaks a long-standing school record.
- *Experience*: Interesting experiences come in two varieties. First is participating in a one-time event such as an Olympic trial; second is an ongoing experience such as serving as a summer intern on Capitol Hill.
- *Vocation/avocation*: Persons with unusual jobs and hobbies might be fair game for profile articles. Examples: Interview a storm chaser, a documentary filmmaker or a collector of James Dean memorabilia.
- *Anniversary*: These stories often involve a person looking back on an event or an era. Examples: Profile a professor who recalls the changes he has witnessed on campus as he marks 30 years of teaching; or profile an eyewitness to the 9/11 disaster who is willing to talk about how the event changed his life.

SIDEBAR 12.1

profiles that emerge put subjects on pedestals for readers to admire. These stories are most at home on the pages of fan magazines, religious publications, internal newsletters, company magazines and other sponsored periodicals.

Idealized profiles can be dangerous to a magazine, its readers and even to the personalities who serve as subjects for stories that gush. Here are three reasons why overwritten profiles are not as harmless as they seem:

- Readers are savvy enough to know that no one is perfect, and they question the honesty and ethics of a publication that perpetuates such a myth. The public will not take the magazine seriously and may categorize its writers as lightweights. If the publication is sponsored, the writers risk being labeled "spin doctors."
- Readers who believe the pumped-up portraits often feel in awe of the people who are profiled. These readers measure themselves against the featured personalities and, compared to perfection, they always come up short. A working mother feels guilty when she reads about the "super mom" who successfully balances home, career, family, friends and community service. The high-school student loses self-esteem when she reads about the teenage rock star who manages to get great grades, wears a size 4 and just signed a movie deal.
- People who fall off pedestals sometimes never recover from the injuries they sustain to their reputations. This is especially true of highly visible religious figures, who too often are depicted in the religious press as practically flawless. If the personality slips and makes a human error, the secular world responds with a loud "Aha!" The "sin" may be as common as getting a divorce or as innocent as an inspirational vocalist "crossing over" to the pop charts. Whatever the problem, the blame rests less with the personality and more with the publication for holding the personality to an unattainable standard of perfection.

PURSUING WARTS AND ALL

As a writer, you aren't writing to please the person you write about; you are writing to inform your reader. For that reason, many editors stipulate they don't want "portrait" articles but rather "warts and all" profiles. This suggests a story that is a written version of a black-and-white news photograph that hasn't been manipulated on the computer screen. It honestly represents the person, flaws (warts) and all. This does not mean that you, the writer, must dig around in a subject's background trying to unearth controversy. Your goal is merely to present the profiled person as normal, real and worthy of readers' interest.

Striking the right balance between a person's positive and negative qualities requires skill. Just as the writer and editor want to avoid elevating the personality to sainthood, so do they want to avoid discrediting or embarrassing the person. The goal is honesty, but the transition from creating word portraits to crafting word photographs can be clumsy at first. The tendency is for writers to mention one human shortcoming and then drone on about five attributes to offset it. Some writers attempt to humanize their subjects by passing off a positive quality as a negative one. For example, "He admits to being overly generous with his family" or "She can't say 'no' to a good cause, especially if it involves children."

Tuning into a subject's "humanity" requires a serious investment of time. You cannot merely sit down with a person, run through a short list of questions and then expect to create an in-depth profile from the answers. You're going to have to use your power of observation and ask open-ended questions during the interview portion of your research.

Shadowing the person for a day allows you to immerse yourself in his world. It also reveals insights into the way he relates to co-workers, family, friends and even pets. Is he shy? Funny? Are people relaxed when they are in his company? Ride in his car with him. Does he drive too fast? Is he often late for appointments? Is he constantly on his cell phone? What kinds of music does he like? (Check out his CD collection in the car.) Take note of his personal space (home, office, dorm room). Is it messy? What pictures hang on the walls? Do you see any indication of a hobby—a motorcycle helmet, a tennis racquet, computer games, a guitar? As your recorder captures his words, your notebook becomes a receptacle of colorful but unspoken details.

If your interview includes a meal in a restaurant, how does your interviewee treat the server? What does she eat? Is she watching her weight? Is she a vegetarian? These are observations to explore in your conversation with her. If she's on a diet—and who isn't—she is on common ground with many of your readers. If she admits to an addiction to chocolate, there's another connection.

Twelve Open-Ended Questions

Create a stash of open-ended questions that you can use after you've established a rapport with your profile subject. Employ them sparingly to reveal the person's deeper or more whimsical side. Here are a few examples:

1 Recall a major turning point in your life and how it affected you.
2 Walk me through a typical day.
3 Describe what, in the past year, has given you the most pleasure.
4 What was the best piece of advice you ever received?
5 If someone were making a film of your life, what part would you want to omit?
6 What have you learned from your biggest failure?
7 Just for fun, let's say someone gave you a great deal of money and told you that you had to splurge on something for yourself. What would you buy?
8 What tops your "bucket list" (list of things you want to accomplish or experience before you die)?
9 What do you like/dislike most about yourself?
10 Fast forward a decade. Where are you? What are you doing? What do you hope to accomplish in the next year?
11 What makes you cry?
12 How would you describe yourself in a single adjective?

ASSEMBLING THE PICTURE

Ideally try to shadow your subject before you sit down for your "formal" interview. While you tag along for a day, engage in casual conversation and take notes on topics you want to pursue when you conduct your question-and-answer session. As you prepare your list of questions, review the clues you've gathered during the shadowing experience. If you spotted a guitar in the corner of your subject's office and you know that country music dominates the CD collection in his car, ask about it. Your reward might be a great anecdote about how he once spent a summer in Nashville trying to make it as a studio musician. By including the story in your article, you let readers know that your subject has had lofty dreams and has experienced disappointments. With one brief anecdote you succeed in humanizing him and making a link to readers.

Peter Jacobi, an author and contributor to numerous magazines, suggests that a good profile article is a combination of A-B-C-D factors. First, it is an *authentic* portrayal of a person—honest in tone and accurate in facts. Second, it provides a *bridge* between the reader and the profiled person; the reader makes a link or finds common ground with the article's subject. Third, the article presents a *challenge* because it can't cover every aspect of the person's life but should nudge the reader to continue to think about the information presented. Fourth, the profile should offer a sense of *discovery* as the reader gains new knowledge or appreciation after becoming acquainted with the profiled individual.[1]

Keep these factors in mind as you continue to gather information and schedule secondary interviews. Constantly review your notes and compile a list of unanswered questions. This list will help you determine additional people you need to consult as you attempt to create a well-balanced representation of your subject.

OFFERING DIFFERENT PERSPECTIVES

One of the major differences between a "portrait" article and a warts-and-all "photograph" kind of story is the number of interviews that the writer conducts. Imagine watching a full-length motion picture that was shot from one angle with one camera that never zoomed in for close-ups or panned the room to show the person in the context of the environment. This would be the ultimate "talking head"—boring, one-dimensional and predictable.

An article based on a single interview with the profiled person can be equally tiresome and superficial. Readers see the individual from only one perspective—his own. Even if the person is candid, witty and wonderfully quotable, he can't make up for the absence of other viewpoints. The article may be good, but probably won't be as good as it could be if you included insights from other sources.

By conducting support interviews with a variety of people who know your subject, you move your camera back and forth and up and down. In short, you capture your subject from different angles. How many support interviews are enough? That depends on your time constraints, the availability of sources, the projected word count of your article and the number of personality traits you hope to explore. Beware: It's possible to talk with too many sources and end up with a collection of disjointed comments. Also, avoid support sources that give only "cheerleader quotes" such as "she's a wonderful friend" without any insights into your subject's character or personality.

The point is, you should choose your interviewees carefully and strive for quality rather than quantity. If an interview subject fails to bring something fresh to the profile, you shouldn't feel any obligation to include the comments.

How to Avoid Cheerleader Quotes

Asking a tightly focused follow-up question is the key to gathering information from a secondary source that goes beyond superficial "cheerleader" responses. Some examples:

Interviewee's Comment	Follow-Up Question
"He's a very good leader."	Describe a moment when he showed his leadership skills.
"She has a great personality."	Tell me your impression of her when you met for the first time. How did she win you over?
"She's an excellent student."	How do her study habits differ from those of other students?
"He's a lot of fun; you never know what he's going to do or say next."	Give me an example of something outrageous that he's done or said.

SIDEBAR 12.3

When identifying support interviewees, you should go back to the idea of the roving camera. You'll probably want at least one close-up. The person's spouse or some other member of the family can best provide this angle. If you want a "view from the top," set up an interview with the person's boss. If you want to focus on the person's hobbies or interests, talk with her tennis partner, roommate or best friend.

Support interviews usually don't require a lot of time, and you can sometimes conduct them on the telephone. (We strongly discourage trading e-mails.) This doesn't mean support interviews aren't important or don't deserve careful planning. You don't want responses that are generic affirmations that could describe almost anyone. The best way to get past one-size-fits-all comments is with questions that invite anecdotal answers. (See Sidebar 12.3.)

Some veteran profile writers conduct their support interviews first, then schedule their shadowing experience and, last of all, sit down for their in-depth, one-on-one sessions with their primary subjects. This makes sense and can save time. Conversations with secondary sources often uncover routine information that might have eaten up valuable minutes if you'd had to gather it during your in-depth interview. ("How long have you been married?" "Where did you go to college?" "How many children do you have?")

More important, secondary sources and the shadowing experience often result in great questions that you otherwise might miss. A best friend might tell you a funny story that you can recount to get a reaction from your primary interviewee. A wife might tick off several awards that her husband won, whereas the husband would be too modest to mention them. You can play one person's comments against another's and end up with a humorous he-said/she-said kind of anecdote.

ADDING COLOR TO THE PICTURE

As an example, let's say you are writing a profile of a prominent leader in your community. Before you sit down for your in-depth interview with him, you spend some time talking with his wife of many years. As part of your conversation, you ask her to recall their first date. She supplies a colorful anecdote, complete with lots of details. Of course, the story is told from her point of view. A few days later you sit face to face with the husband, and you want to hear his side of the story. The dialogue with the husband might go something like this:

INTERVIEWER: Your wife tells me that your first date was a disaster because you neglected to warn her that you were taking her to a football game . . . in the rain. She says that she spent the first half wrapped in a plastic trash bag and the second half under the bleachers. True story?

INTERVIEWEE: Yeah; she thought we were going to see a play, but at the last minute a friend gave me tickets to the Bears' season opener. The weather was brutal. But it was a great game, and the Bears won in the fourth quarter.

RESULTING ARTICLE EXCERPT: Their relationship got off to an icy start when he swapped front-row theater tickets for a couple of passes to a Bears-49ers game. The soft drizzle turned into a Chicago-style downpour and caused her to seek refuge first in a plastic trash bag and then under the bleachers. "We couldn't leave," he explains, adding as justification: "The score was tied, third down and goal to go." The Bears got the win, she got the flu and he got the cold shoulder for two weeks. They now have season tickets . . . to the theater.

Obviously the resulting excerpt would have required a bit of extra research on the part of you, the interviewer. Since the couple's first date occurred many years ago, both the husband and wife were fuzzy in their recollection of the facts. You compensated for this by asking a lot of follow-up questions and then by visiting the library and finding on microfilm the *Chicago Tribune*'s account of the Bears' season opener. You scribbled down a few notes about the weather and the final play of the game and blended these details with the memories that your interviewees supplied. A great little story emerged.

FILE FOR THE FUTURE

If collecting strong comments and anecdotes from a variety of sources has a negative side, it's the fact that you can't include all the material in a single profile article. Most editors don't want a chronological rehashing of a person's life. Instead, they expect you to weave in just enough background to give context to the interesting and timely focus of your profile. This requires you to sift through your notes and transcripts (if you recorded your interviews) and select the information that fits the article's focus, temporarily setting aside the material that doesn't make the cut.

But don't throw anything away. Chances are you'll be able to fold your interviewee's "discarded" comments into any number of future stories.

Here's how it works: Say you research and write a profile about a student who just completed a summer internship in the White House press office. Although you include some background—she's a junior, majors in political science and hopes to go to law school after graduation—the focus of your story is on the eight weeks that the student spent in the West Wing. The other material you gathered, such as the way she found out about the internship in the first place, doesn't fit the focus and never makes it to print.

Later, you tackle a how-to article assignment that offers tips on how to land dream jobs in a tight economy. Your primary interviewee is the director of the campus career center, who emphasizes that internships attract a lot of attention on résumés. To answer the logical question about how students discover internship opportunities, you pull from your files the comments from the student who beat out the competition and spent a summer in the White House. Whereas she dominated the profile article, she now plays a supporting role in the how-to article and occupies only a paragraph or two. Her contribution is important, though, because she provides an anecdote that illustrates a key point.

PUTTING A FACE ON AN ISSUE

A profile is a great way to put a "face" on an important issue and cause readers to get involved and care about a topic they might otherwise dismiss. Many magazine and newspaper writers use this tactic in preparing in-depth articles about complex issues. For some journalists who do this, the reward has been the lofty Pulitzer Prize for feature writing. (The full texts of Pulitzer Prize-winning feature articles from 1995 to the present are available online at Pulitzer.org. They also are compiled in an anthology produced by Iowa State Press.) Some examples:

- We've all heard the criticism that Americans live in such a fast-paced society that too few stop to smell the roses and enjoy the moment. *Washington Post* feature writer Gene Weingarten won a Pulitzer Prize in 2008 when he tested the validity of this statement by shadowing world-class violinist Joshua Bell. The good-natured Bell agreed to go incognito and give an impromptu performance for commuters during rush hour in Washington, D.C. Playing his $3.5 million violin, Bell filled a well-trafficked subway station with incredible music as Weingarten looked on, taking notes about commuters' reactions to the anonymous street musician. The resulting article proved a point even as it gave readers insights into one of the world's finest virtuosos.

- Child abuse was the focus of a gripping feature called "The Girl in the Window" that won the 2009 Pulitzer Prize for *St. Petersburg Times* feature writer Lane DeGregory. The story, divided into three chapters because of its length, told the story of Danielle, a "feral child" who was kept in a closet without any human interaction for the first six years of her life. The author traced the history of this kind of neglect, educated readers on the importance of nurturing and documented the challenges that adoptive parents face when they take a severely damaged child into the family. By the end of the third chapter, readers have deep compassion for Danielle and a better understanding of a social problem that has no simple solution.

Of course, not all profiles have the potential to explore complex issues and win Pulitzer Prizes. Some articles merely provide a quick snapshot of a person for the purpose of entertaining or informing readers.

FROM QUICK TAKES TO ROUNDUPS

The New Yorker invented the term "profile" with its in-depth articles about 1920s personalities. When the magazine celebrated its 75th anniversary, its editor, David Remnick, collected some of its best profile articles and created a 530-page anthology called *Life Stories*. In his introduction, Remnick admitted that writing a great profile is difficult and that profiles suitable for *The New Yorker* sometimes require months or even years to produce.[2] The problem is, of course, that not every writer—or publication—has the luxury of such open-ended assignments. Also, not every writer—or publication—is interested in producing comprehensive life stories. The result? "We are awash in pieces calling themselves profiles that are about the inner thoughts of some celebrity; more often than not they are based on half-hour interviews and the parameters set down by a vigilant publicist," notes Remnick.[3]

He may be right. But "quick takes" (we call them snapshots) are mainstays of some publications and are very popular with readers. Why else do magazines such as *People* and *Entertainment Weekly* boast large circulations? Why else are the inside front covers of *USA Weekend* and *Parade* among the best-read pages of those Sunday tabloids?

A snapshot profile can range from a one-paragraph blurb to an article that fills a single page. The story focuses on an interesting aspect of an interesting person's life. It might be little more than an update or an announcement or a breezy comment about a timely issue. In the case of a celebrity, it might result from a half-hour interview that a "vigilant publicist" has set up and monitored.

But not all snapshots have to be lightweight efforts with limited journalistic value. A writer can assemble a series of snapshots into an "album" and publish the results as a round-up article. As an example, *Marriage Partnership* magazine won a first-place award from the Evangelical Press Association in 2003 for a round-up article called "Happily Even After." The writer, Paul Kortepeter, wrote short profiles (about 500 words each) on four married couples who had stayed together and lived "happily even after" experiencing a variety of hardships.

Other round-up articles composed of several short profiles might be: Five entrepreneurs offer advice on how to start a home-based business; four female members of Congress explain what it's like to be "Ladies of the House."

Round-up articles can give comprehensive coverage to a topic by including various points of view from people who see the issue through a range of lenses.

EXPERIMENTING WITH THE Q & A

A profile article can take many shapes and forms, and the versatile and marketable writer is able to tune into a publication's style and produce the kind of profile that the editors and readers want. As different as portrait, photograph and snapshot profiles are, they should share three characteristics: accuracy, truthfulness and timeliness.

That said, a writer has flexibility in deciding which quotations to integrate into the story, which characteristics to emphasize, how many details to include and what kind of tone to adopt. Those decisions will determine whether the profile emerges as a quick take, a positive glimpse or an in-depth study. The writer, in consultation with the editor, also will decide whether the profile will take the form of a traditional article or a question-and-answer conversation.

Many newspaper and magazine editors include one or more question-and-answer articles in each edition of their publications. Often these are placed strategically as back-of-the-book features. They're easy to find, easy to read and serve as a strong finish to an issue. As an example, *Vanity Fair* typically publishes a one-page Q & A article with a well-known personality who is in the news for one reason or another at the time the magazine arrives in subscribers' mailboxes. Actor Ralph Fiennes answered questions as he was making his debut as a director; author P.D. James was featured to coincide with the release of her latest novel; and musician Wynton Marsalis responded to *Vanity Fair*'s questions as he celebrated his birthday with a national tour.

An article that follows a Q & A format typically begins with a narrative paragraph (or several) that sets up the conversation. This introductory section serves a variety of purposes. It gives you, the writer, an opportunity to describe the backdrop against which the interview took place. You can weave in enough biographical information about your subject so readers will understand who the person is and what makes her an interesting subject for a profile article. You also set the tone for the interview—casual, chatty, formal, academic—with your choice of language and the "attitude" that comes forth in your questions.

The article that we offer as an example is a Q & A interview with Julie Andrews, an Academy Award-winning actress whose career spans decades. The opening paragraphs (fewer than 400 words) accomplish at least three goals. First, they remind readers who Andrews is. Older readers might remember her as the star of *My Fair Lady* on Broadway or from classic films such as *The Sound of Music* or *Mary Poppins*. Younger readers might identify her with the three *Shrek* or the two *Princess Diaries* films. Second, the paragraphs emphasize what is new in her life. They let readers know that this article won't be a rehash of past triumphs but rather an update on a career that is taking a different direction. Third, this introductory section establishes the tone of what will follow. The first-person point of view and the use of contractions ("We've seen her as Mary Poppins . . .") help create a feeling of informality. Most Q & A articles have a casual tone because the publication is offering readers the opportunity to sit in on a conversation between an interviewer and interviewee. Sentence fragments, slang and occasional pauses may be part of the exchange.

As you read the article, be aware of the timeliness factor. Andrews' autobiography, *Home*, was newly released and was on the best-seller list. Pay attention to the questions that the interviewer asks and how these questions steer the conversation. They aren't random. They have direction and are tightly focused. They mention Andrews' high-visibility career as an actress and singer but the emphasis is always on her passion for reading and creating books. They also show that the interviewer had done enough research to elicit thoughtful responses from the interviewee.

At home with Julie Andrews[4]

With several best-selling children's books to her credit, everyone's favorite Fair Lady is finding new ways to promote her lifelong passion—reading.

We've seen her as Mary Poppins, descending from the heavens, feet pointed out, with one hand gripping a serviceable black umbrella. We've watched her as Maria, arms outstretched, filling the hills with the sound of music. More recently, we've heard her as Queen Lillian, mother-in-law to *Shrek*; and we've loved her as Queen Clarisse Renaldi, veddy refined grandmother to actress Anne Hathaway in the *Princess Diaries* films. But these days Julie Andrews is spending more time creating characters than portraying them.

Collaborating with her daughter, Emma Walton Hamilton, she has some 15 picture books, novels, and Early Readers to her credit. Her memoir, *Home*, is her first "adult" effort and earned five-star reviews as it leapfrogged to the top of the bestseller list this summer.

"Writing has taken front and center," Andrews says of the two careers that compete for her attention. "I write in the morning, certainly four hours a day, if not more. When I get toward the middle of a book, the story begins to assume its own momentum. At that point, I write by day and edit by night. As an author you never let go of a story; it's always in your head."

At age 73, she exudes enthusiasm as she talks about her passion for books and her belief that children should read more of them. She and Emma oversee The Julie Andrews Collection, a publishing program that includes high-quality works by established and emerging authors as well as "out-of-print gems worthy of resurrection." She admits that the books featured in the collection might be a tad old-fashioned, but they emphasize virtues—integrity and creativity among them—that never go out of date.

"We're not as edgy as some authors," she admits, "but we believe in all the decent things that we hope will help children find their place in this world."

Andrews recently took a break from her writing regimen to talk with *The Saturday Evening Post* about *Home*, Whangdoodles, and a new fairy princess who is still in incubation.

Although you've been writing books since 1971, most people think of you primarily as a performer. Do you find that it's harder to interpret someone else's words as an actress or to create your own words as a writer?

Andrews: Hmmmm, good question. This may sound odd, but I think it's more difficult to create words as a writer because there's always that feeling of insecurity. It's true that I've been writing for more than 35 years, but those are my children's books. *Home* is my first adult attempt, and I feel like I'm still learning. For me, writing is a joy, but it's also hard work. There are days when I get horribly stuck. I've heard people say that writing is a lonely profession, but I never feel lonely when I'm working on my children's books. I have companions the whole way because I'm creating things that I love, like Whangdoodles. [Explanation: A whangdoodle is "a fanciful creature of undefined nature" and the subject of Andrews' classic *The Last of the Really Great Whangdoodles.*]

In your memoir, *Home*, you manage to recall your early years very vividly. Did you keep a journal when you were growing up?

Yes, but somewhere along the line the very early diaries went missing. As Eliza Doolittle says, "Somebody pinched them!" So, I wrote *Home* in fits and starts—writing passages as the memories came back to me, then putting them all together later. I remember thinking that I wanted to write about the sights, sounds and smells. Of course, there is such a variety of smells in England, from the terrible railway trains to the beautiful spring lilacs.

How difficult was it to relive the past and confront some events that might have been painful? Did you learn anything about yourself that you hadn't realized before?

It was an interesting experience and, yes, there were moments when it was painful. But much of what I write about happened 50 years ago, so I've had time to put it into perspective and then put it to bed. A lot of it was surprising to me . . . things that I discovered as I wrote. For example, I had always thought that I had a very happy childhood. I was an optimistic girl, and I had a lot of nice things happen to me. It wasn't until I started writing that I said to Emma, "Gosh, this seems awfully depressing!" I had forgotten how dark it was at times.

Did you fear a negative response from fans who might prefer to believe you had a fairy-tale existence? Did you wonder how they might react to learning about your mother's alcoholism and the fact that your biological father was someone other than the dad you adored?

The people who mattered were my family, and since I had never mentioned some things to my brothers and sisters, I first cleared the book with them. After all these years, we are brothers and sisters, whether I'm a half sister or a whole sister. The truth is, I cannot be absolutely certain that what I wrote is the truth. I only wrote what was handed down to me. I can't prove it without taking DNA tests or whatever. So, the family and I talked about it, and in some ways that brought us even closer together because we realized that it doesn't really matter . . . our bonds are so strong.

Since *Home* only takes us through 1962, can we assume a second book is in the works?
I don't know if I could do it. The sad truth is that so many people I wrote about are no longer with us. They've passed away, so I felt I could write honestly but truthfully and not hurt anybody. We'll see . . . .

Your daughter, Emma, helped with *Home* and has been your collaborator on many of your children's books. How did the partnership start?
My publisher asked if I had any book ideas for very small children. At the time Emma had a young son, so I said, "Emma, if you went to the library to find a book for Sam, what would you choose?" She said, "No contest, Mom! It would be about trucks." She told me that the only truck books that she found were the very practical variety rather than the whimsical or family-oriented kind. "Well, shall we have a crack at trying to write one?" I asked her. That led to our first series about Dumpy the Dump Truck.

Every team has to have a leader. Who's the boss, you or Emma?
[laughs] We're both fairly bossy people, and so at first we wondered if we would be compatible. We discovered, to our delight, that we have an absolutely wonderful time. We laugh a lot, and when we talk, we even finish each other's sentences. Still, we're very different. I think she's a better writer than I am; she's very structured, whereas I'm given to flights of fantasy. We defer to each other when one of us feels passionately about an issue.

In spite of your busy performing career, you obviously instilled in Emma a true love for books. What advice would you offer parents who want their children to grow up with an appreciation of literature?
Reading to children, even before they're verbal, is so important. Sit a child on your lap, hug her close, and read. Take a picture book or a magazine and

trace the words with your fingers. Talk about what you see; discover together the wonders that are under our noses every day.

What new wonders are you working on now? What should we be looking for in the future?
We're doing an anthology of some unusual poems, songs and lullabies that I love. It's been a joy to pull it together. Right now Emma is typing madly to meet our first deadline. We've also been asked if we could do something in the princess genre for young children. We came up with the title *The Very Fairy Princess* about a girl who is convinced that she's a princess and that she can do anything. Everyone around her says, "No! You can't be!" She proves that she just might be a princess if she looks at things in a certain way. We hope it will evolve into a series.

Do you anticipate your two careers intersecting at some point in the future?
It's happening already. A number of our books are packaged with CDs containing songs, and now a couple of the stories—*Simeon's Gift* and *The Great American Mousical*—are being adapted for family theater. When I began writing, I wanted to combine all the lovely things I used to treasure as a child . . . the written word, the spoken word, and fine quality artwork. I think to some degree, we've succeeded.

IN-CLASS ACTIVITIES

Students: After watching the film *Almost Famous* in class, discuss the tactics that the young journalist used to produce his profile article. The magazine's staff rejected his first attempt. Why? What did he do wrong? What did he do right in the second version? What lessons can future writers learn from the film?

Students: Reread the question-and-answer interview with Julie Andrews at the end of this chapter. If the author had not used the Q & A format, who else could she have interviewed to get another perspective on Andrews? What questions might she have asked? Would you categorize the Andrews profile as a "portrait" or a "photograph"? Why? If the article had run too long for the space allotted it and the author had had to delete two Q & A sequences, which ones would you have recommended?

ASSIGNMENTS

Students: Shadow a person for a day. Meet at breakfast and follow the person through dinner. Leave your recording device at home and take notes on your subject's quirks and habits. Pay attention to how he or she interacts with people, drives, eats, relaxes. From your notes, create a couple of anecdotes to fold into a profile article.

Students: Develop three profiles from one. First, research and write a profile article that resembles a black-and-white news photograph—an honest, accurate, "warts and all" portrayal. Second, revisit the profile, delete all negative aspects and turn it into a "portrait" article—100 percent positive. Third, take an excerpt of about 300 tightly focused words and produce a "snapshot" of the person.

NOTES

1 Peter Jacobi, *The Magazine Article* (Bloomington, Ind.: Indiana University Press, 1991), 217.
2 David Remnick, *Life Stories* (New York: Random House, 2000), ix.
3 Remnick, *Life Stories*, xi.
4 Holly G. Miller, "At Home with Julie Andrews," courtesy *The Saturday Evening Post*, Oct. 2008, 49–50.

13

WRITING NONFICTION NARRATIVES

KEY POINTS

- Characteristics of a good narrative
- Types of plots
- Where to find good stories
- Tips on telling stories

Ray Towler was convicted of rape and sentenced to the Ohio Penitentiary when he was 24 years old. During his first years in prison, Towler filed appeals and legal challenges, applied to the governor for commutation, wrote letters to the parole board and continued attempts to prove his innocence. For 23 years, he was unsuccessful. In 2002, the Ohio legislature passed a bill allowing DNA testing for incarcerated felons. After Towler submitted the paperwork, a judge approved his request for testing. Volunteer attorneys from the Ohio Innocence Project sent Towler's DNA to a Texas lab for testing against remains from the victim's clothing. On May 3, 2010, his attorney received an e-mail with the result: "NOT RAYMOND TOWLER." Two days later, after 28 years, 7 months and 19 days behind bars, Raymond Towler, 52, was free. After his release, he formed a band call Spirit and Truth with other exonerated men and played at Innocence Project fund-raisers. His next goal is to record an album.[1]

"The Correction," first published in *Cincinnati Magazine* and later in *Reader's Digest*, offers a good example of a nonfiction narrative. Popular

Feature and Magazine Writing: Action, Angle and Anecdotes, Third Edition.
David E. Sumner and Holly G. Miller.
© 2013 David E. Sumner and Holly G. Miller. Published 2013 by John Wiley & Sons, Inc.

with many magazines, these true stories tell how a central character encounters a complex challenge that he or she overcomes.

These true-life stories don't usually make national headlines. In most cases, they happen to ordinary people in small towns and cities. If they get reported at all, it's in a weekly or community newspaper and not a big-city daily. Don McKinney says he published hundreds of these types of stories during his years as a magazine editor:

> Some of these writers were inexperienced in writing for magazines, and their first tries were pretty shaggy. But because they had good stories to tell, we wanted very much to help them succeed. We gave them detailed rewrite instructions, talked to them a number of times about their problems and helped them through several rewrites.[2]

This genre of writing has roots in the 1960s when *Esquire*, *Harper's*, *The New Yorker* and *Rolling Stone* pioneered the "New Journalism." Later called "literary nonfiction" or "nonfiction narratives," its distinguishing characteristic applied the use of fiction techniques to nonfiction reporting. Led by Truman Capote, Joan Didion, Gay Talese, Hunter Thompson, Tom Wolfe and others, its writers took stories about people and reported them using the fiction techniques of character development, narrative, dialogue, description and immersive reporting.

For example, Tom Wolfe wrote *The Right Stuff*, which chronicled the story of the seven Mercury astronauts, who were the first Americans launched into space and a new frontier. Wolfe's story later became a movie by the same name that won four Academy Awards in 1983. Pulitzer Prize-winning author Tracy Kidder took these storytelling techniques further with his books *Among School Children* and *Among Friends*. His first book chronicled a difficult year in the life of a third-grade teacher, while *Among Friends* told about the year-long tribulations of two men living in a Massachusetts nursing home.

The plot of a good story looks like this: You introduce a main character who possesses admirable qualities that attract the empathy of readers. You introduce a situation that throws an obstacle or conflict in the person's path. You give your character a goal and show him trying to reach it. This same type of structure forms the plot of thousands of movies and novels. If you want to learn how to write true-life stories, then watch movies based on real events. Or read novels and study carefully the techniques that the writers use. Most novels have a lot of action, dialogue and character development.

"A good story is an experience. That's why we like it," says Jon Franklin, author of *Writing for Story*. "Our minds are made to draw information from experiences. Experiences are narrative. So we give the reader experiences that they don't actually have to live through."[3]

In "83 Minutes of Life Delivers Lifetime of Memories, Grief for Parents," *Milwaukee Journal-Sentinel* writer Crocker Stephenson tells the story of Sara-Rae and Josh Remmel, whose newborn son, Lincoln Ray, lived for 83 minutes. Five months into her pregnancy, they learned their unborn child had a kidney defect and would likely not live long after his birth. Deciding against an abortion, the Roman Catholic couple began planning not only for the baby's birth but also for his funeral. Later they had another child and found ways to support other couples whose children died young.[4] The story is reprinted at the end of this chapter.

The nonfiction narrative can have a chronological span ranging from minutes to years. Lincoln Ray Remmel's life lasted only 83 minutes, while Ray Towler's story spans almost 29 years from the day he was sentenced to prison to the day he earned his freedom. "We live in a world of narratives. I believe everybody has a story to tell. Most of those narratives go unrecognized and untold until journalists give them a voice," said Crocker Stephenson.[5]

The Nieman Center for Journalism at Harvard University offers a wealth of resources for learning about nonfiction narratives in its Nieman Storyboard (www.niemanstoryboard.org). The website publishes stories from newspapers and magazines around the world, audio and video narratives, interviews with authors, blogs and essays about the craft from well-known writers, and Twitter and e-mail updates.

CHARACTERISTICS OF A GOOD NARRATIVE

The following characteristics help you recognize a good story. First, a good story has one or two admirable main characters. Good stories are about people. Second, it has a plot. That means the main character confronts and overcomes an obstacle to achieve a desired goal. Third, it has a resolution, which means the main character solves the problem. And fourth, it begins and ends at a specific time in a specific place.

Novelist Kurt Vonnegut offered these five rules that apply to the writing of narratives:

1   Use the time of the reader in such a way that he or she will not feel the time was wasted.
2   Give the reader at least one character he or she can root for.
3   Every character should want something, even if it is only a glass of water.
4   Every sentence must do one of two things—reveal character or advance the action.
5   Start as close to the end as possible.[6]

Main character

The best stories tell about something that happened to one or two people, not to a group. Stories about a group, such as a team, should be told from the viewpoint of one main character. The best stories also focus on sympathetic characters—people who are easy to like because of their admirable qualities. Skilled interviewers write questions that elicit quotes that reveal character. Their interviews bring out qualities such as courage, honesty or persistence—and they display these qualities through their stories.

Does that mean you can't write a good story about bad people? Not at all, but it's more difficult. In 1966 Truman Capote, who had already written several novels, wrote his first nonfiction book, *In Cold Blood*, which chronicled the murder of a Kansas farm family by two drifters. This best-selling book became one of the pioneers of the "New Journalism" and later became a movie. Capote spent hundreds of hours interviewing the two murderers during their five years on death row prior to their execution. His compelling character development in this story revealed their deranged lives and gave the reader at least some sense of why they did what they did.

In "Disarming Viktor Bout" *The New Yorker* writer Nicholas Schmidle tells the story of the rise and fall of the world's most notorious weapons trafficker. It begins with the Russian-born Bout's entry into the weapons business in the early 1980s, follows his rise to international notoriety and ends with his conviction on conspiracy and terrorism charges in a New York City courtroom in 2010. The story has a resolution because justice came to a man described as "the personification of evil" by one of Schmidle's sources. Bout became so notorious that the 2005 movie "Lord of War" starring Nicolas Cage was loosely based on his life.[7]

A good narrative should focus on a specific series of events in a person's life with a beginning, middle and end. It isn't a broad-brushed profile.

Guideposts advises prospective contributors in its writers' guidelines on its website:

- Don't try to tell an entire life story. Focus on one specific happening in a person's life. The emphasis should be on one individual. Bring in as few people as possible so that the reader's interest stays with the dominant character.
- Don't leave unanswered questions. Give enough facts so that the reader will know what happened. Use description and dialogue to let the reader feel as if he were there, seeing the characters, hearing them talk. Dramatize the situation, the conflicts, the struggle, and then tell how the person was changed for the better or the problem was solved.

The Difference Between a Profile and a Dramatic Story

SIDEBAR 13.1

Don't confuse writing a profile with writing a nonfiction narrative. Think about the differences this way:

Profile	Nonfiction Narrative
describes a person	tells a story
mixed chronology of events	specific beginning, middle and ending
eclectic structure	
assorted quotes and experiences	chronological structure
	contains a plot and an outcome

Plot

The deepest, oldest conflicts are few and simple: We struggle against nature, against ourselves and against each other. No one enjoys a sugary-sweet story that is all goodness and light because life doesn't happen that way. On the other hand, no one enjoys a story full of suffering and evil that ends in sadness. We look for realism but also hope for redemption. The tension between the way things are and the way things ought to be creates the most compelling and powerful stories.

Jon Franklin, in *Writing for Story*, describes this obstacle that the central characters overcome as a "complication." Another word is simply "plot." The plot drives the story's action by motivating the central characters. "The idea of a character complication is simply something that makes a character exert an effort. Now often this is a conflict . . . but you can have a complication without a conflict."[8] The plot may be a problem, an accident or illness, a failure or an inspirational challenge faced by the central character. As Kurt Vonnegut said, the main character must "want something" that drives the action.

Whether it's called a plot or a complication, it's simply any challenge encountered by a man, woman or child. To create a story with literary value—meaning an interesting story that people want to read—a problem must meet two criteria. First, it must be a basic problem that everyone can relate to. "Basic" in this sense means about issues everyone faces: love and hate, life and death, war and peace, sickness and health, joy and sadness, deprivation and abundance. The reader must be able to say, "I can relate to that."

"You can write about someone who has a peculiar problem. Not everyone has to have that particular problem, but the reader must identify with the dilemma itself or what it does to the person's family," says New York-based writer Judith Newman.[9]

The second criterion for a good complication is that it must matter enough to the central character that he or she is willing to take action to deal with it. That means a major problem and not simply an annoyance. Getting a flat tire is a complication. But it's not life-threatening and doesn't require a major effort to solve.

Resolution

The problem must have a resolution, or it won't fly with readers. That sounds harsh because everyone knows that life presents many sad problems without seeming solutions. That's okay because it's life, but readers of articles and books expect resolutions. A "resolution" doesn't necessarily mean a perfect or happy solution. It simply means the central character figures out a way to deal with it. Sometimes the resolution means the central character simply accepts an unhappy situation in life and decides to move on to other things.

In "83 Minutes of Life," Sara-Rae and Josh Remmel didn't have a happy ending when their son died before he left the hospital. They even knew before his birth that he would not live long. Yet they found a resolution. Their Catholic faith gave them the resources to find meaning in the experience and a way to go on living. At the end of the story, they participated in the "Wisconsin Walk for Hope" to benefit other families who had lost children.

The resolution for "The Correction" is more clear-cut. A DNA test clearly proved that Ray Towler was innocent and he went on to find reasons for living after spending 29 years in prison.

Chronology

A good story has anchors in real time and a real city or town. The dramatic story tells what the main character did as he or she grew up in Atlanta during the 1980s, went to college in Hawaii in 1995 and started her career in Singapore in 2000. The story's time span stretches from its beginning at a particular time and ending at a particular time. The amount of time within a good story can range from a few hours, as in "83 Minutes of Life," to dozens of years, as in "The Correction." Beginning writers sometimes write a story that seems like it hangs in space. While it may be full of quotes and even some good anecdotes, the writer never mentions any dates or places. Readers need these anchors. Readers need tangible dates and specific places to help them visualize the characters and understand the surroundings in which the story occurs.

TYPES OF PLOTS

All good plots serve to create suspense and make the reader wonder how the story will end. These themes, therefore, begin with the type of problem or complication and end with the type of resolution. Good stories can have hybrid plots that involve two or three of these descriptions. What all plots have in common is a central character who has a goal and works hard to achieve it. The nonfiction narrative is a chronology of events that describes how that happened. The following plot themes run the risk of over-simplification because life isn't always this neatly plotted. They do, however, characterize the most common types of plots found in stories.

Rising to the challenge

A typical "rising to the challenge" story involves a central character who discovers a new goal in life and rises to the challenge of achieving that goal. That goal could range from starting a business to becoming a successful brain surgeon or defense attorney, achieving an Olympic gold medal or graduating from college. Candice Millard, a former writer for *National Geographic*, told an inspiring "rising to the challenge" story in her historical book *River of Doubt: Theodore Roosevelt's Darkest Journey*. After his humiliating 1912 presidential re-election defeat, Theodore Roosevelt set his sights on the most punishing physical challenge he could find: the first human exploration of an unmapped, rapids-choked tributary of the Amazon river. Roosevelt, with his son, Kermit, and a band of explorers, survived physical hardship, near-starvation, disease and injuries. Roosevelt himself came close to dying from malaria. His success resulted in a widely heralded accomplishment and the remapping of the Amazon's tributaries.[10]

Failure to achievement

Failure-to-achievement stories involve aspects of life as diverse as succeeding in losing weight, going from poverty to riches or earning a college degree after dropping out of high school. One of our students wrote a story about a woman who had lost 100 pounds. In another example, in "The Art of Rebounding," *Men's Health* profiled Randy Pfund, who achieved his lifetime dream of becoming head coach of a professional basketball team. However, after two dismal losing seasons, he was fired as head coach of the Los Angeles Lakers. After spending time reassessing his life, he decided to try something different. He went into sports management and became a chief executive for the Miami Heat team.[11]

Victim to survivor

A victim experiences unfair suffering inflicted by either the negligence or malevolent intent of others. Victims result from incidents of crime, ignorance or simple accidents. In the best-selling book *Unbroken*, World War II veteran Louis Zamperino survived not only a plane crash in the Pacific followed by 43 days on a raft but also two years of torture and deprivation in a Japanese prisoner-of-war camp. He returned home to California as a war hero.[12] The best victim/survivor stories have specific causes that you can easily describe. A corollary theme is "danger to safety," involving people who overcome injuries, illnesses, danger and natural disasters. These stories tell not just what happened but also how it happened because of the victim's determination and courage.

Chaos to meaning

In these types of stories, change occurs inside the central character more than in his or her outward circumstances. "83 Minutes of Life" is a good example of a "chaos to meaning" story. These stories are more difficult to write because you have to describe psychological, emotional or spiritual changes. A "chaos to meaning" story frequently describes how someone finds new meaning after the death of a spouse or child. For example, in "The Tender Mercy of Cheryl Kane" (*Good Housekeeping*), a Boston nurse "lost all zest for life . . . the pain was just excruciating" after her middle-aged husband died. Cheryl Kane found new meaning in life working in a street outreach program giving medical care to the homeless.[13]

Saving the world

A "one person can make a difference" story has a positive, inspirational quality. In this type of problem-resolution, a motivated citizen confronts a social problem and organizes the resources to bring about a solution. *Reader's Digest*, *Clarity* and other magazines told the story of Debi Farris, a Los Angeles woman who founded "The Garden," a cemetery for babies who have been abandoned by their mothers in dumpsters and trash bins. Faris lobbied the California legislature to pass a "safe haven" law that allows young mothers to give up their babies for adoption without fear of retribution. In another example, *The New Yorker* told the remarkable story of Zeil Kravinsky, who grew up as the son of a poor Russian immigrant. After starting out as an inner-city school teacher, he began investing in real estate and eventually earned millions of dollars. After he gave away almost his entire $45 million real-estate fortune to charity, he felt he needed to do still more for humanity. So he donated a kidney to a complete stranger—something only 134 other Americans had ever done.[14]

Love conquers all

These stories follow a separation-reunion theme and also have a positive, upbeat tone. They can tell the story of the separation and reunion of lovers, of siblings, of parents and children or even of long-lost friends. Dozens of stories have been published about adopted children who located their biological parents after a long search. Many newspapers and magazines have published features telling about couples who were high-school sweethearts and, after graduation, married someone else. Many years later, their marriages ended in death or divorce. Then the sweethearts found each other, often with the help of the Internet, and rekindled their romance and married.

WHERE TO FIND GOOD STORIES

You can't write a great story until you find a great story. No amount of careful editing or literary polish will make a mundane story fascinating.

Reading local newspapers for short stories you can develop with more reporting is one way. You will more likely find these stories in a small-town newspaper (or its website) than in an AP, Reuters or CNN story. Local newspapers frequently publish short "end of the story" articles. A city official is convicted of a crime, a teenager survives a terrible auto accident, a young woman starts a clothing bank to help the poor, or a high-school teacher earns an "outstanding teacher" award. These short reports tell you "what happened" at the end of the story, but they don't tell you *how* or *why* it happened. They don't reveal the inner motivations or characteristics of people who end up in the news. They don't tell you what actions they took to create this outcome.

Many writers figure out the type of story they want to write and then look for referrals to someone who can tell and illustrate that type of story. Crocker Stephenson was writing a series of stories on infant mortality and he wanted to find a couple whose baby had died soon after birth. So he asked a nurse who worked in the neonatal intensive care unit, and she referred him to the couple whose baby had lived only 83 minutes. You can ask a local United Way agency for referrals to people who have "made a difference" in their communities. You can ask the Chamber of Commerce for referrals to someone who has moved from "failure to achievement" with a business success story. Hospitals and other nonprofits may have privacy policies and not immediately give you contact information, but will check with suitable sources for their permission to have a writer or reporter call them.

Watching local TV news reveals similar stories. Newspaper and television reporters don't have the time or the space to give in-depth reports. They can't do "character development" on the people they write about. They are producing one to three stories daily, moving from one deadline to the next. Taking the idea for a story and doing your own reporting and interviews does not involve any type of plagiarism as long as you don't steal direct quotes. You must do your own interviews.

Most people know someone within their immediate circle of friends and family who has survived cancer, an automobile accident, bankruptcy or failure, or has achieved a remarkable success. If you can't immediately think of someone, ask for suggestions from one of your parents, siblings or teachers. They may know an aunt, uncle or co-worker who has a remarkable or inspiring story. If you hear a story that moves, inspires or touches your heart, then you've probably found a good one that others will want to read.

TIPS ON TELLING STORIES

Do in-depth interviews

First, interview the central character several times and do supporting interviews with several friends and associates. You cannot write a powerful story based on one or two interviews. Remember that people, not places or things, create a story. Develop interview questions that will bring out not only the action but also your subject's values, beliefs and feelings. Create complex, multidimensional characters. Reveal the faults and weaknesses of your heroes and the admirable qualities of your villains. No one is all saint or all sinner.

When you interview your sources, ask them to tell you what they thought and felt at the time, not just what they said and did. Look for the problem, conflict or tension that will provoke readers' curiosity and keep them involved with the story. Here are 10 generic questions you can adapt for the main character in your story.

1 Describe the most critical turning point in your ordeal or journey.

2 Describe the moment when you felt most discouraged.

3 What was most difficult for you about getting through this time in your life?

4 How did people put obstacles in your way either intentionally or unintentionally?

5 What accomplishment gives you the most satisfaction as you look back?

6 What kinds of criticisms did you face from others? Give me an example.

7 What do you get complimented for most often?

8 What are the rewards of doing what you're doing now?

9 What would you do differently if you could go back and do it over?

10 What advice do you give others who face the same kind of challenge?

Besides formal interviews, record little details about people and the physical surroundings in which they live. However, use only those details that reveal character and move the story along. Don't include description just for the sake of exercising your literary talents. Spend time with the people you are writing about in places where they live and work. Hang around. Observe. Capture the mood and ambience of their lives.

Support interviews are crucial to the story. Most people are too humble to tell you everything they have achieved, much less describe their personal qualities. Sometimes people don't know all the facts about an illness or disease. That's why every good story needs support interviews from people who can add new dimensions and facts to the story.

"You need to interview other people. If you don't the person exists in a vacuum," says Judith Newman. "Sometimes you interview someone whose experiences of what they're going through seems different from what their family is going through and that should be reflected in the story. A lot of times people tell you a story about their illness and they really don't know all about it."[15]

Here are 10 questions you can adapt for support interviews.

1 How would you describe [your friend, etc.]?

2 What values or beliefs motivate him/her the most?

3 How did he/she deal with the pain or frustration?

4 What is his/her strongest quality? What else?

5 How does he/she deal with failures and setbacks?

6   What surprised you the most about how he/she dealt with the challenge?

7   How has he/she been recognized by others? Can you give an example?

8   What did the doctor say at the time about his/her condition or illness?

9   Can you give an example of a situation in which his/her best qualities were visible?

10   What do you think was the hardest thing for him/her to do?

Find the meaning or "take home" value for readers in your story. What is the point of the piece? What moral engine drives the story? Make it more than simply a factual chronology. Finally, set your story in its wider context. For example, if a person suffers from a rare disease, then do some research to provide details and context. Research the facts, statistics, issues or history of the larger issue that your story involves.

Build suspense

Predictability kills a good story. The problem that you introduce must make the reader wonder how the story will turn out. That's why good mystery novels are best-sellers. People love "page turners" that hook them and cause them to read past midnight to see how the story turns out. That's why the plots described earlier introduce an element of unpredictability by their nature. For example:

- Rising to the challenge: Will Roosevelt make it?
- Failure to achievement: Will Randy Pfund succeed?
- Victim to survivor: Will Louis Zamperino survive?
- Chaos to meaning: Will Sara-Rae and Josh discover new meaning?

Meg Grant is a former *Reader's Digest* editor who has edited some of its "Drama in Real Life" stories, which appear in every issue. She says, "These stories have to be told in a dramatic way in the same way a fiction writer would. The piece has to be crafted to be suspenseful and not give it all away in the first couple of paragraphs. You have to take the reader on this journey."[16]

Chronicle the events

Your job as a writer is to skillfully lead the reader step by step through the actions taken by the central character to confront and resolve the problem. These events can be physical or psychological. Psychological events are more difficult to describe than physical events. Meg Grant edited a *Reader's Digest* story about a kayaker who was lost in the ocean for three days. She says, "There was some question about whether there would be enough sustained action—because basically he sat on a kayak for three days. There wasn't a whole lot that happened. But it had the mental action, the hallucinations, that really carried the piece."

She adds, "Sometimes you have these things happen too fast, and you can't make that work either. You can have a helicopter crash and everything happens in an instant. That wouldn't work as a dramatic narrative because you have to have some time that elapses and some different things that happen."[17]

The plot point is a central part of the story. It's the moment when the central character recognizes what he has to do to solve the problem that he faces. After Debi Faris learned that the county cremated and dumped abandoned babies in a communal grave, she realized that she needed to raise money and find land to create a cemetery for them. After Sara-Rae and Josh discovered that their newborn likely would not survive, they started planning his funeral and even ordered a hand-crafted casket.

TIPS ON CHARACTER DEVELOPMENT

Character development is what fiction writers do well. Journalists who are accustomed to news and factual reporting need practice in revealing the traits of the people they write about. Character development means creating empathy. Character development will result from several interviews preceded by skilled question-writing and development. Not only must you get your subject to describe what happened but you must also ask questions that will bring out her motivating values and beliefs. You must ask her not only what she said and did but also what she thought and felt as these events happened.

Revealing character may involve these dimensions of a person's life:

- *Work habits.* What people do for a living may not reveal as much about them as their work habits. Look for such characteristics as ambition, perfectionism, carelessness or laziness.
- *Family relationships.* Whether a person is single, married or has children is basic information. The details of those relationships, however, are more revealing of character. For example, are they close and intimate or aloof and estranged?
- *Social affiliations.* Affiliations reveal character because someone who belongs to the American Civil Liberties Union, the Sierra Club or the United Auto Workers may possess different values than someone who is a member of the Rotary Club or the National Rifle Association.
- *Religion.* A person's religious affiliation or lack of affiliation also hints at their values and beliefs. A Roman Catholic differs in outlook and values from a Mormon or a Muslim. A practicing Buddhist evokes a different image from someone who is a practicing Baptist.
- *Moral beliefs.* Nothing is more basic to character than a person's ethical beliefs and practices. You have to look at what people do, as opposed to what they say, to show their moral character. Anecdotes and stories that reveal honesty are always refreshing to read. One of the frequently told stories about Abraham Lincoln is that he once walked a mile to return money to a store clerk who had given him too much change.

Character is revealed through effective and frequent use of dialogue. Dialogue and quotations are not the same. Dialogue occurs when two people talk to each other. Monologue, which originates from one person, is what writers normally call "getting quotes." Good quotes are better than no quotes, but conversation between two people really brings a story to life. Conversation also brings out the character of the people whose story you are telling.

Meg Grant says that *Reader's Digest* is trying to emphasize character development more in its stories. "Sometimes the action in these stories received more emphasis than the character development. Part of what we're trying to do now is put the character back in and make the character important. The mental and emotional journey is part of the story." When a freelance writer proposes one of these stories, "We need to know that the writer can focus on one or two characters, get in their heads and sort of go through what they went through psychologically," she says.[18]

Create an emotionally satisfying ending

Happy endings are more fun to read than sad endings. Can a true-life story have a sad ending? Many human stories do, and we could all tell a few of our own. The more relevant question is whether readers accept an unhappy ending. Can you publish a story that has an unhappy ending? You can, but it's tricky, and you have to handle it skillfully.

Think about yourself. When are you willing to watch a movie with an unhappy ending? Some sad movies end with a sense of closure and resolution, but others simply end. You leave the theater feeling like something was missing.

Readers will accept an unhappy ending if it leaves them with a sense of closure, resolution and meaning. The central character learns from his mistakes and decides to move on. The parent accepts the death of a child and finds new meaning. The victim of an accident accepts her disability and discovers a new talent that allows her to earn a living.

Just as there is no one right lead, there is no one right ending. Don't leave the reader hanging and feeling that the story is not over. While it doesn't have to be a happy ending, it must leave the reader with a sense of closure and resolution. Find an image, quote or anecdote that ties together the theme of the story and brings it to an emotionally satisfying ending. The ending should leave the reader feeling satisfied, inspired or moved. For example, "83 Minutes of Life" ends this way:

> So Sara-Rae continues to carry Lincoln. As she once carried him in her womb, she now carries his memory in her heart. It is memory that is not without pain, but it helps sustain her, and she will carry it until the day she dies.

IN-CLASS ACTIVITIES

Instructor: Discuss with your students some popular movies that display one of the six common plots discussed in this chapter: (a) rising to the challenge; (b) failure to achievement; (c) victim to survivor; (d) chaos to meaning; (e) saving the world; (f) love conquers all. Visit the websites of some current films to look at the trailers/previews.

Students: Write a 250-word summary of a dramatic, funny or interesting story based on your personal experience. Write with a narrative structure that includes the plot, resolution, time and place.

ASSIGNMENTS

Students: Find a true short story in a newspaper or blog from your campus or local area that you could develop into a nonfiction narrative with additional reporting and interviewing. Identify the missing elements in the story, the kinds of sources you would seek and questions you would ask.

Students: Find six stories from newspapers, magazines or websites that display each of the six types of plots discussed in this chapter: (a) rising to the challenge; (b) failure to achievement; (c) victim to survivor; (d) chaos to meaning; (e) saving the world; (f) love conquers all.

83 Minutes of life delivers lifetime of memories, grief for parents[19]

by Crocker Stephenson

Lincoln Ray Remmel was born at Froedtert Hospital on July 8, 2009. He died in his mother's arms 83 minutes later.

His parents, Sara-Rae and Josh, knew for months that their time with Lincoln—if he lived at all—would be brief. Devout Roman Catholics, they prayed for a miracle. Begged for one. Pleaded.

Sara-Rae says she carried her hope in that miracle the way she carried Lincoln in her womb: She nurtured it, and by its mere presence, hope sustained her.

But the moment doctors clipped the umbilical cord, separating child from mother, Lincoln's heart rate began to drop. He was placed in Sara-Rae's arms, Josh beside them. A priest wrapped in a yellow surgical gown baptized Lincoln before doctors finished closing Sara-Rae's C-section.

Dozens of family and friends attended Lincoln's birth, and the minutes that remained were filled with celebration. A crumb of birthday cake was placed on his lips. There was music. Kisses. Lincoln met his 13-month-old brother, George. He met both sets of grandparents. He met aunts and uncles and cousins.

Sara-Rae wanted Lincoln to know nothing but love, kindness and joy. Then heaven.

426

Lincoln was one of 70,824 babies born in Wisconsin in 2009.

That year, 426 babies died before their first birthday. A disproportionate share came from Milwaukee.

One could easily estimate the financial cost of infant mortality to our community. Tally the dollars and cents.

But how does one measure the loss of a particular child? Where are the instruments that might weigh the grief, map the scope of the injury or count the people the loss touches?

Sara-Rae is a former recruiter for Marquette University. Josh is a pharmacist. They live on a grassy cul-de-sac in a suburb west of Milwaukee.

They are ordinary people.

To them, Lincoln was not one of 426. He was their son.

Photograph

Taken just after the moment of Lincoln's death, a photograph shows Sara-Rae collapsed against the pillow of her hospital bed. Her hand covers one side of her face. She appears to have been slapped by sorrow.

Her brother, on her right, and her father, on her left, reach toward her. A yellow visitor's pass is clipped to her father's shirt. His shirt appears freshly pressed. His face is wrinkled, lined with anguish.

Lincoln—5 pounds, 4.6 ounces, 17 1/4 inches—is tucked among the plastic tubes and monitors affixed to his mother's left arm. He is swaddled in a blanket decorated with infant footprints. A fold in his blanket and a tiny cap obscure most of his face.

His eyes, having never opened, are closed.

Now I Lay Me Down to Sleep

The image was taken by Les Wallack, a semiretired photographer who lives in Slinger.

Wallack is a volunteer at the Now I Lay Me Down to Sleep Foundation, a chain of 7,000 photographers worldwide who attend and record the birth of terminally ill babies. The images are presented to the parents free of charge.

Over the past six years, Wallack has photographed about 30 births for the foundation. He's taking a break. It's too much, he says.

"Too much sadness."

Ultrasound

A fetus floats in a sac of amniotic fluid. This fluid gives the developing baby room to grow and helps his or her lungs develop properly.

Kidneys are essential to the production of amniotic fluid. During the early weeks of pregnancy, amniotic fluid is mostly water from the mother's body. After 20 weeks, most of the fluid comes from the baby's urine.

Sometimes embryonic kidney cells fail to develop, a condition called renal agenesis. One kidney can produce enough amniotic fluid to give a fetus an excellent chance of surviving. But the prognosis for a fetus missing both kidneys is bleak.

Without enough amniotic fluid, growth within the womb is impaired. Lungs do not mature. About 40% of these infants are stillborn. The lives of those who survive are measured by hours and minutes.

The condition, which occurs in about 1 in 4,000 births, is commonly called Potter syndrome, named after Edith Potter, a physician who first described its mechanics in 1946 at the Chicago Lying-in Hospital.

About 19 weeks into Sara-Rae's pregnancy, an ultrasound revealed that her baby was a boy and that he had only one kidney. That kidney was cyst-encrusted and would soon disappear.

Sara-Rae remembers a somber neonatologist telling her: "He's not going to make it."

Sara-Rae was alone. Josh was home taking care of George.

She remembers thinking—praying—"Why are you doing this to my son? What did we do?"

Chosen

Sara-Rae and Josh never contemplated terminating their pregnancy.

As long as Lincoln didn't suffer, Sara-Rae would carry him and, perhaps, she and Josh would get to meet him.

Sara-Rae had once thought about becoming a nun. She decided, instead, to marry and raise a family. That would be her ministry.

Josh shares her convictions, and together they try to understand their lives in the context of their faith.

And so, though they felt wounded by the God they loved, Sara-Rae and Josh believed their pregnancy was intrinsically meaningful.

"We were chosen for a reason," Sara-Rae says.

Sara-Rae and Josh say they felt a subtle but unmistakable pressure from Sara-Rae's doctor to end the pregnancy. They remember feeling that her doctor did not support their wish to carry a child to term who had little, if any, chance of leaving the hospital alive.

They say their doctor told them: "Well, call me when he stops moving."

License plate
The license plate on the Remmels' white 1999 Jeep Cherokee reads "Luke 1: 38."

It is a citation to the New Testament story of the Annunciation, when, according to the Book of Luke, the angel Gabriel appeared to Mary and announced that she would conceive and give birth to the son of God.

Mary, a virgin engaged to Joseph, tells the angel she does not understand how this is possible.

"For with God nothing shall be impossible," the angel answers.

The verse found at Luke 1:38 is Mary's response:

"And Mary said, 'Behold the handmaid of the Lord; be it unto me according to thy word.' And the angel departed from her."

Marcia Koenig
Within weeks of Sara-Rae's grim ultrasound, she and Josh placed their pregnancy in the care of the Fetal Concerns Program at Children's Hospital of Wisconsin, where they met Marcia Koenig.

Koenig is a mother of three who spent 15 years as a nurse in the neonatal intensive care unit before joining the staff of three other nurses in fetal concerns. The program, which has about 40 women enrolled at any given time, treats pregnancies complicated by fetal anomalies, lethal or not.

"What we do here," she says, "is an honor."

"We are with families at the most delicate, special, terrible part of their lives."

In Lincoln's case, Koenig helped the Remmels, as she puts it, "celebrate his birth, honor his life as brief as it might be, and prepare for his death."

Thursdays were the days the Remmels went in for ultrasounds. Sara-Rae would arrive in a state of anticipation—she would get a cloudy glimpse of her son—and of hope: Lincoln will have sprouted kidneys, amniotic fluid will have expanded her womb.

"It would break my heart," Koenig says.

"She would come in so hopeful for her miracle, and it hadn't happened."

Sara-Rae would swallow her disappointment. She would not let it spoil the moments she had looking at Lincoln within her.

"I would think," she says, "That is my child. He is so alive—so alive inside me."

Plaque
Near the hospital's birthing center is a room hardly big enough to accommodate a couch, a few chairs and a table.

Beneath the couch is a box of plaster. The plaster is used, if parents wish, to make molds of their terminal newborn's hands and feet.

Koenig reaches to a shelf above the couch and takes down a small object wrapped in tissue paper. There are several packages much like it.

A name is written on the paper. Inside is a heart-shaped plaque decorated with silver glitter. Attached to the plaque, the white plaster cast of a startlingly tiny foot.

"Some families don't come back for them," she says.

"We save them, though."

She refolds the tissue around the unclaimed plaque.

"Someday someone may come back."

"The Shack"

"The Shack" is a novel by William Paul Young about a man whose young daughter is slain by a serial killer.

Most of the novel takes place in a shack where the child was killed and where the man goes to confront God about an ancient question: How can a loving and all-powerful God allow the innocent to suffer?

Sara-Rae read the book during her pregnancy. She brought her copy with her to the hospital and stamped an imprint of Lincoln's left foot on the inside cover.

On Page 55, she has underlined a passage that occurs as the father contemplates his loss:

"He was swept away in the unrelenting and merciless grip of growing despair, slowly rocking back and forth. Soul-shredding sobs and groans clawed to the surface from the core of his being."

Casket

Rick Sturtz, a woodworker in Neillsville, built Lincoln's casket.

Much of it is made of walnut, from a tree that grew on the front lawn of the home where Sturtz's father-in-law lived for more than 60 years.

One of Sturtz's mentors was George Nakashima, a founder of the American craft movement. Nakashima believed planks of wood expressed the soul of the trees from which they were harvested.

In a letter to the Remmels, Sturtz explained that Nakashima worked primarily with walnut.

"Every walnut tree has, at its center, a 'hollow' vein that Nakashima referred to as the 'pitch center,' a physical manifestation of that tree's 'soul,'" he wrote. "You may note that the 'soul' of one of the walnut boards is revealed upon the interior of the box I have created for you."

Sturtz wanted the Remmels to understand the significance of all the materials he used to create Lincoln's casket.

The box's cherry top was a memento a woman gave him in 1997, Sturtz wrote. The cherry board had once belonged to the woman's father.

The birdseye maple in the bottom of the box came from a tree cut in the 1800s and retrieved in the 1990s from the bottom of Lake Superior within sight of the Apostle Islands. The planks were cut and dried by Sturtz himself.

"So," Sturtz wrote, "there are many 'meanderings' in this little box and also many reminders that every object is part of the circle we call life."

Father Peter

Father Peter Etzel, who was then pastor of the Church of the Gesu, was the yellow-gowned priest who baptized Lincoln at the hospital. Less than a week later, he presided at his funeral.

"This was a beautiful child," he says.

"What a gift he was."

He calls the Remmels' decision to carry Lincoln to term "a remarkable act of love." He says that in death "life has changed but not ended for Lincoln." He believes that Lincoln and his family will someday be united.

But how would he answer those who might ask: How can God allow the innocent to suffer? To what purpose?

"I wouldn't even try," he says.

"Because I don't know."

Delayed mail

Sturtz had never met the Remmels.

He is the brother of a woman who works part time as a receptionist at Becker Ritter Funeral Home, where—even as they made plans for Lincoln's birth—the Remmels made plans for his funeral. When the receptionist heard that the Remmels wanted a wood casket, she suggested her brother.

Sturtz did not charge Sara-Rae and Josh for the box he made for Lincoln. He asked only that they consider making a donation to the Christine Center, a Catholic retreat in Willard in Clark County.

"There are many ways in which one is compensated for his work," Sturtz wrote in his letter to the Remmels.

"You have given me my most 'lucrative' commission yet, and I thank you for the privilege and honor it has been."

The language of Josh's letter in response is nearly ecstatic. He calls Sturtz's gift "a most humbling and gracious offering that initially rendered us trembling with tears in our eyes."

In his letter, Josh tells Sturtz that his gift helped calm his and Sara-Rae's anger toward God and steadied their faith in his goodness.

"We unequivocally believe Providence's hand lovingly entrusted your sapient hands as instruments of God's peace and mercy."

Josh's letter is dated Jan. 22, 2010.

But he didn't mail it until that May.

The reason for delay is explained in a postscript.

Later that January day, Josh and Sara-Rae discovered that they were again pregnant. Josh held off sending the letter until he could announce the news and the results of an ultrasound that indicated their baby, whom they would name Paxton Abraham and who would be born Sept. 11, 2010, was perfectly healthy.

Walk

On a recent late summer day, several dozen people release balloons into the clouds above Lake Michigan.

One of the balloons, blue and smudged with a red kiss of freshly applied lipstick, bears the message: "Mommy loves you, Lincoln." Sara-Rae watches it rise with all the others.

Sara-Rae is with her mother, Bonnie Schalow; with Josh's mom, Mary Remmel; and with her sons George and Paxton. George, who is 3, waves at the balloons. Pax, not yet 1, is in his mother's arms.

The group has gathered at the lakefront for the Wisconsin Walk for Hope, a five-kilometer walk for families who have lost a child. Most are wearing T-shirts and buttons with photos of their loved ones. Tables have been set out beneath tents. A man with a microphone tells participants they better get going, before the rain comes.

Sara-Rae and her family walk south from Discovery World. To the west, storm clouds build in the darkening sky. The walkers hear thunder and most turn around and head back to the tents.

When Sara-Rae turns around, she nearly bumps into Dawn Kellner. Sara-Rae recognizes the name and smiling face printed on Dawn's T-shirt: Jared Kellner.

Jared was crushed on June 24, 2010, by a 13 1/2-ton concrete panel that fell on him from the O'Donnell Park garage.

The garage is just blocks from where the two women embrace and weep.

The women continue to hold each other even after fat drops of rain begin smacking the ground around them.

Entwined

Bonnie Schalow, Sara-Rae's mother, had a friend who, dying of ovarian cancer, told her: "I'll never know any of my grandchildren."

When Lincoln died, Schalow thought about her friend.

"I felt she could hold mine," she says.

Another woman she knows has a son who drowned. The woman could not bear to leave her home. The first time she did so was to join the Remmels to celebrate Lincoln's first birthday.

"The sources of our strength come from places you wouldn't expect," Schalow says.

"We are all so entwined."

"A new normal"

Sara-Rae and Josh call Pax their "rainbow baby."

"He came to us after a terrible storm," she says.

Pax has not replaced Lincoln. To the Remmels, he is the youngest of their three sons. A symbol of Lincoln is always present in family portraits. Usually it is in the form of a dolphin, one of Sara-Rae's nicknames for Lincoln during her pregnancy.

But if Pax is their rainbow baby, the truth is that the storm has never quite blown over. Sara-Rae has come to accept what she calls "a new normal," and one of the characteristics of that new normal is grief.

A few nights after the Walk for Hope, while the rest of the house was asleep, Sara-Rae got up, went into the living room, and—as she puts it—"let it out."

"I can't say I was trying to make sense of it all," she says. Mostly, she just wept.

"I was just feeling it. I need to feel it. It reminds me how much I love him, how integral he is to our family. Sometimes you just have to let yourself feel it."

So Sara-Rae continues to carry Lincoln.

As she once carried him in her womb, she now carries his memory in her heart.

It is memory that is not without pain, but it helps sustain her, and she will carry it until the day that she dies.

NOTES

1 Paraphrase of Jacob Baynham, "The Correction," *Cincinnati Magazine*, Nov. 2010, www.cincinnatimagazine.com/features/Story.aspx?id=1449769 (accessed July 7, 2012).

2 Don McKinney, *Magazine Writing That Sells* (Cincinnati, Ohio: Writer's Digest Books, 1993), 104.

3   Jon Franklin, "Structuring Stories for Meaning," *Nieman Foundation for Journalism.* www.nieman.harvard.edu/reports/article/101487/Structuring-Stories-for-Meaning.aspx (accessed July 7, 2012).

4   Crocker Stephenson, "83 Minutes of Life Delivers Lifetime of Memories, Grief for Parents," *Milwaukee Journal-Sentinel*, Oct. 1, 2011.

5   Speech at Ball State University, Muncie, Ind., April 11, 2012.

6   Kurt Vonnegut, *Bagombo Snuff Box: Uncollected Short Fiction* (New York: G.P. Putnam's Sons, 1999), 9–10.

7   Nicholas Schmidle, "Disarming Viktor Bout: The Rise and Fall of the World's Most Notorious Weapons Trafficker," *The New Yorker*, March 5, 2012.

8   Franklin, "Structuring Stories for Meaning."

9   Telephone interview with David E. Sumner, Dec. 11, 2003. Reconfirmed as accurate by e-mail on May 2, 2012.

10 Candice Millard, *River of Doubt: Theodore Roosevelt's Darkest Journey* (New York: Doubleday, 2006).

11 Bruce Schoenfeld, "The Art of Rebounding," *Men's Health*, Jan.–Feb. 2003, 114–119.

12 Laura Hillenbrand, *Unbroken: A World War II Story of Survival, Resilience, and Redemption* (New York: Random House, 2010), 119.

13 Elizabeth Gehrman, "The Tender Mercy of Cheryl Kane," *Good Housekeeping*, Jan. 2004, 79–83.

14 Ian Parker, "The Gift," *The New Yorker*, Aug. 2, 2004, 54–63.

15 Telephone interview with David E. Sumner, Dec. 11, 2003. Reconfirmed via e-mail May 2, 2012.

16 Telephone interview with David E. Sumner, Nov. 29, 2003. Updated correspondence April 16, 2012.

17 Telephone interview with David E. Sumner, Nov. 29, 2003. Updated correspondence April 16, 2012.

18 Telephone interview with David E. Sumner, Nov. 29, 2003. Updated correspondence April 16, 2012.

19 Reprinted with permission of the *Milwaukee Journal-Sentinel* © 2012. Original publication date Oct. 1, 2011.

14

ELIMINATING THE HO-HUM
FROM THE HOW-TO

KEY POINTS

- A four-part formula for service articles
- Tangible vs. intangible results
- Where to look for ideas
- Finding credible experts

The easiest way to break into print today is by offering an editor a timely and tightly targeted how-to article. Why? Because we live in an "er" world. Everyone is trying to be thin*er*, rich*er*, smart*er*, happi*er*, healthi*er* and saf*er*. Some people want to look young*er* long*er*; others hope to achieve professional success fast*er* so they can buy a larg*er* home and bigg*er* car soon*er*. This insatiable hunger for improvement has resulted in best-selling books with upbeat titles (*The Charisma Myth: How Anyone Can Master the Art and Science of Personal Magnetism*), popular television networks (HGTV and the Food Network) and hundreds of how-to articles in magazines and newspapers. The instructions can be as lightweight as how to "prettify" your potting shed, included in a spring issue of *Country Living*, or as serious as "How to Save the Christian College," offered by *Christianity Today*. Forget the old advice that writers should write about what they know. How-to articles enable curious writers to research and write about what they and their readers would *like* to know.

It's a fact: How-to articles sell magazines. Imagine that you're walking through an airport en route to catch a flight. You pause briefly at a

Feature and Magazine Writing: Action, Angle and Anecdotes, Third Edition.
David E. Sumner and Holly G. Miller.
© 2013 David E. Sumner and Holly G. Miller. Published 2013 by John Wiley & Sons, Inc.

newsstand to pick out a couple of magazines to pass the time between naps. How do you choose between this month's issues of *People, Vanity Fair* and *Elle*? What causes you to reach for *Fitness* rather than *Self*? Your flight is boarding; you only have a few seconds to make your decision, so you can't linger over the tables of contents. If you're like most magazine buyers, you make your selection based on two factors.

- First, the face featured on the cover tells you that a profile article is inside the issue (see Chapter 12). If the person—usually an A-list celebrity—interests you, chances are you'll buy the magazine to learn more about the personality behind the photo.
- Second, the cover lines highlight the most provocative contents. We mentioned these four-to-six-word blurbs earlier, but now it's time to consider the psychology behind them. One editor we know describes cover lines as little "marquees"—usually arranged on either or both sides of the celebrity's cover photograph—that showcase key articles inside. Editors write cover lines carefully because they know the impact that the blurbs have on single-copy sales.

Among the most successful cover lines are those that promote how-to or informational articles. Many newsstand browsers will buy a publication because a how-to article, touted on the magazine's cover, has succeeded in its mission to grab the attention of shoppers.

LOOKING FOR ANSWERS

How-to articles fall into the general category of "service articles" because they promise to be of benefit or service to readers. Some service articles impart information in standard paragraph form; others take a more instructional approach and walk readers through detailed steps arranged in a 1–2–3 or bulleted format. The unspoken message of a how-to article is: "If you buy this magazine, read this article and follow this advice you'll be better, smarter, happier, thinner, richer" or some other desirable characteristic. How-to articles are mainstays of home remodeling and dec-orating magazines—think *This Old House* or *Decor*—but they're equally appropriate for publications that focus on fitness, business, women, travel, gardening, sports or investments. Editors like them because they invite readers to get involved and experiment with the advice that the authors share.

Some magazines use bullets to cluster entire packages of advice, which they tout under single headings on their covers. The assumption seems to be that, if one bulleted story doesn't grab your attention, perhaps the next one will. As an example, an issue of *Kiplinger's Personal Finance* packaged four separate money-related success stories under the title "How They Did It."[1] Each piece of the package was written by a different author, was short (one page of text) and was presented in a question-and-answer format. Each story briefly profiled a person who had (respectively):

- built a million-dollar business
- paid for college on his own
- erased $70,000 in debt
- saved $1.4 million for retirement

Although the words "how to" aren't used, the message to readers is: Here's how one person solved a problem or dealt with a situation; if you face a similar problem or situation you might follow the advice and enjoy the same results. The strength of the package was its variety. Older readers would be interested in the person who had amassed a sizable nest egg. Younger readers might skip the retirement segment and go directly to the story about the college student who will soon graduate debt-free.

THREE CHARACTERISTICS OF SERVICE ARTICLES

The most effective service articles share three important characteristics: their topics are specific and timely; the author shapes the information to meet the needs of a tightly defined audience; and the advice is fresh and comes from credible sources.

The more specific and timely the how-to article is, the more irresistible the reader will find it. An article that promises to tell golfers "How to Shave Five Strokes off Your Game This Winter" is more powerful than merely "How to Play Better Golf." An article that outlines "Three Steps to Beating the Holiday Blues" is more engaging than "How to Overcome Depression." Whatever the words, the underlying promise is that this article will give readers information that they can use in their lives *right now* to reap quick, positive results.

Editors and readers seem to love numbers in cover lines, and the most popular numbers seem to be three, five, seven and 10. If you can come up with three, five, seven or 10 original ways to do anything, you may have the beginning of a good how-to article.

Because how-to articles address readers' current concerns, the writer must tune into the issues that are on the minds of the target audience. A cover line in *Marie Claire* magazine touched a nerve at a time when many companies were downsizing and distributing pink slips to employees: "How to Survive a Layoff—and Spot One Coming." The topic was especially pertinent for the publication's readers, whose median age is 33 and 76 percent of whom are working women.[2]

Shaping an article to fit the audience often involves doing research on the topic followed by additional research on the anticipated readership. When novelist Shirley Jump was launching her career as a freelance journalist, she looked for how-to topics that she could sell and resell to a variety of publications. As an example, she would research a broad subject such as "How to Buy Health Insurance for Your Employees" and then tweak it for different audiences. "Every industry has to buy health insurance," she explains. Her core research on health insurance would remain the same, but one article might advise small-business owners on buying health insurance whereas a second article might offer tips on buying insurance for a large, blue-collar workforce.[3]

Another way to shape an article to fit its readers is by writing in a style and tone that is conversational for the audience. Aware that the *Marie Claire* article on surviving a layoff would be read by young, professional females, author Lea Goldman chose this lead: "Here's a stark news flash: The pink slip is back, big time. Call it the latest grim reminder of these hard times, alongside gas prices inching to $4 a gallon and higher prices on everything from Cheerios to chicken wings."[4]

The final key characteristic of effective service articles—fresh advice from credible sources—is the one that students frequently ignore. Beginning writers too often cast themselves as the "experts" who are sharing information with readers. A writer may have a genuine interest in and some knowledge about a topic, but that doesn't qualify him as a quotable expert. In addition to facts gathered during interviews, the service journalist also uncovers statistics and other data from recent studies, surveys and reports. As an example, the article about "How to Survive a Layoff" contained current unemployment numbers and the names of well-known companies that had cut jobs in recent months.

THE FOUR-PART FORMULA

Popular how-to articles are often very specific and relatively short—1,200 to 1,500 words—and usually contain four parts, the last of which is optional. Here's the formula that many writers follow:

- introduction
- transition
- steps/tips
- wrap-up (optional)

Because the goal of a how-to article is to instruct or educate readers, the author wants to get to the tips as quickly as possible. The introduction is sometimes the only place that the writer can exhibit creativity; even so, the opening paragraph should be short and tightly written. The "job" of the introduction is to set up the rest of the article. Let's look at two examples of effective introductions.

The first example involves asking a question. Aimed at women who feel stalled in their careers, an article in *O, The Oprah Magazine* challenged readers to apply nine strategies that would push them to a creative break-through. Before sharing the strategies, the article's author, Lindsy Van Gelder, introduced the topic in this way:

> Whether you're an aspiring acrobat, an emerging jewelry designer, or a budding environmentalist, there comes a point when you require a special kind of strategy to jet propel yourself to the next level. Maybe you've hit a motivational wall and need to get back on track. Or maybe it's time to head down another road entirely. But how? What you're looking for is a breakthrough. Here are nine ways to make it happen.[5]

The advice that follows comes not from the author but the research she's uncovered and the experts she's interviewed. Each of the nine strategies is packaged as a separate element; the "glue" that holds the elements together is that they answer the question posed in the introduction. If readers follow the advice, they may be motivated to turn their dreams into reality.

A scenario, or creating a scene, is a second good way to introduce a how-to article. An introduction that describes a brief moment that readers can relate to is particularly effective if they've been in a similar situation. Example: Say you are writing an article titled "How to Make a Speech . . . and

Survive!" Chances are, readers who have suffered wobbly knees and near-panic-attacks when standing in front of an audience will want to learn how to ease their nervousness. The writer establishes additional common ground with readers with this introduction:

> Your heart was pounding as you took a final gulp of ice water and blotted your mouth with the napkin. Breathe deeply, you told yourself. Inhale . . . one, two, three . . . exhale . . . one, two, three. Why had you ever accepted the invitation to speak at the mother-daughter banquet?
>
> The waiter cleared the last dish from the head table, and the emcee began her introduction. There was no turning back. You were on.[6]

Having grabbed the reader's attention with the scenario, the writer next creates a transition sentence or paragraph and introduces the expert. This person might assure readers that they can survive the ordeal of making a speech if they follow five (or whatever number you choose) easy steps. These steps, often packaged in a bullet format, offer specific strategies to help readers through their next public-speaking obligation. The bullets, containing words of advice from one or more experts whom you've interviewed, might look like this:

- *Slow down.* Sometimes nervousness causes you to speak too fast. Prof. John Smith suggests that when you rehearse your speech you should keep an eye on the clock. "Try to talk at a rate of about 120 words per minute," he recommends.
- *Dress code.* Strive for a look that is slightly more formal than your audience, says fashion coordinator Mary Brown. A navy-blue suit and crisp white shirt will help you feel like the cool professional that you are. As an added benefit, the jacket will provide a dark background that will hide the inevitable clip-on microphone.

The most credible experts are those with impressive titles, important positions and a wealth of experience. Strive for variety. In the bulleted pieces of advice above, the sources have a blend of professional training and field experience. Note, too, that each piece of advice is supported by a quote or by an illustration.

The final element of a how-to article is the optional conclusion. If you have a strong wrap-up comment from one of your expert sources, this is where to use it. Otherwise, you can merely end the article with the last step or tip. Remember: It was the advice rather than your clever introduction or closing paragraph that attracted the reader to your article in the first place.

DELIVER THE GOODS

A how-to article must deliver what it promises. If a title and cover line promise an article that will explain how to kick a career into high gear or how to survive a public-speaking ordeal, the article inside should offer new information from reliable experts. You damage your credibility by luring readers into an article with a provocative title and then rehashing information that is common knowledge or easy to find on the Internet. This was the case several years ago when a women's magazine offered this cover line on a December issue: "How to Look Like You've Lost 10 Pounds Overnight." Readers who bought the magazine were dismayed by the article's tired suggestions: Wear something black and remember to stand up straight.

The Internet contains tens of thousands of free how-to articles published by businesses for their customers, the government for consumers, and educational institutions for their students. How-to articles from novice writers frequently fail to pass the "common sense" test. They rehash common-sense information everyone knows or can easily figure out with a Google search. To get published and paid for what you write, you must come up with original information readers can't find anywhere else. The only way we know to find original information is by interviewing experts.

A good service article should cause readers to clip and save the steps and tips. These steps should be so creative that readers cut them out, tack them on bulletin boards, tuck them under magnets on their refrigerator doors or stuff them into their wallets and purses.

TANGIBLE VS. INTANGIBLE HOW-TO ARTICLES

Most how-to articles fall into either the tangible or the intangible category. The tangible variety offers steps that, if followed, will lead to the creation of an object or an event. The results are visible. Three examples of this type of service article are:

- "How to Plan a Garden Wedding Under $500"
- "How to Launch a Home-Based Business"
- "How to Create a Low-Maintenance Garden"

Keys to writing a successful tangible how-to article are to keep the directions simple and illustrate the directions with examples and anecdotes that connect with the publication's audience. Too many steps can overwhelm and confuse readers. One way to avoid a complex topic is to narrow the focus. Example: "How to Plan a Garden Wedding Under $500." This variation of a broader article—"How to Plan the Perfect Wedding"—limits the focus by season (summer), location (garden) and budget ($500).

Intangible how-to articles often are described as "self-help" articles and reap results that may not be visible. Instead, they may involve personal changes. Three examples of this popular category are:

- "How to Be More Content in Your Job"
- "How to Control Your Jealousy"
- "How to Cope with Failure"

The types of expert sources will vary widely, depending on which type of how-to article you write. For the tangible service article you will want to talk with persons with first-hand experience and a great deal of expertise in the topic—a wedding planner, a small-business owner, a landscape architect who has created dozens of low-maintenance gardens. Remember, your best friend isn't a quotable expert on weddings just because she planned her own ceremony. She may make a good anecdote or an example, but she does not have the credentials necessary to serve as your expert source.

For an intangible how-to article you typically will interview a person with impressive academic degrees or formal training in the topic—a counselor or a psychologist. Otherwise, the article will have what we call the "authority problem." This means that the author writes in his or her own voice, doesn't give examples and fails to quote experts or authorities about the subject of the article. The reader may distrust the information and react by thinking, "Who says so?" As an example, we recall a writer who once wrote about how to overcome a food addiction. Since she had no training in counseling or nutrition, we questioned her authority in giving advice on the issue.

HOW-TO ARTICLES AS SIDEBARS

Editors often want article packages. These packages generally include a main story plus related sidebars, graphics and other illustrations. Taken together, a package can be more visually attractive than a single article because it involves several elements that break up a text-heavy page. The package also benefits readers because it offers variety and choice. A reader can read any or all of the elements on the page. How-to articles often make good sidebar accompaniments to long articles. Here are some examples:

Main Article	How-To Sidebar
Five Off-Season Honeymoon Cruises	How to Pack for a Week at Sea
Road Rage Heats Up	How to Keep Your Cool
Training Tips for Your First Marathon	How to Choose the Right Shoes for a Marathon

When packaged as a sidebar, a how-to article should not exceed one-fourth the length of the main story. It shouldn't repeat any information or quote the same sources as the article that it accompanies. It should complement the main story and is placed in close proximity to the major feature. Many readers choose to read sidebars before they decide whether to read the longer story. Because of their short length, sidebars seem less intimidating and require less of a time commitment on the part of readers.

WHERE TO LOOK FOR HOW-TO IDEAS

Because the how-to article is in demand at most magazines and newspapers, writers interested in earning bylines and building portfolios should master the format. Where are the best ideas for how-to articles found? A writer's personal experience is the most obvious place to begin the search for topics. For example, we know an animal activist who created a series of how-to articles aimed at pet owners, pitched the articles to the features editor of her community's daily newspaper and was rewarded with a weekly column. Even with her extensive knowledge of animals, this writer probably couldn't sustain a column for several months (or years) if she were to depend only on her personal experience. She supplements her knowledge by frequently interviewing veterinarians, trainers and other experts who provide a stream of fresh insights and information.

Another idea is to brainstorm with friends about problems they would like someone to solve or questions they would like someone to answer. *More* magazine came up with a list of 18 "things you should know by now" for their target readers (female, age 40+). The result was a package of short how-to articles that told readers how to bluff at poker, make an entrance, get a passport at the last minute, overcome writer's block, put out a fire, make a sales call and so on. Each standalone article contained a nugget of valuable advice from an expert. A television actress offered tips on how a woman can make a dramatic entrance to a room; a successful novelist provided ideas on beating writer's block; a Georgia firefighter suggested ways to put out a fire.[7] For the most part these were the "tangible" type of how-to articles. A more recent issue of *More* magazine promoted on its cover an example of an "intangible" how-to article: "Making Peace with an Angry Childhood."[8]

Another way to discover viable how-to topics is to think in terms of crossroads. People typically face many crossroads in their lives—decision points when they must choose to follow one course of action or another. They look for help in making the right decisions at these crossroads, and help can come in the form of how-to articles. Here are several examples:

Crossroad	How-To Article
Graduation	"How to Master the Job Interview"
Serious relationship	"How to Know if You're Compatible for Life"
First full-time job	"How to Evaluate the Benefits Package"
Buying a home	"How to Avoid Hidden Closing Costs"
Retirement	"How to Know When to Go"
Family illness	"How to Choose the Right Nursing Home"

Because today's magazines are so specialized, you can tune into a publication's demographics and surmise the decisions—minor and major—that its readers are likely to face. For instance, *Brain, Child: The Magazine for Thinking Mothers* might explore how to avoid obesity in children, and *Parents Magazine* might share tips on how to spot learning problems early on. On the other end of the age spectrum, *AARP Bulletin* appeals to older Americans and typically offers readers how-to articles about choosing a retirement community, re-entering the job market after age 60 or shopping for affordable health insurance.

An obvious place to look for how-to article ideas is the back issues of the publications that you plan to approach. Many magazines publish perennial how-to topics and are always looking for fresh angles and new sources. For example, *Prevention* magazine runs a variation of a "how to lose weight" article in almost every issue. *Runner's World* frequently revisits the topic of how to cross-train in the off-season. *Consumer Reports* tells readers several times a year how to purchase some kind of computer hardware.

Another place to look for strong how-to article ideas is in broadcast and print media that typically report new research and surprising statistics. A retirement bulletin, for example, revealed that in the next 18 years an American will turn 50 every 18 seconds and that more than 22 million Americans are in their 50s. The smart writer takes those bits of information and asks: What kinds of help will these people need to cope with all the changes they will face in the upcoming years? What crossroads will they encounter? What how-to articles will they be interested in reading? A feature in *The Wall Street Journal* claimed that late December is one of the busiest times of the year for cosmetic surgeons who perform elective procedures on patients. The creative writer might take this snippet of news and use it as a springboard for articles that explore how to shop for a doctor, decide on the right procedure and trim costs by going to an out-patient clinic. A single idea can keep a writer busy for a long, long time.

PULLING IT ALL TOGETHER

The following article is an evergreen—it never goes out of season—and can be tweaked for a variety of audiences and times of the year. This version is appropriate for spring (pre-vacation) and is geared to parents of children in the 8–12 age range. The author interviewed only one source, but that source had credibility as an "expert." Like many how-to features, this one uses the second-person voice ("you") to create a certain intimacy with readers. The tone is conversational, which explains why the expert is referred to by her first name after her introduction. The length is short (about 500 words) and the bulleted format gives an editor the flexibility to lop off a bullet if space is limited.

Hospitality begins at home[9]

Your intentions are the best. You want your kids to appreciate diversity, interact with people from other cultures and be willing to sample food they didn't access through a drive-up window. There's just one problem: The family budget won't cover a trip to an exotic destination this summer.

Not to worry, says Donna Stanley, whose international ministry has taken her to 79 countries—often with her sons, and now her grandchildren, by her side. Author of two books that help parents raise culturally-savvy children, Donna insists that families can travel to faraway places and still sleep in their own beds at night. The success of such adventures hinges on preparation . . . lots of discussions around the dinner table. Kids need to have a healthy curiosity about the world and not shy away from people simply because they look or dress differently. "That, plus a friendly smile, can break down all sorts of barriers," says Donna. She suggests four "field trips" that enable children to experience diversity, practice hospitality and learn a thing or two about geography.

Browse the mall
Stop by the mall, wander the shops, and ask your kids to read the labels on their favorite products. Where were those running shoes made? How about that cell phone? What country sent those neat super-hero action figures? Make a list of "countries of origin," and when you get home, find the countries on the map.

Eat at an ethnic restaurant
Thai? Italian? Mexican? Chinese? Greek? Choose a family-owned eatery—or a franchise—in an ethnic neighborhood and patronized by locals. Encourage your children to ask questions of the wait staff about the menu, the décor and the language they hear. "Don't worry if they sound impertinent when they ask, 'Why do you wear that funny hat?'" says Donna. "Kids are kids, and people rarely are offended by them."

Take in an international festival
Sometimes supported by churches as fundraisers, international festivals offer total cultural immersion. At a Greek festival your family will nosh on

wonderful pastries; the Irish may teach you to line dance; and the Germans will entice you with brat, kraut and an oom-pah-pah band. If the sponsoring church is open for tours, you might be able to duck into the sanctuary and take note of the architecture, stained-glass windows and religious icons.

Visit a college campus

Most college and university campuses have international student programs that are actively looking for host families. The number of international students studying in the United States is at an all-time high—more than 670,000, with India sending the largest group. Because many visiting students are on tight budgets, they can't go home for holidays, spring breaks and summer vacations. Sadly, some spend years here and never see the inside of an American home. "Ask to be put in touch with a couple of students who might need help with English," suggests Donna. "Invite them for dinner and suggest that they bring their friends." In the days leading up to the dinner, have your children do a crash course in the students' country. Plan a mixed menu by serving an all-American dish complemented by something from their cuisine.

IN-CLASS ACTIVITIES

Students: Work in teams of two and compile a list of five timely how-to/ service articles that you would read if you saw them listed in a magazine's table of contents. Give each article a catchy title that would make a good cover line. Determine what kind of expert a writer would need to interview to produce each article.

Students: Choose a "crossroad" (decision point) that people in their 20s are likely to face. Come up with three how-to articles related to the crossroad.

ASSIGNMENTS

Students: Research and write a 750-word how-to article that offers advice that, if followed, will lead to the creation of a tangible object or an event.

Students: Research and write a 750-word how-to article that offers advice that, if followed, will result in an intangible personal change or improvement.

NOTES

1 *Kiplinger's Personal Finance*, "How They Did It," April 2011, 59–65.
2 *Marie Claire*, July 2008, cover.
3 Presentation by Shirley Jump, July 26, 2008 at Midwest Writers Workshop, Muncie, Ind.
4 Lea Goldman, "Surviving a Layoff," *Marie Claire*, July 2008, 94–97.
5 Lindsy Van Gelder, "How to Spark a Breakthrough," *O, The Oprah Magazine*, Oct. 2011, 186–189.
6 Dennis E. Hensley and Holly G. Miller, *Write on Target* (Boston, Mass.: The Writer, Inc., 1995), 71.
7 Rebecca Adler et al., "18 Things You Should Know by Now," *More*, Oct. 2007, 137–148.
8 *More*, March 2012, cover.
9 Holly Miller; a version of this article appeared at Kyria.com.

15

MAKING A TIMELY CALENDAR CONNECTION

KEY POINTS

- Looking beyond the obvious
- How to tune into anniversaries and observances
- Creating a seasonal link
- Giving new life to old topics

A special double issue of *Newsweek* in 2012 carried the cover line "Welcome back to 1965." Motivation for the retro edition of the magazine was the launch of a fifth season of *Mad Men*, the popular TV series about the male-dominated advertising industry of the 1960s. In her introductory column that set up the theme, editor Tina Brown welcomed readers to *Newsweek's* "time machine" and explained that "the content of this issue is new and about today, but there are echoes aplenty from the past, all uncannily like the present."[1] Some of the "echoes" were subtle—the *Newsweek* nameplate on the cover and the type fonts used on the interior pages were resurrected from 1965. Other "echoes" were obvious—the advertisements featured women wearing bouffant hairstyles and men wearing two-inch neckties. The author of the cover story was a veteran female reporter who began her journalism career in the decade that the TV show recreates. Photos showed her as she looked then . . . and now.

The *Newsweek* gimmick worked because it was both extreme and clever. It also made two important points. First, magazine editors are

Feature and Magazine Writing: Action, Angle and Anecdotes, Third Edition.
David E. Sumner and Holly G. Miller.
© 2013 David E. Sumner and Holly G. Miller. Published 2013 by John Wiley & Sons, Inc.

Asking Pertinent Questions

Knowing that a story has a connection to the calendar helps a writer create questions to ask interviewees. As an example, Holly Miller once accepted an assignment to write a brief personality profile article (650 words) about Robin Roberts, former college basketball standout, ESPN sportscaster and co-anchor of ABC's *Good Morning America* (GMA) show. What made the story interesting and timely were three calendar-related facts. The article was slated for a magazine's October issue because October is Breast Cancer Awareness Month; the issue would hit the newsstands close to the one-year anniversary of Roberts' public announcement of her breast cancer diagnosis; and the interview coincided with the release of Roberts' new book, which dealt with her cancer experience. These factors gave the writer a clear focus for the story and assured her that the article would occupy a prominent place in the magazine and on the magazine's website. Knowing the story's angle helped the writer to come up with several open-ended questions to ask during her interview with Roberts. Some examples:

- As you mark the one-year anniversary of your cancer diagnosis, how are you different? What did the experience teach you?
- In your book you talk about your family's strong religious beliefs. What role did your faith play in your treatment and recovery?
- You will be making many public appearances linked to the release of your book. What message will you carry to your audiences? What do you hope people will take away from your experience?[2]

always looking for ways to ramp up the relevance of their publications by publishing articles that relate to whatever their readers care about right now. Many *Newsweek* readers eagerly anticipated the return of *Mad Men* after the show's hiatus of more than a year. Second, the magazine's feature articles weren't limited to nostalgia. Readers of news magazines aren't interested in revisiting history unless the past gives insights to the present. *Newsweek*'s editors successfully used events and newsmakers of the 1960s as springboards to events and newsmakers of 2012. The advertising industry as portrayed in *Mad Men* was compared to the ad industry of today. A profile article about presidential candidate Mitt Romney contrasted him with his father, George, who was a political force in the 1960s. Because the retro issue was a rarity and a surprise, it generated much favorable publicity for *Newsweek*.

To a lesser extent, editors work hard to include what we call calendar-related content in most issues of their magazines. By "calendar-related" we're referring to stories that tie into a season, a holiday, an anniversary or a special observance. This challenges writers, who must research and write articles weeks or even months in advance of publication so their stories will seem timely when they appear in print. Christmas comes in July and barbecue season arrives in December for magazine editors, who follow a six-month production schedule.

FAST FORWARD FOUR TO SIX MONTHS

Timing is everything in magazine journalism, and an article linked to Breast Cancer Awareness Month (see Sidebar 15.1) needs to land on an editor's desk in early spring (April or May). With lead times that vary from four to six months, writers and editors generally work at least a season or two ahead of the calendar. This means they're planning back-to-school issues in March, considering Christmas fiction submissions in July and looking for spring gardening features in November. Since monthly and quarterly magazines can't compete with the Internet, television, radio, daily newspapers and weekly magazines in reporting breaking news, the staffs at these publications must be creative if they are to ensure relevance in the material they offer readers.

Some calendar-related features are perennial favorites, and readers look forward to them year after year. *Sports Illustrated*'s famed swimsuit edition has become a pre-summer tradition since its launch in 1964; *Vanity Fair* does a popular Hollywood issue every March that coincides with the Academy Awards presentation; and *Yankee* produces its special New England travel issue each May–June.

Beyond these well-known themes, calendar-related material includes articles that are linked to events and activities (June weddings, October tailgate parties), stories that mark anniversaries (the 9/11 terrorist attacks,

Martin Luther King Jr.'s death) and features that call attention to special observances (Father's Day, Mother's Day, Labor Day). The smart writer looks to the calendar for timely article topics and submits them to publications at precisely the right moment.

To tune into the creative ways that editors tie content to the calendar, simply visit the library or stop by a well-stocked newsstand and take note of the seasonal articles promoted on the covers and listed in the tables of contents. For example, an April issue of *Bon Appétit* offered "Spring Chicken: 5 Easy Recipes to Start the Season."[3] Eight months later, a cover line on the same magazine promoted "Our Guide to an Easy, Stress-Free Christmas Party."[4] Just in time for midterm exams, the feature section of *The Wall Street Journal* published an article aimed at college students. The headline asked, "What Is the Best Way to Study?" and the article provided answers as to the recommended time to review the toughest material (right before you go to bed) and the best breakfast to eat the morning of an important test (oatmeal).[5]

Calendar-linked articles can deal with serious or lightweight topics. A spring issue of *Scholastic Instructor*, a magazine geared to teachers, suggested "Poolside Picks: Top Professional Titles" for subscribers who wanted to catch up on educational reading during their summer vacations.[6] Because the first issue of any year is a logical time to help people make their annual resolutions, *Smart Money* once urged readers to "Set Your Course Now for the Year Ahead."[7] April is an appropriate month to publish articles related to finances because readers are feeling the pinch as they prepare their income-tax returns. Thus, "Get the Paycheck You Deserve" drew attention to an April issue of *Self*.[8] *Smithsonian*, known for its serious journalism, had fun when it marked the 30th anniversary of Elvis Presley's death by running an article about Elvis impersonators, or "tribute artists" as they call themselves.[9]

CREATING A SEASONAL LINK

Occasionally a writer tweaks an article to make it seem seasonal. A visit to a southern spa once resulted in a feature story for a November issue of *The Saturday Evening Post*. It began with the question "Time for a winter tune up? Florida's newest spa will strip you of stress, wrap you in luxury and send you home fit for the holidays." Had the writer offered the same article for publication in a May issue of the magazine, she might have changed the introduction to "Time to shape up for swimsuit weather? Florida's newest spa will strip you of stress, wrap you in luxury and send you home fit for long afternoons at the beach."[10]

A creative writer with a good topic can "adjust" a feature story to make it seem appropriate for any season. An article about home security—"How to Burglar-Proof Your Home"—might point out that intruders often take note of houses left vacant during the summer vacation season. A different spin on this same topic might remind readers that winter weather keeps neighbors inside, where they're oblivious to the sights and sounds of nearby break-ins. Since the topic is an evergreen—of perennial interest to readers— it takes on an element of importance with the insertion of a few sentences that link it to the season.

Some months lend themselves to easy content-calendar connections. December is the most obvious because of the holidays. Every year readers can expect to see cover lines such as "50 Great Gifts Under $25" and "Newlyweds Blend Family Yule Traditions." Other months, such as February and March, seem to challenge writers and prompt them to stretch to come up with timely ideas. Two competing magazines—*Parents* and *Parenting*— once featured similar cover lines for their February issues. The title of one article was "Be My Valentine: Sweet Ways to Make Your Kids Feel Special."[11] The title of the competition's article was "I Love You: Little Ways to Make Your Child Feel Special."[12] Apparently the editors were on the same wavelength.

When brainstorming topics with a calendar connection, writers need to keep a magazine's demographics in mind. As an example, the majority of readers of the short-lived *Hallmark Magazine* were female, married and age 35+. Those subscribers probably liked a February issue that had red roses on the cover and cover lines that promoted three seasonal stories: "One-of-a-Kind Valentines," "Romantic Dinners" and "12 Real-Life Stories of How We Met."[13]

FORGET "THE FIRST THANKSGIVING"

If the calendar is a good place to begin hunting for timely article ideas, it's only a starting point. You have to look beyond the obvious and avoid predictable topics that sound like retreads from your sixth-grade spiral notebook of essays. No editor is interested in your take on "The First Thanksgiving," musings about "What Christmas Means to Me" or recollections of "How I Spent My Summer Vacation." One of our writing colleagues used to warn her students against "I-strain," her label for the dangers of writing from a first-person point of view.

An easy way to move beyond predictable article ideas is to brainstorm with a calendar in front of you. For January, move past the general topic of New Year's resolutions and think about specific changes that you've heard people say that they want to make in their lives. January gives them the feeling of a fresh start, a clean slate, a new beginning. Perhaps this is the year they hope to get out of debt, go back to school, lose weight, start exercising, kick a bad habit or strengthen a key relationship. Each resolution can lead to a how-to feature (see Chapter 14). For example, readers who resolve to get out of debt and be more fiscally responsible this year might want to read an informative article titled "How to Cut Your Credit Card Debt in Half." Its timing seems right on target in January.

For a June publication, a student writer might ask a handful of college professors, college administrators and prominent alumni to offer parting words of wisdom to the senior class that is about to graduate. The writer might follow up with this question: "What do you know now that you wish you had known when you walked across the stage and picked up your diploma so many years ago?" (Beware: Some interviewees, when asked such open-ended questions, can't resist delivering lofty sermons.)

For September, commemorate Labor Day by reminding readers that Henry Ford announced the eight-hour, five-day workweek on Sept. 25, 1926. Then leave history behind and interview current experts for their responses to these questions: Is it possible to abide by Henry Ford's proposed workweek if you're a corporate trainee competing for a management position? How many hours is a young lawyer expected to put in if he hopes to become a partner? And what about the entrepreneur who operates a one-person shop? If he works at home, is he always on duty?

CONNECTING THE DOTS

Three of the best websites for calendar-related ideas are Butlerwebs.com/holidays, History.com and Gone-ta-pott.com. Plan to spend a good deal of time exploring these resources, and be prepared to let your imagination run rampant. The first website (Butlerwebs.com/holidays) allows you to choose a month and then scroll down day by day to learn of holidays, special observances, anniversaries, and the births and deaths of prominent people.

For example, among its many designations, May is Better Sleep Month. Combine this bit of trivia with recent research that found that too many Americans aren't getting the recommended seven to eight hours of sleep a night; add the fact that most colleges and universities schedule their final exams during May; and you come up with an ironic conclusion: Many students become sleep-deprived zombies during Better Sleep Month. Could this be the beginning of a feature story? Start your background research by visiting the websites of the National Sleep Foundation (www.sleepfoundation.org) and the American Sleep Association (www.sleepassociation.org). Next, conduct interviews with faculty and students to elicit their advice and anecdotes about prepping for finals—the right and the wrong way. Create a sidebar that lists the value of caffeine, energy bars and other products that inhibit sleep. The result is an informative and timely article.

The second website (History.com) makes it easy for you to connect the past with the present and come up with some colorful story ideas. For example, you can type in an area of interest such as "women's rights" and learn that one of the founders of the women's rights movement (Elizabeth Cady Stanton) was likely the first bride to omit the word "obey" from her marriage vows. Use that as a springboard to a feature article about contemporary couples who are writing their own vows and tailoring their wedding ceremonies to express their personalities and beliefs. Make the point that this trend is nothing new; in fact, it dates back to Elizabeth Cady, who promised in 1840 to love, honor but not necessarily *obey* her husband. Interview two or three couples as well as a sampling of clergy who officiate at these unique ceremonies. Offer it for publication in a June issue of a magazine.

The key to a successful anniversary article is making the topic interesting to present-day readers—much like *Newsweek* did with its retro issue. Whereas writers should weave enough history into a feature story to educate readers on the event's significance, they should avoid merely retelling what historians have already documented in textbooks. Among the most interesting calendar-related stories are those that bring to the forefront anniversaries that are unknown to most people (Gone-ta-pott. com will help you here). Let's look at several diverse examples culled from various websites.

Historic event: In 1849, Elizabeth Blackwell became the first woman in America to earn a medical degree. She went on to open a hospital just for women and children and was instrumental in starting a medical college to provide training for women in 1867.

Anniversary article idea: Almost 150 years after Dr. Blackwell helped to educate women for careers as physicians, what kind of progress have women made in the medical profession? How many women make up the student bodies of medical schools today? Are they as successful as men when they establish their practices? Remember that Elizabeth Blackwell would not be the focus of this article; she would merely be a way of getting to the issue.

Historic event: Sometime between 1832 and 1839, a man named Robert Anderson invented the first electric carriage that ran on rechargeable batteries.

Anniversary article idea: Here we are, so many years later, and Americans still haven't embraced the idea of the electric car. In light of the rising cost of fuel, why are 21st-century Americans so reluctant to trade their traditional gas guzzlers for hybrids? What alternative means of transportation are in development?

Historic event: Almost 80 years ago, "The Original Amateur Hour" debuted on radio and quickly became one of the highest-rated programs on the air. During the broadcast's long history, first on radio and then on TV, more than a million amateur acts auditioned for the chance to compete for audience votes.

Anniversary article idea: The popularity of "Star Search," "American Idol," "America's Got Talent" and "So You Think You Can Dance" are proof that Americans still love the idea of helping to discover the next big act. What is the lure of these shows? Is there a "performer" in all of us yearning for a chance at stardom? Interviews with a psychologist, a media expert and a couple of fans could provide answers.

Historic event: In 1995 the first item was sold on Amazon.com. Two years later the popular website became the first Internet retailer to secure a million customers.

Anniversary article idea: Twenty years later, what has been the impact of online shopping? How can small, independent businesses compete?

Sample Calendar-Related Query Letter

The following query letter pitches a timely idea that relates to the 100th anniversary of the Girl Scouts of the USA. The author proposes a total package—a main story plus sidebars—that allows the editor to make refinements according to the available space and the interest level of the publication's readers. As you read the letter, notice how the author weaves in some history without getting bogged down in the past.

Dear _____:

It's time to break out the Tagalongs®, Trefoils and thin mints—the Girl Scouts of the USA are turning 100! With more than 50 million alumnae and 3.2 million current members, the Girl Scouts and their Girl Scout Promises have become cultural icons in the United States.

I'm proposing an article in which five women will share their stories on how Girl Scouts shaped their lives. From a trip to Japan to running a local council, these women's tales provide both modern perspectives and glimpses into Girl Scouts 50 years ago.

In addition to these chronicles, sidebars will include a whimsical timeline of Girl Scout cookies throughout history and a serious conversation with current leaders on the challenges that Girl Scouts face today.

May I send you this nostalgic roundup on speculation to commemorate the March anniversary? When Juliette Gordon Low founded the Girl Scouts, she wanted to help girls develop and connect outside of isolated home environments. One hundred years later, this message still resonates with young women and still influences the Scouts of yesterday.

Sincerely,
Kelley E. Frye[14]

SIDEBAR 15.2

NEW LIFE FOR OLD TOPICS

Even a tired topic gains new life when it is tied to an observance or an anniversary. Many writers have probed the serious issue of teen pregnancy, but Mother's Day provides an appropriate time to revisit the topic. The resulting article—call it "Moms Too Soon" or "Premature Moms"—might update readers on current teen-pregnancy statistics and on new efforts to discourage the trend of kids having kids. The Mother's Day connection also might prompt an article about professional women who delay motherhood until they've successfully launched their careers. Again, the topic isn't new, but the calendar connection makes it seem worthy of another look.

The idea of one generation passing its wisdom on to the next may be tired, but, if the advice is offered in conjunction with Father's Day, it still can work. Consider interviewing three or four successful people from different walks of life who credit their adult success for their fathers' influence when they were children. Include lots of anecdotes as you tell their individual stories in a round-up article. Or talk with a handful of well-known people and ask them to recall the best advice their fathers ever gave them. *AARP* magazine did this for a May–June issue and called it "Tops of the Pops." The secondary title explained: "Some of our favorite people recall the lessons they learned from their dads."[15]

Major historic anniversaries often serve as the foundations of major magazine articles. Hundreds of publications in the United States and Europe recognized the 100th anniversary of the sinking of the *RMS Titanic* on April 14, 1912. When the United States observed the 60th commemoration of D-Day (the Allied forces' invasion of Europe during World War II), the story made the cover of *Time*. Much more than merely reminding readers of the date and recapping the event, *Time* made the statement, "D-Day: Why It Matters 60 Years Later."[16] A second story featured the recollections of 10 veterans who witnessed the Normandy landings.

The anniversaries of landmark Supreme Court cases give writers good reasons to revisit hot topics. *Brown vs. the Board of Education of Topeka, Kan.*, which led to public-school desegregation, was decided in May 1954. Fast forward 60 years and many writers will likely be taking another look at education in America and assessing whether schools are offering equal opportunities to all students. Another important case, *Roe vs. Wade*, legalized abortion in the United States. The court handed down its decision in 1973, and writers have revisited the controversial issue on subsequent anniversaries.

BIRTHDAY ISSUES REAP REWARDS

Sometimes editors create anniversary issues that directly or indirectly celebrate the publications that they edit. These often generate extra advertising revenue and attract record newsstand sales. *Time* has commemorated its 25th, 50th and 75th anniversaries with special issues. *Rolling Stone* produced three special issues in 2007 that celebrated the magazine's 40th anniversary. In 2008, *Esquire* began a year-long commemoration of its 75-year history. While most anniversary issues mark the birth of a magazine, at least one served to memorialize the end of a publication. This was the case in April 2008 when *CCM* produced its final print edition on the 30th anniversary of its founding. It survives as an online magazine (www.ccmmagazine.com).

Typically, magazines use five-year markers to call readers' attention to anniversaries of all kinds. A 10th, 15th, 20th or 25th anniversary is more appropriate than a 17th, 23rd or 51st anniversary. Of course, some calendar-related events are so extraordinary that magazines begin the celebration well in advance. This was the case when the millennium approached. Starting in April 1998, *Time* issued a series of editions that cited the most influential people of the past 100 years. The project, according to managing editor Walter Isaacson, was "more popular than we dared dream."[17] These themed editions not only sparked lively conversation but also prompted readers to buy and save them as keepsakes. For its last magazine of the century, *Time* announced its choice as "Person of the Century"—Albert Einstein.[18]

IN-CLASS ACTIVITIES

Students: Brainstorm and come up with three feature article ideas with a connection to autumn. Come up with three ideas linked to May. Come up with three ideas related to Christmas. Come up with three ideas related to college graduation.

Students: From your list of article ideas, choose the one you think is most marketable. What kind of research would you need to do? Whom would you need to interview? Are there any sidebar possibilities? What title would make a provocative cover line?

ASSIGNMENTS

Students: At the library, choose a favorite monthly magazine and review all 12 issues from one year. Jot down the calendar-related cover lines that you see.

Students: With the help of an almanac or one of the websites mentioned in Chapter 15, identify at least two historic events that will mark either 25- or 50-year anniversaries in the next 18 months. How might you give a current spin to the anniversary? How can you make it meaningful to today's readers?

NOTES

1 Tina Brown, "This Special Issue," *Newsweek*, March 26 and April 2, 2012, 2.

2 Interview with Holly Miller, June 25, 2008.

3 *Bon Appétit*, April 2012, cover.

4 *Bon Appétit*, Dec. 2011, cover.

5 Sue Shellenbarger, "Toughest Exam Question: What Is the Best Way to Study?" *The Wall Street Journal*, Oct. 26, 2011, D1.

6 *Scholastic Instructor*, May–June 2004, cover.

7 *Smart Money*, Jan. 2004, cover.

8 *Self*, April 2007, cover.

9 "Elvis Lives," *Smithsonian*, Aug. 2007, 64.

10 Holly G. Miller, "Southern Comforts," *The Saturday Evening Post*, Nov.–Dec. 2001, 62–63.

11 *Parents*, Feb. 2004, cover.

12 *Parenting*, Feb. 2004, cover.

13 *Hallmark Magazine*, Feb.–March 2008, cover.

14 Used by permission.

15 Al Roker and Friends, "Tops of the Pops," *AARP*, May–June 2005, 29–30.

16 *Time*, May 31, 2004, cover.

17 Walter Isaacson, "Why Picking These Titans Was Fun," *Time*, Dec. 7, 1998, 6.

18 *Time*, Dec. 31, 1999, cover.

WRITING ABOUT TRENDS AND ISSUES

KEY POINTS

- Definition of trend stories
- Definition of issue stories
- Five characteristics of trend and issue stories
- Where to look for trend and issue stories
- How to choose the best angle
- How to do the reporting

In "Digital Music's Cloud Revolution," *Rolling Stone* explained the rise of music services by saying, "This year the digital-music revolution took its biggest step since iTunes launched in 2003." The story told about the launch of MOG, Spotify, iTunes Match, Google and Amazon's cloud-based music services in 2011. Spotify's founder and CEO told *Rolling Stone*, "We've seen a bit of a perfect storm this year. The world is getting more connected, and it's becoming more and more obvious that music belongs in the cloud."[1]

"Going by the numbers, America is gaga about ballroom dancing. The nonprofit USA Dance, Inc., reports a 35 percent spike in the number of people taking lessons and attending ballroom events over the past ten years," wrote Holly G. Miller in her *Saturday Evening Post* article "America Goes Dance Crazy" (reproduced in full at the end of this chapter).[2]

Trends occur in pop culture, politics and plenty of other places in life. Strong feature stories explain these trends by using facts, numbers, quotes

---

Feature and Magazine Writing: Action, Angle and Anecdotes, Third Edition.
David E. Sumner and Holly G. Miller.
© 2013 David E. Sumner and Holly G. Miller. Published 2013 by John Wiley & Sons, Inc.

and plenty of anecdotes and examples. They explain how, where and why trends occur. Trend stories differ from news stories because they don't report on a single event but on a complex series of events that come together to form a trend. They go beyond telling "what happens" to explaining "why" and "how" events happen and how they affect readers. For example, the *Rolling Stone* story included a sidebar with the pros, cons and cost of each of the five most popular cloud music services. Miller's story says that the dance craze can be attributed to the rise in TV dance shows and Americans' improved desire for health and fitness. A desire for personal contact in a digital-crazy world is another reason that Miller documents through the use of examples and expert quotes.

Trend, issue and controversy stories don't have clear-cut boundaries, and some stories may contain elements of all three. These definitions and examples will, however, help you understand the distinctions.

DEFINITION OF TREND STORIES

A trend is any social phenomenon or type of behavior that is increasing or decreasing in frequency. Trends always have a numerical dimension, such as growth or decline, and can occur in society, pop culture or any field of endeavor. For example, around 410,000 unmarried teenage girls aged 15 to 19 gave birth in the United States in 2009, a 30 percent decline from 20 years earlier. *The Wall Street Journal* reported that autism diagnoses in children have increased 78 percent in the past 10 years.[3] The causes remain unclear. Students have written about autism and teenage pregnancies by personalizing them with local examples and explaining them in the context of the national trends.

Writers can produce trend stories about these serious topics or lighthearted pop culture trends. A recent YouTube and pop culture trend is "the cinnamon challenge," which involves contestants competing to swallow a spoonful of cinnamon without gagging or choking.

"If you see it once, it's interesting. If you see it twice, it's a trend. If you see it three times, you can report on it," said Gail Belsky, a Fordham University journalism professor and former magazine editor.[4]

Trends vary and change according to the economy, said Belsky. She said five years ago she asked one of her classes how many of them bought organic foods. About 90 percent of the class raised their hands. When she asked why, most of them said for health reasons. Five years later, she asked the same question and only about 10 percent of the class raised their hands. When she asked why, most of them cited the economy and said they could no longer afford organic foods.

DEFINITION OF ISSUE STORIES

An issue is a phenomenon or development that threatens some segments of the public at the same time that it may benefit others. Consequently, it has opposing sides. Issues evolve into controversies and a prolonged, intense debate without an immediate or easy solution. For example, many Americans are concerned about illegal immigration; specifically, the unsecured borders and the 11 million estimated illegal immigrants. Immigration offers economic benefits for the new arrivals but critics argue that these people strain the social services and education budgets of the states. Several states have passed laws allowing state and local police to check the immigration status of suspected illegal immigrants. Civil rights activists protest that these state laws result in ethnic profiling.

Another controversial issue in the United States, Canada, France and Australia is fracking, a technique used by natural gas producers. It involves the "fracturing" of shale to release the natural gas contained within rocks. The newly discovered technique has produced a plentiful supply of natural gas at record-low prices. Critics, however, argue that when multiple "fracks" are done in adjacent wells the risk for contaminating drinking water rises, according to "The Truth About Fracking" in *Scientific American*.[5]

FIVE CHARACTERISTICS OF TREND AND ISSUE STORIES

These five common characteristics of trend and issue stories will help you conduct research, do interviews and write the stories:

1 Their purpose is to inform and educate readers about a trend, issue or controversy and how it affects them. They can be characterized as "lighting a candle instead of cursing the darkness."

2   They must quote the views of expert sources and experiences of people who are affected by the trend or issue. These stories are challenging to report because they require multiple sources—not a single person or a single interview.

3   They must document the trend or issue with factual evidence, which often includes statistical data to prove that a trend or issue exists. Anecdotal evidence and miscellaneous quotes are not sufficient.

4   Issues that evolve into controversies often benefit one sector of the population while hurting others. Both sides must be reported fairly.

5   Trends and issues can quickly become outdated. You must continually look for fresh angles and approaches to these topics.

WHERE TO LOOK FOR TREND AND ISSUE STORIES

A trend story can start with anecdotal evidence in the behavior of people around you. You may notice more people taking online courses, which leads to an investigation into the rise in online-only degrees. You may notice more people using their spring breaks to engage in volunteer mission trips, which can lead to a story about the trend. You may notice fewer people pledging sororities and fraternities, which leads to an investigation as to whether it's a national trend. One student wrote about the 400 percent rise in vinyl LP album sales since the trend originated in 2005.

"Don't just limit it to the people sitting next to you or around you," said Gail Belsky. "Move out demographically and look at people a few years older than you or a few years younger. Notice what they are doing. What seems commonplace to people in one generation may be a feature story for people in an older generation," said Belsky.[6]

Some trends may be dangerous or controversial while others are positive or light-hearted. In his article "What's Up, Doc? The Prestige of Honorary Degrees Falls to Record Lows," Joseph Epstein poked fun at the decreasing prestige of honorary doctorates because so many universities have offered them to nonqualified celebrities and donors.[7]

In "Why U.S. Workers Are Losing the Tug of War Over Toilet Paper," *The Wall Street Journal* reported on the "controlled delivery" trend in company and public restrooms. They save on paper costs by making dispensers tricky to use. The story quoted a building-services manager who defended the practice, and included statistics related to the most popular complaints about public restrooms.[8]

Trends with harmful consequences turn into controversies as people debate solutions to the problems they bring. For example, *Jane* reported on "Women Who Rape: A Scary Trend You Don't Hear About: Female Sex Offenders." This story reported on the increasing number of female sex offenders. In "Why Some Brothers Only Date Whites and 'Others,'" *Ebony* quoted experts who attributed the rise in interracial dating and marriage partly to the cross-racial hip-hop culture.[9]

"Those trend stories can start with the anecdote or the big picture. Trend stories can come from statistics and can come from having a friend who is having some problem," said Ted Spiker, a University of Florida journalism professor and former senior editor at *Men's Health*. Spiker said that anecdotes bring a story to life but the statistics add credibility.

"If you don't have a number there, you haven't proven to me there's a trend," he said. "You don't need a ton of numbers. The anecdotes can drive a story, but you have to have at least one or two numbers. You can use government statistics or even polls or surveys."[10]

For the United States, one of the best sources to start with for "the big picture" and to look for trends in numbers is www.fedstats.gov. More than 100 government agencies gather statistics on every conceivable aspect of American life. You can browse the site by dozens of subject areas ranging from crime, cancer, employment and unemployment to birth, death, marriage and divorce rates. Fedstats.gov offers overviews of the country as well as state-by-state breakdowns in each topic area. Trends in the divorce rate, for example, can be localized for your area.

Writer-editor Gail Belsky said that trend stories originate in everyday life before they show up in statistics. "When I was the executive editor of *Working Mother*," she says, "the census had just come out that showed for the first time in 24 years that the number of women who returned to work after having a baby went down."

Yet she says she already knew about it. A couple of years earlier, a young colleague had told her at lunch that she did not have a single friend who had gone back to work after having a baby. Belsky continued:

To me, that speaks volumes. That is the trend, far more than waiting for the census bureau to spit out a number. You see that kind of anecdotal information once you start looking around and seeing what's going on. You see it once, you think "hmmm." You see it twice and you know there must be a third one. You know if you do a little walking and talking, you're going to come up with more.[11]

CQ Researcher, as explained in Chapter 4, offers a great source for ideas and background for articles on current events issues. It provides a balanced overview of issues the media and public are discussing, such as human rights in China, the accuracy of the Internet, cyberbullying, the gender pay gap and the future of airlines.

For example, a recent edition focused on "College Football: Is the Drive for Prestige and Profit Out of Control?"[12] Revenues at the top six athletic conferences had increased by more than 50 percent in the past six years, with the Southeastern Conference revenue topping $1 billion. More than 10 coaches earned an annual salary of at least $3 million—many times what college presidents earn. The Bowl Championship Series bowl selection system remains controversial because it excludes lesser-known teams from the most prestigious bowls.

Another edition of *CQ Researcher* focused on "Crime on Campus: Are Colleges Doing Enough to Keep Students Safe?" A federal law requires colleges and universities to report the number of major crimes that occur on their campuses each year, but critics say the data fail to give a complete picture of offenses by or against students, which frequently occur off-campus.[13] You can localize a campus crime story by comparing data from your university against the national data.

Some trends and issues turn into controversies because people disagree intensely about their causes, solutions or both. Sometimes the opposing groups are clearly defined, such as labor and management, faculty and administration or Republicans and Democrats. At other times, supporters and opponents come from less clearly defined coalitions. For example, rising fuel costs motivated public support for ethanol, which in turn made more farmers start growing corn. But, as demand for corn rose, food prices rose, shortages resulted and a controversy developed over whether tax-subsidized ethanol production was the cause and whether it did any good to alleviate high gasoline prices. Some newspapers and magazines ran "pro" and "con" articles about whether ethanol was causing rising food prices and shortages.

Voter identification laws are controversial in the United States. The first voter ID laws were passed in 2003, and 30 U.S. states currently require some form of photo or nonphoto identification before allowing people to vote. The issue generally divides along partisan lines with liberals opposing the laws and conservatives favoring them. Liberals argue that they discourage low-income voters from coming to the polls, while conservatives argue that they prevent voter fraud and "voting by dead people."

Newspaper feature editors want balanced stories with comprehensive, equal coverage of opposing points of view. Magazine editors may permit writers to argue a point of view, depending on the magazine's tradition. *National Review* is one of the most conservative commentary publications, while *The Huffington Post* is among the most liberal. Each covered the issue of voter IDs from its own point of view. In "Not a Race Card: Photo IDs Are a Necessity to the Integrity of the Voting Process," *National Review* argued that voter IDs make sense because Americans are required to have a photo ID to get a library card, drink a beer, cash a check, board an airplane, buy a train ticket or check into a hotel.[14] In "Voting Rights Are Under Attack", *The Huffington Post* argued that photo ID cards restrict the voting rights of 5 million Americans who are disproportionately low-income, disabled or minority voters.[15]

Controversies and trends begin behind the scenes before they turn into news stories or statistics. You can get a real "scoop" if you're the first to report them. These stories often begin with a hunch based on personal observations and conversations. Following that hunch into interviews and research can give you the scoop. For curiosity-filled writers, it's the most exciting and interesting type of story to write.

Ted Spiker recommends that a good way to spot a trend is to "Call up a retail store and say, 'What's your latest, greatest thing that's selling and why?'"[16] Visit auto dealers and find out which cars are selling quickest and slowest as gas prices reach record levels. Visit food pantries or rescue missions and ask the staff whether high unemployment is straining their resources.

HOW TO CHOOSE THE BEST ANGLE

For trends, the first question is, "Where does the real story lie?" Is it in the trend itself, the causes of the trend or the consequences of the trend? You can look at the people it hurts or the people it helps. The answer may not be obvious and you may need to do some research and interviews before you know which angle to pursue in depth.

The second question to ask is whether you have specific examples that demonstrate how and why this trend is occurring. You can focus on one person who illustrates the situation or gather quotes from several people for a "round-up." Your best material will come from those with the closest exposure to the trend and those whom it most directly affects. Beware of casual quotes from observers that reveal no insight into what is going on.

Third, can you find an expert who can give an overview of the subject area? Besides individuals directly affected by the subject, you will need to interview someone with an overview, a neutral expert who is knowledgeable about the subject.

Every issue or controversy offers a dozen angles to pursue. To help in choosing the best angle, start by analyzing the issue from these three perspectives: central development, benefits to those who support it and harm to those who oppose it.

- *Central development.* Something begins to happen. For example, electronics companies begin exporting jobs and factories to countries with cheaper labor.
- *Benefits for some.* As the development advances, it affects people, places or institutions in specific ways. Consumers get cheaper televisions, DVD players, smartphones and other gadgets. Developing countries get new jobs and a higher standard of living.
- *Harm to others.* As the effects take place, impacted groups react to this development. Labor groups may pressure legislative bodies for import restrictions. Some communities lose factories and jobs and look for ways to rebuild their economies.

Each of these three phases of development, however, involves four directions for the writer. For each one you can look at *magnitude* (how much, how many, how often); *location* (which regions or countries are most affected); *diversity* (which groups of people are affected); or *intensity* (to what degree or extent they're affected).[17]

HOW TO DO THE REPORTING

Feature stories on trends and issues can't depend on a single source. They require reporting from four different sources:

1 *People who are the players.* The players in the events are the principal sources—the people involved at street level in the nitty-gritty of the

action. They may include the mother of an autistic child or a couple that takes ballroom-dancing lessons.

2   *People who are experts.* The experts earn a living from finding, fixing or dispensing information. They may be as diverse as college professors and auto mechanics.

3   *Hard facts.* The facts add background, context and depth. They can let you know where, when, why or how these types of events occur.

4   *Numbers.* These convey the magnitude, enormity or frequency of any phenomenon. Numbers are especially important in trend stories. They add credibility to your main points and demonstrate that you did your homework.

A solid story may require dozens of hours in the library followed by dozens of interviews. It depends on background research for context and interviews for color. Too much secondary research without interviews will make it dull. Likewise, interviews alone with too little background research will make it irrelevant or outdated.

Hal Karp, a former writer for *Reader's Digest*, says the first step is to read everything published on your topic:

> The most important thing I can do is locate what's already out there. I have to do as much research as possible, which is incredibly time consuming. I ask myself, "Who's looked at this topic?" and "What science is behind it?" I will really dig into the research and find all the primary materials.

Karp says that good features require a combination of anecdotes and hard factual evidence:

> You have to have both. Anecdotes bring it to life and make readers see themselves in the topic. You can read statistics all day long about how many kids die in car crashes, but you may not think about it much until you read about a mother who lost her kid in a crash. It's really important to have both.[18]

Almost every type of social issue, medical disease, industry, product group and political issue has trade or special-interest groups representing it. If you're writing about the rise in autism, for example, a quick online search will reveal three national associations and dozens of regional and state organizations. If you're writing about organic foods, there are two groups: The Organic Trade Association and the Organic Consumers

Association. If you're writing about illegal immigration, you can consult the American Immigration Council. These organizations may have research reports and statistical data on their websites and full-time staff members whose jobs are to work with the media.

"A lot of the time those people are going to be my best finders," says Karp. "They're interested in getting the word out because that's their job. They want to help journalists." You can find thousands of these groups in the three-volume *Encyclopedia of Associations, Regional, State and Local Organizations* available in most libraries or the Internet Public Library's Association Directory (www.ipl.org/div/aon).

Stories can contain too few or too many quotes. Stories with too few quotes run the risk of boring readers or overwhelming them with too many facts. Stories with too many quotes can make readers work hard to interpret what's being said. Most readers prefer a healthy balance of interpretive reporting by the writer and colorful and insightful quotes from sources.

Hal Karp says, "I use quotes kind of like exclamation marks as the final point—the point that really drives it home. I also use quotes to balance an article. People like reading articles that contain some quotes and some paraphrases. Sometimes you quote because you just need to break it up."

Finally, good pacing depends on the logical movement of ideas throughout the article. You can improve the pace of these stories by ensuring that your paragraphs or sections thematically progresses from one to the next in a logical fashion. Sentences and paragraphs should follow one another in logical sequence. And each paragraph must contain a significant or unique idea that in some way develops your main theme.

Earlier in this chapter we used the phrase "It's better to light a candle than curse the darkness." Adlai Stevenson, former American ambassador to the United Nations, made the statement when he praised Eleanor Roosevelt during an address to the UN General Assembly in 1962. "She would rather light candles than curse the darkness, and her glow has warmed the world," he said.[19] Think of writing trend, issue and controversy stories as "lighting a candle in the darkness." You perform a public service for readers and make a crazy world easier to understand.

IN-CLASS ACTIVITIES

Instructor: Display on a screen the website of a popular news site, such as BBC.com, Reuters.com or CNN.com. Look at breaking news stories and ask students to create some feature story ideas that are related to the news but with a potential shelf life of several months.

Students: Bring an example of a trend story to class from a magazine, newspaper or website. In groups of two or three, summarize your story and discuss whether you can find another story idea based on the *causes* or *consequences* of the trend.

ASSIGNMENTS

Students: Choose a recent trend and develop three angles based on the approaches discussed in this chapter: (a) central developments, (b) causes and (c) consequences.

Students: If your library has a full-text or online subscription to *CQ Researcher*, choose an issue discussed in the last two months and write a 500-word summary of key facts and viewpoints about this topic. Use this as a starting point for developing an article idea targeted at a niche magazine whose readers have specialized interests.

Steppin' out: Americans give ballroom dancing a whirl—again![20]

By Holly G. Miller

At age 66, Donna Thomas was an unlikely candidate for dance lessons. Raised in a conservative church, she had graduated from a college that frowned on anything that resembled what it categorized as "rhythmic activity." Yet two years after becoming a widow, Donna summoned her courage, walked into a studio near her Springboro, Ohio, home and announced, "I want to dance." It was a smart move.

"I needed to be with people," she recalls. "I figured I had a choice: either withdraw and stay in my shell or step out and try something new." The "something new" included mastering the waltz, samba, cha-cha-cha, and jive. Her timing—on the dance floor and off—was perfect. At home, she was learning to operate solo and make all the decisions that she and her husband used to make jointly. In the studio, she felt the pressure ease and the responsibility shift as she became part of a team again. "I didn't have to be in charge," she says. "All I had to do was follow my partner's cues and react to the music. That lifted my spirits."

Professional dancers share Donna's enthusiasm but use different terms to express it. They talk less about lifting spirits and more about boosting endorphins. Then they tick off the many perks of working up a sweat while dialing down the stress. "It's the most joyful way for me to get my exercise, get my heart rate up, and get the endorphins I crave," says actress Jennifer Grey, who has done as much for dancing as it has done for her. As costar of the 1987 hit film "Dirty Dancing," she motivated millions to head for the ballroom. Last year she had a similar effect when she earned top honors on ABC's *Dancing with the Stars* (*DWTS*) and proved, at age 50, it's never too late to strap on 4-inch heels and out-perform competitors 20 years her junior. "Dancing takes me out of my busy monkey mind and dumps me in a physical space where I can be free from thinking," she says. "It's the best way for me to feel connected and alive. I take one dance class every week, but it's not enough. I want to be able to do it everyday."

Although ballroom dancing has never lacked for fans, its popularity is on the upswing thanks to shows like *DWTS* and its FOX-TV counterpart, *So You Think You Can Dance*. Statistics confirm that Americans are giving ballroom dancing another whirl. USA Dance, Inc., the nonprofit group that promotes competitive and social dancing across the country, reports a 35 percent spike in the number of people taking lessons and attending ballroom events. The organization now has 180 chapters and sponsors programs that reach out to more than 200,000 people. Motivation for getting involved varies, often influenced by the age of the dancer. Teens like the pace—the faster the better. Seniors cite the research that shows dancing keeps the body agile and reduces the likelihood of developing dementia.

"People are *definitely* getting off their sofas and starting to dance again," emphasizes Carrie Ann Inaba, one of *DWTS*'s three professional judges. "During our first season on television people would come up to me on the street and say, 'I watch the show every week.' By the time the second season rolled around they were saying, 'I'm talking my husband into getting into a dance class.' Now they're telling me, 'We're taking lessons and having a ball!'"

They're also dancing in unlikely places. One of the most colorful offshoots of the trend is the "flashmob," best described as a spontaneous outbreak of dancing in very public settings such as shopping malls, school cafeterias, hotel lobbies, food courts, and train stations. Participants, alerted to a planned flashmob through social media, congregate and wait for their cue.

"People are just milling around when all of a sudden one or two start dancing," explains Angela Prince, a spokesperson for USA Dance. Others join in and before long—in a flash—the mob's toes are tapping, hips are swiveling, and bodies are gyrating. "I remember being on a Caribbean cruise when a couple of passengers started a flashmob while we were eating dinner," recalls Angela. Everyone, including waiters and crew, caught the spirit and formed a conga line of about 300 people that snaked its way around the dining room. "There's an element of surprise to a flashmob," she says. "You look for a unique place where people least expect it and you just have fun."

Although Angela agrees that reality shows such as *DWTS* have encouraged the ballroom craze, she credits other factors as well. "Dancing seems to experience a bump in popularity after events that change our lives," she says, using the years following World War I and II, Vietnam, and 9/11 as examples. "Music is great therapy, and dancing gives people the opportunity to come together."

Technology also may have a hand in the revival. Mary Murphy, a studio owner and frequent choreographer and judge on *So You Think You Can Dance*, says dancing provides a degree of human connection that is missing since people have come to rely on the Internet as their primary mode of interaction. She works with elementary and middle school students to introduce them to what she calls the "language" of dance. "Some of the kids come kicking and screaming into the classes, but teachers tell me that they see positive changes within a few weeks." The idea of a young couple joining hands as the boy guides his partner and the girl follows his lead, is appealing. It allows students to communicate without the pressure of finding the right words. "Kids who have behavior problems have calmed down and found new ways to express themselves," says Mary.

When it comes to the therapeutic benefits of dancing, Mary can speak from first-hand experience. She underwent treatment for thyroid cancer a year ago and faced the possibility of losing her ability to talk. Today she is cancer-free and as exuberant as ever. She used dancing to help prepare for surgery, and she integrated it into her recuperation regimen. "Getting that diagnosis and hearing the word 'cancer' was the one time in my life I just wanted to shut down and have a major pity party, which I did for a couple of days," she admits. "Then I decided I absolutely had to keep my body moving. So I added a lot of activities to my pre-surgery program to increase my lung capacity. I did yoga, pilates, and dance exercises every day. I wanted to be in the healthiest condition possible." Her plan worked. She says that she "sailed through" the operation and the recovery that followed. The reason? "I absolutely believe it was because of dance," she says.

Fans of the TV shows can attest to similar dramatic effects that dancing has had on several of the competitors. "Kirstie Alley immediately comes to mind," says Carrie Ann Inaba. Dubbed "the incredible shrinking Kirstie" because of the weight she lost during Season Ten of *DWTS*, Kirstie decided to wear the same costume on the show's finale as she wore for the initial competitive round. This proved to be a challenge for the wardrobe staff because the dress had to be downsized by 38 inches. The combination of a healthy diet and rigorous dancing had caused her to lose almost 100 pounds.

"A lot of times our self esteem is determined by the shape we're in and how good we feel about ourselves," says Carrie Ann. "Dancing brings you back to a place where you feel physically confident about your body because you're strong again. Your core muscles are working; you're in shape; and you're in tune with your body. I watched Kirstie rediscover her confidence last season."

Dancing also can replenish a zest for life. Donna Thomas discovered this when she stepped out of her comfort zone and signed up for ballroom lessons back in Ohio. "I was searching for a new direction and I thought, 'Why not?'" recalls Donna, who occasionally goes dancing almost 20 years later. She took private lessons until she felt confident enough to enroll in a group class where she met new people and made many friends. Friday night dance parties came next, and eventually her instructors encouraged her to enter competitions. She still has the sassy black dress and high heels that she wore when performing, and somewhere there's a scrapbook of photos, certificates, and ribbons. Her favorite memory, though, doesn't involve winning prizes or gaining recognition. It's more personal. "I remember the night I invited my kids to attend a dance with me," she recalls, with a laugh. "They were surprised at how good I was!"

NOTES

1   Steve Knopper, "Digital Music's Cloud Revolution," *Rolling Stone*, Dec. 22, 2011–Jan. 5, 2012, 16.

2   Holly G. Miller, "America Goes Dance Crazy," *Saturday Evening Post*, Nov.–Dec. 2011, 40.

3   Shirley S. Wang, "Autism Diagnoses Up Sharply in U.S.," *Wall Street Journal*, March 30, 2012, A5.

4   Telephone interview with David E. Sumner, April 5, 2012.

5   Chris Mooney, "The Truth about Fracking," *Scientific American*, Nov. 2011, 305, 5.

6   Telephone interview with David E. Sumner, April 5, 2012.

7   Joseph Epstein, "What's Up, Doc? The Prestige of Honorary Degrees Falls to Record Lows," *National Review*, May 26, 2008, 10.

8   Jared Sandberg, "Why U.S. Workers Are Losing the Tug of War Over Toilet Paper," *The Wall Street Journal*, Sept. 10, 2003, B1.

9   Zondra Hughes, "Why Some Brothers Only Date Whites and 'Others,'" *Ebony*, Jan. 2003, 70–72.

10 Telephone interview with David E. Sumner, April 5, 2012.

11 Telephone interview with David E. Sumner, April 5, 2012.

12 Kenneth Jost, "College Football: Is the Drive for Prestige and Profit Out of Control?" *CQ Researcher* 21, no. 41, Nov. 18, 2011.

13 Peter Katel, "Crime on Campus: Are Colleges Doing Enough to Keep Students Safe?" *CQ Researcher* 21, no. 5, Feb. 4, 2011.

14 Hans A. von Spakovsky, "Not a Race Card—Photo IDs Are Necessary to the Integrity of the Voting Process," *National Review*, Aug. 29, 2011.

15 Christina Pelosi, "Voting Rights Are Under Attack and We Must Organize to Get Them Back," *The Huffington Post*, April 1, 2012. www.huffingtonpost.com/christine-pelosi/voting-rights_b_1394706.html (accessed July 8, 2012).

16 Telephone interview with David E. Sumner, April 5, 2012.

17 Credit to William Blundell in *The Art and Craft of Feature Writing* (New York: Penguin Books, 1986) as the original source of these concepts.

18 Telephone interview with David E. Sumner, Nov. 15, 2003.

19 *The Phrase Finder.* www.phrasefinder.co.uk (accessed July 21, 2008).

20 Reprinted with permission from *The Saturday Evening Post*, Nov.–Dec. 2011. ©.

PART V

EXPLORING DIGITAL OPPORTUNITIES

"I'm convinced that there are only so many words per day in the human body: If you do some longish e-mails and a few tweets, you feel done."

Anna Quindlen, Pulitzer Prize-winning journalist

While the basic principles of reporting and writing remain unchanged, digital publishing venues have proliferated exponentially. We now have creator blogs, critic blogs, conversationalist blogs and collector blogs. Cinematic storytelling involves using video, audio and digital graphics to tell stories that people can read anywhere and anytime on their smartphones and mobile devices.

17

BUILDING A STORY BLOG

Brad King

KEY POINTS

- What type of blog?
- Creator blogs
- Critic blogs
- Conversationalist blogs
- Collector blogs
- Beyond the page
- Podcasts
- Vlogs
- The fear

The magazine world has moved beyond the printed page. Regardless of their personal stance on print publishing, writers must be able to operate within the digital world if they hope to carve out a meaningful career. The days of the single-platform feature writer spending months on one exclusive story are gone. Instead, modern writers are expected to think about the distribution of their stories on multiple platforms. Freelancers are hired based upon their ability to deliver content to a digital audience.

Sites such as Gawker.com pioneered the pay-per-page-view model of journalism, the type of model that pushed a rolling string of short posts built around search-optimized topics. More traditional magazines such as *The Atlantic* have adopted digital blogging networks with a vast online reach around big-name writers who have a strong point of view.

Feature and Magazine Writing: Action, Angle and Anecdotes, Third Edition.
David E. Sumner and Holly G. Miller.
© 2013 David E. Sumner and Holly G. Miller. Published 2013 by John Wiley & Sons, Inc.

Both models have opened new avenues for writers to make their way into the magazine world, but to become successful it's important to understand the layout of the online landscape. Essentially, this new world gives writers two distinct benefits they didn't have before the advent of social technologies: Once writers have a dedicated audience, they are in better position to negotiate payment for stories, and they can build their careers writing about topics that interest them.

Dan Gillmor, a former technology columnist at the San Jose *Mercury News* and one of the United States' most influential technology writers, says in his book *Mediactive* that journalists need to consider creating a "home base" for their personal brand.[1] In the age of social media, when ideas can circumnavigate the globe in hours, writers and reporters need a place where they can respond to criticism of their work in order to maintain credibility. Without that home presence, he argues, writers have a hard time responding to controversies.

WHAT TYPE OF BLOG?

While launching a blog may seem like an obvious choice, one of the hardest decisions new bloggers make is determining what they want to post. On the surface, it seems like a rudimentary problem that should be easy for a writer to figure out. After all, writers are paid to find stories and share them with a larger audience, which is exactly what we have come to expect on blogs. The problem comes when you start to consider the day-to-day operation of the site. For instance: How often should you post? How much time should you spend building and interacting with an audience? How much of your writing should you give away for free, and how much should you hold back for story pitches? Who owns the story you've written for a magazine, and how does that affect your ability to grow that story beyond a single article?

In just a short time, you can find yourself frozen with fear when it comes to building your blog because you don't understand what is happening across the Web. Fortunately, there are some good frameworks for analyzing what's happening online. One excellent framework comes from Josh Bernoff and Charlene Li, authors of *Groundswell*,[2] a book that examines how corporations should use social media to reach customers. While the book's target audience isn't writers, the authors' "sociotechnographic profile"—a framework for understanding how people interact on the

Web—is helpful to writers trying to figure out how they should go about building the home base that Gillmor says is so important.

While we won't go into the entire profile, we will examine four *Ground-swell* personas as a way to help writers begin to craft a personal blog. Those four personas are:

- creators, who make original content
- conversationalists, who largely respond on blogs or forums
- critics, who offer criticism, expert or amateur, on topics
- collectors, who gather information from various sources[3]

CREATOR BLOGS

You can approach a blog built around original writing in several ways. For long-term projects, you may want to build a community site around the reporting you are doing, posting bits and pieces of news related to the idea of a specific story. For instance, when John Borland and Brad King were building the blog for their book *Dungeons and Dreamers*, they launched the site a year before the book came out.[4] Once the site was running, the two writers posted seven to 10 short pieces each day. Built around computer games and popular culture, the site's purpose was to supplement the book and create a community of people interested in their book's topic.

Running a site like that takes at least two hours a day, but long-form topics may end up in a book. It's the most effective way to create an audience. By the time the book was published, Borland and King had a dedicated readership of 50,000 people for the blog. Certainly, building that network was a long, slow process, but it helped the writers flesh out their ideas, talk with the gaming community and find new leads.

Obviously a full-blown community site might be too big an undertaking for a general-interest feature writer whose work changes each month, but, for those ideas that have staying power, these types of creator blogs are worthwhile.

However, not every creator blog has to be dedicated to one subject. For instance, *The New Yorker* writer and author Malcolm Gladwell (www. gladwell.com) built his site around the body of his work instead of one idea. His site has individual pages dedicated to his books (*Tipping Point, Blink, Outliers, What the Dog Saw*), an archive of his work at *The New Yorker* and a blog where he writes about whatever is on his mind: from childhood memories to literary responses to those who have taken offense to his work. While the site encompasses a variety of writing formats—books, magazines, blog posts—it's all built around the identity of Gladwell. It's his home base.

CONVERSATIONALIST BLOGS

When *The Atlantic* repositioned itself as a digital-first publication in 2010, not everyone was convinced the magazine—which has been published since 1857—would survive. After all, few other publications at the time had managed to navigate the every-changing landscape of new media. The company, though, made one important editorial choice: launching *The Atlantic Wire*, a daily blog network where its writers and editors can talk about news of the day.

Unlike creator blogs, which focus on posting ideas and thoughts related to one subject, conversationalist blogs allow a magazine to respond to daily happenings in a smart, informed way. Whereas good long-form feature writing helps to set the agenda for conversations, T*he Atlantic Wire* is a great example of how writers can engage in conversations that others have started.

To really master this type of blogging, writers need to deploy a series of digital tools to help them understand the tenor of conversation. This means using tools such as RSS readers, Google Alerts, Twitter search filters, blog searches and other automated search tools to keep up with the daily flow of information. Setting up some of these can take time. For instance, Brad King's personal Google Reader has more than 250 publications, research firms, conferences and bloggers' information aggregated into one place. Naturally this took time to complete; however, once the Reader is set up, writers can get an up-to-the-minute snapshot of what's being published by scores of sites.

Understanding how to sift through the deluge of digital stories is just the first component of a conversationalist's blog. Once a post has been published, writers must turn their attention to engaging with their readers. Before a writer launches this type of blog, he must consider two elements:

1   You must always remember that conversations are two-way streets. If you engage in a conversation online, expect responses and don't expect them to be deferential simply because you are a writer.

2   You can't simply speak into the void. To build a conversation, you must spend time engaging with your readers and responders, moderating the activity on your site and ensuring that interactions remain civil. If you neglect this part of the conversation, you'll quickly find your voice drowned out (or worse, ignored) on your own site.

CRITIC BLOGS

Similar to traditional critic sections, critic blogs should be built around a special interest and used to build some area of expertise. Unlike those traditional spaces, however, the critic blog is a curated response to a particular subject, a fact-checking site that tries to find objective fact within the constant flow of information across the Internet. Think of the best critic blogs as a way to bring order to the chaos of the open marketplace of ideas that is the Web.

One of the more respected critic blogs is that of Dr. Ben Goldacre, who writes BadScience.net, a site dedicated to correcting factual errors that creep into news reports about scientific studies. Goldacre has parlayed his blog into a gig at *The Guardian*, one of the United Kingdom's largest newspapers, and has also became a best-selling author.

Another critic blog that has achieved notoriety among public relations professionals is The Bad Pitch Blog (http://badpitch.blogspot.co.uk), run by P.R. professionals Kevin Dugan and Richard Laermer. The two collect the worst public relation pitches they've seen, and then explain what's wrong with them on the site. Normally they don't use the names of the offending company or professional; however, the two are not above outing professionals who continue to violate basic rules of the news and information game.

What both these blogs have in common is a dedicated viewpoint toward objective truth. They are not concerned about giving "equal weight" to all sides of an argument, an attitude New York University professor Jay Rosen describes as "the view from nowhere." In fact, Goldacre's goal is the opposite. His blog cuts through half-truths and subterfuge and attempts to replace it with the best thinking of science today, while Dugan and Laermer shine a light on some of the laziest practices in public relations.

As you might imagine, a writer who steps into the middle of contentious debates must come prepared with facts and a reasoned argument. Unlike conversationalist blogs, which focus on user interaction and should thus be more immediate, the critic blog gives writers time to think about bigger ideas before they weigh in on them.

COLLECTOR BLOGS

One complaint often leveled at the Web is that the sheer size of it keeps users from developing a common understanding that creates a shared experience. Back in the days when large cities had three television networks, two newspapers and a few radio stations, most of the United States experienced the same news flow. You could talk with your neighbors and be reasonably sure they had read, heard and seen the same information you had. That's no longer true.

This gives intrepid long-form writers who are developing deep sources and investigating ideas the chance to compile definitive source lists for readers. During the baseball season, *ESPN Insider* published a weekly column of links and very short summaries of the best local writing from from around the league. This enabled baseball fans to catch up with the entire 32-team baseball league in one place. After all, no matter how dedicated people are, they are unlikely to spend their free time aggregating work from the 31 *other* teams.

However, the writers of collector blogs don't need to hold back their own work. BoingBoing.net, the Internet's "directory of wonderful things," is a group effort. A small handful of writers including David Pescovitz, Cory Doctorow, Mark Frauenfelder and Xeni Jardin sift through user submissions and their personal collections of links to publish a rolling blog about interesting phenomena, which means everything from copyright to robots to gender issues. No matter whether the collector blog is done by one writer or a group, the idea is to create an expert-driven, a contextualized collection of the best information on the Web.

BEYOND THE PAGE

In the digital age, though, choosing a blog type is just the first step in the process. Modern software tools make it easier for writers to explore topics using multimedia elements such as audio and video. As with any other creative endeavor, it takes time and energy to master each craft. Audiences now expect to interact with writers, so writers should consider how they want to engage their readers. Depending on the type of blog you've launched, that interaction may be the key to your success online. Before you begin crafting that blog, though, consider what your possibilities are.

PODCASTS

In 2009, stand-up comedian Marc Maron debuted an interview podcast show. It was released (mostly) twice a week, and it consisted of him sitting down with fellow comedians and talking about their lives and their work. It was a simple idea, one that doesn't seem like it would garner much interest. However, it resonated with audiences and quickly became one the Web's "must" downloads.

The podcast was recorded in several locations, including the offices of Air America, where Maron once hosted a radio program, but by 2011 Maron was recording in his garage. The program is free—anyone can download it straight from the show's website or through iTunes—and soon it will be offered through the Public Radio Exchange, which is a nonprofit distribution platform for podcasts.

If this were a radio program, it likely wouldn't have lasted more than a few weeks. The audience is too spread out for local radio and too small for a national syndication. The program is, however, perfect for Maron, who uses the platform as a way to extend his comedy beyond the stage in much the same way that a conversationalist blog might be used.

Not everyone has time to schedule regular guests for an audio program, particularly writers trying to write feature stories. The benefit to creating a podcast, though, is that the medium allows for the quick creation of conversations around specific topics. These shows can be created using free tools such as Audacity, an audio recording and editing program, or Sound-Cloud.com, a site that enables you to store and publish audio files. And, unlike Maron, who produces a slick show, writers won't necessarily need to find sponsors and elicit donations.

More and more, magazines are producing these types of programs as part of the company's offerings. Publications such as *Slate, Time, Science* and *BBC History* magazine have podcast shows that are part of their monthly site offerings. In the same way that writers who build a loyal blog audience have more negotiating options, those who develop a strong podcasting presence will also give themselves a boost.

VLOGS (VIDEO BLOGS)

In 2004, Amanda Congdon and the Rocketboom team went live . . . on the Web. Their short, cheeky new program was a mix of Internet snark, news and opinion about the biggest stories of the day. While the actual number of viewers was never officially released, at the height of its popularity most estimates put viewers of the daily Web show in the neighborhood of 100,000 people.

The world has come a long way since then, and you now have more tools at your disposal if you want to create video blogs or programming. A quick scan of YouTube's channels will verify that many people are using simple recording tools such as Apple's PhotoBooth or YouTube's My Webcam to create their own channels. Even better for writers without a great deal of multimedia acumen, those files can be uploaded to free video storage sites such as Vimeo or YouTube, giving writers the opportunity to build their own personally branded video channels.

If you're less inclined in getting on camera, though, there are also several tools available for recording others. Vodburner, for instance, lets you record interviews through Skype, giving you the chance to create short interview pieces for blogs. You can also find relatively cheap video cameras such as camera phones or Bloggie Touch, which can hold eight gigabytes of video. The one aspect of those cameras to watch out for is file type. You want to make sure your camera records in the standard MP4 format.

In summary, few—if any—technological barriers hold you back from participating in the modern trend for video blogging. As with all of writing and blogging, the hardest part will be determining what content to put on your site.

THE FEAR

After years of teaching writers, editors and students how to use all of these technologies, we believe the single biggest hurdle continues to be the tiny voice inside that tells you that you can't do this properly. For many, that voice is decidedly louder when it comes time to plant a flag in the digital world because it feels so overwhelming.

It's easy to get caught up in the speed of the Web. It's easy to think you have to write on your blog every day, create a publishing schedule that you stick to without fail or launch multimedia elements regularly. It's easy to find yourself obsessing over your blog as if it's your very own magazine, slated to come out on a certain date, imagining that if it doesn't then thousands of people will send you angry e-mails.

None of that is true. Your blog isn't a magazine. It's an extension of you as a writer and as a person. You should treat it as such. If you miss posting for a day or two, don't sweat the small stuff. Always remember that this is your place to write. It's your home base, and you will make it what you want. Certainly you'd like to spend the time building it up, but that takes time and patience. You won't have a million readers the first day. You may not even have 10. But, if you keep writing and get involved with others on the Web, your readership will grow.

Until that time, though, remember two rules when publishing your blog:

1 Make sure you have thought about which of the styles you'd like to develop with your blog and stick to that.
2 Be authentic with your voice. If your voice sounds contrived or affected, perhaps because of a wish to hide from your readers, people will avoid you on the Web. People gravitate to blogs so they can feel the personality of the writer.

IN-CLASS ACTIVITIES

Instructor: Have your students launch a free WordPress blog (www. wordpress.com). This is a three-step process that takes just a few minutes. Then have them select from a list of predetermined topics and spend 45 minutes reading articles on their chosen topic. Finally, ask your students to write a curated collector post that gives context to each link.

ASSIGNMENTS

Instructor: Launch a free WordPress blog and add each student as a user. Select a local topic on which students can do primary research. Have them record a 3–5 minute video blog, upload it to YouTube and post it on the class blog. Then have the students record video responses to at least one classmate.

NOTES

1   Dan Gillmor, *Mediactive: Creating a User's Guide to Democratized Media* (Dan Gillmore, 2008).
2   Charlene Li and Joseph Bernoff, *Groundswell: Winning in a World Transformed by Social Technologies* (Cambridge, Mass.: Harvard Business School Press, 2011).
3   Li and Bernoff, *Groundswell.*
4   Brad King and John Borland, *Dungeons and Dreamers: The Rise of Computer Game Culture From Geek to Chic* (Emeryville, Calif.: McGraw-Hill/Osborne, 2003).

18

LONG-FORM DIGITAL STORYTELLING

Brad King

KEY POINTS

- The introduction of tablets
- Defining digital storytelling
- Digital storytelling elements
- Producing digital stories
- Interaction vs. engagement
- Keep your navigation simple
- Design matters
- The production cycle
- The future of the magazine

On April 3, 2010, the world of magazine publishing received a long-awaited digital boost when Apple released the first tablet-based computer, the iPad. After years of dealing with the long, slow decline of print advertising, publishers had a platform they hoped would allow them to create a delivery system for long-form writing and storytelling that could also deliver a new revenue stream.

Of course, this isn't to say that Apple's foray into the tablet market was going to single-handedly save the publishing world. Before the iPad, no fewer than 30 eReaders had been commercially available, and Google's Android-based tablets and eReaders would soon follow. Despite the increasing numbers of digital readers, publishers were having a hard time finding

Feature and Magazine Writing: Action, Angle and Anecdotes, Third Edition.
David E. Sumner and Holly G. Miller.
© 2013 David E. Sumner and Holly G. Miller. Published 2013 by John Wiley & Sons, Inc.

enough new revenue to balance out losses in other parts of the magazine business. However, Apple's fiercely loyal customer base, its deep corporate pockets and its substantial marketing power made the tightly controlled platform an ideal testing bed for publishers.

The iPad, though, would do more than create the potential for a sustainable digital publishing model. It also changed the way long-form storytellers would need to consider telling stories. These 10-inch tablet computers were large enough to stream video and display rich graphics and small enough for people to carry with them. This combined functionality and portability meant that deft storytellers working with multimedia designers could create lush stories that a reader could interact with using the touch-screen interface.

The platform introduced an interesting conundrum for magazine writers. The very product that may save the magazine industry threatened to marginalize the craft so many persons had spent years honing. After all, the interactive environment meant publishers could begin to offer substantial subscription packages and create highly interactive advertising, but it also meant that readers would increasingly expect their digital, tablet-based magazines to look more like movies and have game-like interactivity.

In June 2010, the world got a first-hand look at this future when *Wired*, the signature publication chronicling the digital lifestyle, debuted its much-hyped iPad app. Partnering with Pixar, the magazine's teaser video showcased a short video of *Toy Story*'s Buzz Lightyear, several scrolling graphics, image slideshows, panoramas and comics. The breath-taking video captured the imagination of storytellers and sent an ominous warning to writers. The future of long-form storytelling didn't appear to have much room for words.

DEFINING DIGITAL STORYTELLING

In just a few years, millions of people have purchased tablet computers and eReaders, making the digital platform a viable distribution point. The interactivity of tablet computer and eReader environments offers a way to publish stories using multimedia elements on devices that *feel* like magazines. You can read while you're riding on a bus, sitting outside or lying in bed. While that may seem like a minor change, its implications are great.

For instance, prior to the widespread adoption of eReaders, traditional editors often asked writers working on the Web to create story "chunks," a term used to describe the creation of small bits of information that could be separated by links and subheads on the Web. A writer might put together a short 150-word paragraph that would then have a companion audio file of the person quoted in that section. These Web stories, which you read sitting at your desk, were more like elongated bullet points. While they created clean navigation and easy-to-read sections, those "chunks" also created a rather displeasing reading experience.

The new mobile, digital environment meant writers could abandon chunks for a more integrated, multimedia approach to storytelling. Video and audio files were no longer ancillaries to the written text. Now these elements could be embedded within a narrative, replacing the written word where it was most appropriate. Storytellers could use each media element as part of one interactive, long-form digital story that could be experienced in both linear and nonlinear fashion. Since readers used these devices more like books and magazines, storytellers had to worry less about getting a point across as quickly as possible.

This also meant the magazine world was no longer the domain only of writers and editors. Now audio, video and interactive graphic skills were necessary, and these gave rise to the notion of cinematic storytelling, a term often associated with the film industry. Instead of painting pictures with words, digital storytellers were expected to consider *better* ways to tell stories. Writers detailing the events of a bank robbery, for instance, might now include surveillance footage of the robbery in lieu of writing a scene.

In many cases, this meant writers would now be working as part of an interdisciplinary team to develop a story idea, explore how that story might be told and create storyboards for the layout and design before anything was written on the page. Design was now elevated to an equal partner in the content world.

Writers can take heart, however, because story remains at the heart of this new form, and the written word remains integral to the long-form process. Despite the new tools that storytellers have at their disposal, text remains the easiest way to convey information to people who are carrying mobile, digital readers. (Imagine, for instance, a hundred passengers on a plane turning on their tablets and simultaneously interacting with multimedia magazines.)

CINEMATIC STORY ELEMENTS

For those who grew up hoping to write long-form pieces, it was much easier to figure out what these might look like. On any given day, you could simply head to the bookstore and peruse the magazines lining the back walls or the countless numbers of books filling the nonfiction sections. There was a road map that others had followed that gave you some indication of *how* to write.

This new digital publishing world has few antecedents, and what few that exist largely fall outside the traditional world of journalism. For instance, what most aspiring writers haven't likely spent a great deal of time considering is how their reading audience might interact with a story. It's hard to imagine *The New Yorker*'s Malcolm Gladwell obsessing over a sentence wondering whether a reader would click on a link he's provided, or *Esquire*'s Chris Jones debating whether a panorama or an interactive graphic would better replace a scene he's written in one of his stories.

In some ways, the notion that writers don't consider these ideas is comforting. Despite the move to digital publishing environments, writers can still deliver transformative experiences through the written word. However, a new breed of storytellers will experience the long-form world through the lens of the multimedia delivery palette, no longer constrained by the limitations of the printed page. For them, this cinematic world will feel very much as though the shackles of the analog world have finally been thrown off.

These writers, though, won't be operating without some direction. While storytellers have precious few literary analogies to learn from, there are frameworks for thinking about creating stories within this environment.

One of the best thinkers on storytelling in interactive environments is Dr. Henry Jenkins. His work focuses on how writing and storytelling have been changed by interactivity. In 2004, he introduced the concept of "narrative architectures,"[1] arguing that interactive environments don't necessarily need classic story structures as found in "the hero's journey," a narrative framework for mythologies defined by Joseph Campbell.[2] Instead, authors should consider creating elements of story that allow the reader to explore the virtual space. These architectures are:

- *Spatial creation*, which allows for the construction of a narrative, whether complex or not, with a set end (e.g., rescue the princess).
- *Evocative spaces*, which provide a framework for which people fill in narrative spaces (e.g., an amusement park).

- *Enacting stories*, which blur the line between performance (game play) and story (narrative) as players are given control within an environment to act on their own while still progressing the overall narrative forward.
- *Embedded stories*, which appear within larger narratives (e.g., backstory).
- *Emergent narratives*, which take place within structured digital environments without a set narrative (e.g., *The Sims*, the best-selling "real-life" simulation in which players control characters who do little more than live "normal" lives with the digital environment).

Writers should understand that these narrative architectures don't replace the idea of story. Without a well-constructed story, no amount of multimedia or interactivity will keep people interested. Instead, these structures are best considered as part of the story you are constructing.

For instance, stories that contain several main characters can be difficult to manage. Writers are consistently forced to make trade-offs on what action elements take center stage and which characters have the most compelling narrative. In cinematic journalism, an author may create a series of embedded narratives that take the place of exposition within the story. Instead of including the backstory of every character, you might create a series of embedded informational graphics that can be called up whenever a character is mentioned within the story instead of spending precious narrative space introducing even minor characters.

This changes the structure of the story, as you've introduced side narratives into the main story, which might require the creation of interactive graphics. With one decision, then, the writer may have introduced two levels of complexity within the story creation phase.

Like any other craft, though, learning how to use this new storytelling platform doesn't happen overnight. Authors will need to spend time learning the capabilities of tablets and experimenting with different ways to use those capabilities to create narratives.

BASIC HEURISTICS AND GUIDELINES

Heuristics are general rules that give you a starting point in your thinking as you consider these long-form digital stories. When we continue exploring cinematic storytelling, we have some understanding of what works, what readers expect and what causes frustration. Over the years, researchers have spent a great deal of time trying to figure out how people read, interact and learn in digital spaces. What's come from these studies is a series of heuristics, sometimes called "rules of thumb," that can help writers consider how to approach telling a story using these new platforms by giving them some basic rules to follow.

Certainly we'll continue to learn more about how people interact with stories and with each other as more people purchase these devices. For now, much of the data we have comes from small research studies, expert analysis and basic hands-on experience with the devices.

Heuristic 1: interaction vs. engagement

One of the great promises of interactive media was that it would engage readers in ways that traditional media hasn't. We heard that people no longer wanted to be passive consumers of media; they wanted to work. That idea—engagement with the reader—is sometimes true. What really matters, however, is a strong narrative. Readers will be as interactive or as passive as you like, depending on your skill as a storyteller.

In other words, don't get caught up in all the bells and whistles of this new form just because it's shiny. It's not uncommon to see storytellers using interactive environments for the first time making the same mistake novice designers made in the early days of desktop publishing. Amateur publishers would often splash a cornucopia of font styles, sizes, and colors onto the page with little regard for classic form, creating visual eyesores that did little to communicate the intended message. In the digital realm this "feature creep," the term used to describe the addition of new interactive elements for no reason, can torpedo your storytelling efforts.

While it *may* be true that readers learn more when they are engaging with interactive elements (and there's little research to suggest that it is), simply getting people to click buttons or interact with touch-screen environments doesn't lead to a richer, more literate experience. Well-written stories will always trump stories that contain lots of digital features for no narrative reason.

Heuristic 2: keep your navigation simple

Another issue writers and readers have with new technology is gaining an understanding of how it operates. Unless you have a deep understanding of technology and its development principles, developing an accurate, cohesive understanding of what can be done is difficult. Many times we fall back upon analogies and metaphors from the past to help explain the future. For interactive reading environments, the obvious metaphor was the book.

The problem with that metaphor, though, is the lack of interactivity within the "technology" of paper books. Books are author-driven vehicles for a narrative story. There is little for a reader to do other than passively flip the pages, following a journey already constructed by the writer. Interactive environments, however, create a storytelling palette that might include a nonlinear structure, a search-and-share function or user-created content that becomes part of the story.

This metaphor problem then colors the expectations of the writer and the reader. Each assume, one imagines, that an eReader such as Barnes & Noble's Nook Color or Apple's iPad will still have an author-driven experience that may include a few images or sketches. This was probably why the first Kindle was designed to only deliver words and pixel images. This expectation creates two problems:

1 Readers don't understand what a truly interactive reading experience may look like.
2 Authors aren't trained to create truly interactive stories.

We'll talk more about producing these stories later in this chapter, but for now remember that one major difference between traditional print delivery systems and digital environments is the idea of navigation. In digital spaces, readers aren't turning a page. Often, a link within a digital environment takes someone to a different section of the publication or even out to the Web. Without good design, that can be jarring. However, once storytellers begin to understand how navigation can be used as a tool with a narrative, they can use that tool to create deeply rich stories.

This means authors should consider what they are trying to communication and how their readers might experience the story. Many times this involves making low-fidelity prototypes (e.g., sketches) to map the flow of navigation between different elements early on in the story-development process.

Heuristic 3: design matters

We are quickly realizing that design matters. In digital environments, though, design means more than just the look of a story. Design refers to the ability to construct a complex, interconnected relationship that is easy to navigate and leaves people with a pleasurable feeling.

Some design is as simple as giving people the option to modify features (e.g., on/off), interact with information in multiple ways (e.g., charts or text), easily search for terms, access other information or share that information with friends. Other design is about leaving out what readers don't like, such as poor interfaces, an inability to tell where you are in a story (called "agency") and an inability to return to a previous spot in a story if the reader happens to wander off on an intellectually curious tangent.

Design in these environments should focus on searching and sharing while mitigating feature creep and poor layout. Words—or other visual storytelling elements—should take center stage, while navigation metaphors should be divided into two distinct parts: home/library and page/book navigation. Cloud functionality (e.g., multiplatform syncing) and exploratory searches should be done alongside the story and ideally attached within the text, and the note-taking experience should include a social bookmarking setup or a note-sharing capability. However, sociability should include the ability to export personal notes and create a personalized and annotated version of the text.[3]

Of course, you're probably thinking that this particular heuristic certainly *seems* important but that it certainly isn't the job of the writer to consider these types of processes. In the traditional print world that would likely be true (although if you spoke to print designers most would tell you that writers should be more involved in these discussions). In the digital world, writers need to help map these interconnected relationships, define the metadata that will allow people to build serendipitous finding (e.g., clicking on tags that bring up similar stories) and create the navigation structures that will be designed into the story.

Content will continue to be king, but design is part of content.

THE PRODUCTION CYCLE

Writers must adjust to a new production cycle for cinematic stories. Writing is no longer a solitary experience. To fully use all of the interactive functions of tablets, designers must begin working on interactive graphics early in the process; developers and coders may need to build customized database programs; and illustrators and photographers may need to create intricate designs that take hours to render.

This means writers must understand (at the very least) project-management processes that often come from areas such as computer science. One such process, user-centric interaction design, is a basic development process that involves creating a series of user requirements (e.g., an interactive map with embedded video), developing several designs for that requirement (e.g., an illustration, a 3D model), building a series of prototypes and evaluating the effectiveness of each. When done properly, a team comes together in the user-requirements phase and then its members work in parallel—that is, each develops prototypes individually. The team members come back together every week or two, presenting their prototypes and deciding which functionality works best.

This means you may be asked to change the narrative process you've developed based upon a prototype. This process can't happen within a magazine publishing cycle if writers get their assignment and then return several weeks later with a story.

Writers must also learn to think "graphically," exploring different ways to tell a story and what visual elements might replace the written word. One excellent way to conceptualize a story visually is through storyboards. A variety of software programs are available commercially, but small, detailed sketches on paper serve exactly the same function. The point isn't to create a prototype for the designers but to communicate your story visually so you can consider alternatives to words.

Writers must learn how to conceptualize, create and edit audio, video and image files so they can better gauge how long those processes take. If you want to be an effective storyteller, learn the tools of the trade. While you likely won't be creating your own multimedia (there are experts for that), you should get hands-on experience learning the capabilities of software packages such as Premiere, Photoshop, Final Cut, GarageBand and Audacity. If those (or other) programs intimidate you, Lynda.com and VTC.com offer quick, well-done training videos that walk you through a host of software.

The goal isn't to turn writers into multimedia journalists. Backpack journalism, as it's called, may work for breaking news, but it's a poor substitute for long-form, cinematic storytelling. Instead, writers need to understand how all these tools work in the same way that they need to understand grammar: this is the literacy of the digital age.

THE FUTURE OF THE MAGAZINE

While it's fine to study cinematic storytelling and what *Wired* is doing with its iPad app, that's not very helpful for the writer who doesn't have the technical background to create that experience. If the only companies that can create those types of experiences are major international titles, then it's hardly worth worrying about developing that skill set because there won't be any jobs.

At the moment, no tools exist (such as the ubiquitous software Word-Press in the blogging world) that enable stories to be built like this without having a great deal of technical knowledge. However, that is about to change.

Evan Ratliff, a National Magazine Award finalist, has launched a company, The Atavist, that delivers long-form, cinematic stories for the iPad and other interactive environments. The company, which has published more than a dozen titles, will launch a free platform in 2012 that will be available to any writer. Slated to launch in 2012, this cinematic storytelling platform is the first of several being developed. Writer and New York University professor Adam Penenberg is developing a similar platform. And, for those with bit of technical acumen, the Adobe Digital Publishing Suite allows writers the chance to build tablet apps complete with embedded video, audio and pictures for just a few hundred dollars.

In other words, the future of cinematic journalism within tablet environments is almost here. Writers will soon have the tools to create long-form cinematic storytelling without needing much coding or design training, just as writers don't need to learn HTML to blog. As these tools become more ubiquitous and magazines move toward publishing in interactive environments, you will find more opportunities to publish if you have an understanding of how to create compelling stories within this environment.

IN-CLASS ACTIVITIES

Instructor: Have students read a long-form story before class. Spend 5–10 minutes demonstrating simple low-fidelity sketched storyboards. Break into small groups, giving students 15 minutes to create storyboards that encompass a cinematic story that contains embedded and emergent narratives.

ASSIGNMENTS

Instructor: Show a series of videos of cinematic stories (e.g., from The Atavist) and apps (e.g., *Wired*). After a brief discussion, break the students into groups of three and have them design their "perfect" digital magazine app, which must include multiple forms of media. Along with that, have them construct a list of key features that the app and each story should include.

NOTES

1   Henry Jenkins, "Game Design as Narrative Architecture," *Computer*, 44, s3.
2   Joseph Campbell, *The Hero With a Thousand Faces*, 3rd ed. (Novato, Calif.: New World Library, 2008).
3   Craig Mod, "Post-Artifact Books & Publishing," *Craig Mod: Considering the Future Of Books + Storytelling*, June 2004. http://craigmod.com/journal/post_artifact (accessed April 28, 2012).

PART VI

PREPARING THE FINAL DRAFT

"A sentence should contain no unnecessary words, a paragraph no unnecessary sentences, for the same reason that a drawing should have no unnecessary lines and a machine no unnecessary parts."

William Strunk Jr., author
The Elements of Style

Many magazine staffs are downsizing, which means editors may not have time to "clean up" a manuscript that is overwritten, has an abundance of punctuation errors or fails to follow an accepted style manual. Most job interviews today begin with an editing test. Follow the tips and advice in these chapters to create clean and polished final drafts.

19

ADVANCING BEYOND THE SLUSH PILE

KEY POINTS

- Why little details matter
- Seven places to never use a comma
- Seven places to always use a comma
- Seven other punctuation marks
- Seven frequent grammar mistakes
- Seven frequent *AP Stylebook* mistakes
- Concluding thoughts

The "slush pile" is the huge stack of unsolicited articles, manuscripts, query letters and e-mail proposals received by magazines and online content publishers. Some magazines and websites receive thousands of unsolicited articles and query letters weekly. Editors assign the task of reading this pile of material to interns or the lowest-level editorial assistants. These "first-read" editors look for reasons to reject. They choose the best 5 or 10 percent of unsolicited material to forward to the high-ranking editors for serious consideration.

As we remind you in Chapter 20, some of the most common mistakes involve punctuation, grammar and style. Even if you have a great story, these mistakes give slush-pile editors the best reasons to reject your material. Professional writers avoid these mistakes. They know how to advance beyond the slush pile.

Feature and Magazine Writing: Action, Angle and Anecdotes, Third Edition.
David E. Sumner and Holly G. Miller.
© 2013 David E. Sumner and Holly G. Miller. Published 2013 by John Wiley & Sons, Inc.

Jon Gingerich, editor-in-chief of *O'Dwyer's* magazine, wrote, "Experience has also taught me that readers, for better or worse, will approach your work with a jaundiced eye and an itch to judge. While your grammar shouldn't be a reflection of your creative powers or writing abilities, let's face it—it usually is."[1]

These 35 points about grammar, punctuation and style are "necessary but not sufficient" conditions of good writing. They are necessary to advance beyond the slush pile but not sufficient to get published. Only great reporting with great writing will get you published.

Visualize punctuation marks as road signs. The purpose of road signs is to prevent accidents. The purpose of punctuation marks is to avoid confusing the reader. Used properly, they create clarity. A period tells you to "stop" and a comma tells you to "slow down." Colons and semicolons tell readers to "yield right of way." Don't think of using proper punctuation as having to memorize rules; rather, think of it as making ideas and concepts more understandable to the reader.

A professor wrote the following sentence on the board and asked his class to punctuate it:[2]

Woman without her man is nothing.

Half of the students punctuated the sentence this way:

Woman: without her, man is nothing.

The other half of the students responded this way:

Woman, without her man, is nothing.

This common example and many others we could use emphasize that punctuation marks, especially commas, can change the intended meaning of a sentence. Lynne Truss' best-seller *Eats, Shoots & Leaves: The Zero Tolerance Approach to Punctuation* contains dozens of humorous examples. Even its title, "Eats, Shoots & Leaves" (with a comma), has a different meaning from "Eats Shoots & Leaves" (without any commas).[3]

Commas are the most abused and overused punctuation mark. Commas have only one purpose: to tell the reader to slow down. Just as speed limit signs tell drivers to slow down to avoid danger, commas tell readers to slow down to avoid getting confused. Most beginning writers, however, put too many 45 m.p.h. speed limit signs on their Interstate writing. They make their writing poke along and confuse their readers. Therefore, we begin with seven types of word structure that never require a comma.

SEVEN PLACES TO NEVER USE A COMMA

1. Between two complete sentences. Writing run-on sentences is the most common grammar mistake among beginning writers. For example: "Katelin giggles at anything remotely funny, her sunny disposition is contagious." This type of "run-on sentence" is sometimes called a "comma splice" because a comma is used to "splice" two sentences. Here are three acceptable revisions:

Katelin giggles at anything remotely funny, and her sunny disposition is contagious. (add the conjunction "and")

Katelin giggles at anything remotely funny; her sunny disposition is contagious. (separate the sentences with a semicolon)

Katelin giggles at anything remotely funny. Her sunny disposition is contagious. (rewrite as two separate sentences)

2. Between compound verbs in a sentence with only one subject. Compound sentences with two subjects and two verbs require a separating comma, but sentences with two verbs and one subject don't need one. Example:

Katelin's friends give her lots of support after her cancer diagnosis and call her daily.

3. Before or after prepositional phrases. Prepositional phrases begin with words such as "to," "in," "from" or "after" and do not contain a verb. Example:

Katelin's oncologist says he expects her to have a 100 percent recovery after her treatment.

4. To set off clauses beginning with "that." These restrictive clauses restrict the meaning of the nouns they modify to a particular person or thing. If you omit restrictive clauses, sentences lose their meaning. Example:

Katelin responded so positively to her chemotherapy that she still plays club volleyball.

If you omit "that she still plays club volleyball," then the sentence makes no sense. A more detailed explanation of "that" and "which" occurs later.

5. Before subordinate clauses and phrases that occur at the end of the sentence. Words such as "because," "although" and "since" are coordinating conjunctions. When they are used to begin a clause toward the end of the sentence, they do not require a preceding comma. Examples:

Because her tumor was discovered early, Katelin's treatment will likely be successful. (comma)

Katelin's treatment will likely be successful because her tumor was discovered early. (no comma)

6. After a month and year when no specific date is included. Dates are confusing to punctuate because commas follow a year when preceded by a specific date in the month but not when no specific date is included. Example:

Katelin expects to graduate from college in May 2013 and attend medical school.

7. Before "Jr." or "III" when they follow a name. Omitting the comma follows the *Associated Press Stylebook* guideline, but other stylebooks require the comma after "Jr." or "III." Example:

Example: *John W. Williams Jr.*

SEVEN PLACES TO ALWAYS USE A COMMA

1. To separate items in a series. Example:

Dennis Ulrich enjoys ice fishing, moose hunting and gardening.

The *AP Stylebook* specifies no comma before the final item while the Chicago, Turabian and other style manuals do insert a comma before the final item.

2. After the day of the month or name of the state when they occur in the middle of a sentence. As explained earlier, do not put a comma after a year when no date is mentioned, but do use a comma when the date includes a specific month, date and year. You should also use a comma after the name of a state when it follows the name of a city. Example:

Dennis Ulrich left his job on May 13, 2011, after a dispute with his former employer to move to Anchorage, Alaska, to take a new job.

3. Between compound sentences. When two complete sentences are connected with a conjunction, they form a compound sentence delineated by a comma. Compound sentences contain two subjects with two verbs separated by a conjunction such as "and," "but" or "so." Example:

Dennis Ulrich won the lawsuit against his former employer, so he is now a wealthy man.

4. Following introductory clauses that begin a sentence. As explained earlier, words such as "because," "although" and "since" are called coordinating conjunctions. When they begin a clause that precedes the main sentence, a separating comma is necessary. Example:

Because he won the lawsuit against his former employer, Dennis Ulrich is now wealthy.

5. Before and after job titles and other phrases that amplify the meaning of a noun. These are called "appositive" phrases. They explain or elaborate on the preceding noun or name. Example:

Dale Ashton, vice president for legal affairs, said the company would appeal the court's ruling in Ulrich's favor.

6. Before and after restrictive clauses beginning with "which" and sometimes "who." These nonessential clauses add interesting information to the sentence but aren't essential to its meaning. Example:

The judge's decision, which was announced on May 11, awarded $1 million to Ulrich.

7. With direct quotes preceding or following the attribution verb "said." Example:

Dale Ashton, vice president for legal affairs, said, "The judge's $1 million judgment could cause layoffs for the company."

In summary, here is the most simplified rule for comma use: If the reader won't feel confused without the comma, then leave it out. If the reader might feel confused, then use it. You decide. If in doubt, then omit it. After all, who wants to see a 45 m.p.h. speed-limit sign on the Interstate?

SEVEN OTHER PUNCTUATION MARKS

Here are a few quick tips on seven other punctuation marks. Please also consult the back section in the *AP Stylebook*, which contains more detailed and complete explanations for all of these punctuation marks.

1. Periods. Periods are the writer's best friend because they create short, crisp and readable sentences. If in doubt, use a period and you will rarely be wrong. In American usage, periods and commas always go inside quotation marks—both short quotes and long quotes, single quotation marks and double quotation marks. British style places them outside the quotation marks.

2. Hyphens. Hyphens are "joiners." They join together two or more words that form one idea. Use a hyphen to separate compound modifiers that describe a person or other noun. Examples:

Best-dressed professor; first-born child; old-fashioned idea.

Linking compound modifiers with a hyphen helps the reader understand the concept and meaning more quickly.

3. Semicolons. Semicolons separate two complete sentences. While you can always use a period, a semicolon links two or more sentences related to each other in theme or content. Example:

The day is long; the students are tired; it's time to go home.

4. Colons. Colons introduce. Use a colon to introduce a long list of items or names, or a long quotation. While there are no clear rules here, shorter lists ("She went to the store to buy apples, oranges and pears") do not require a colon. Examples:

He made big promises: no new taxes, more social services and less government spending.

Smith had this to say about the changes: "I am in favor of progress, but these proposals will cost too much and take too long."

Both colons and semicolons are like "yield" signs. They tell the reader something is coming up soon that they should pay attention to.

5. Exclamation points. Do not use exclamation points in journalistic writing except when directly quoting someone who speaks in an excited manner. Do not try to use exclamation points to create artificial excitement among your readers. Use good writing to create excited readers.

6. Question marks. Question marks can go inside or outside quotation marks, depending on whether the question is part of the quote or the question is asked by the writer of the article. Examples:

The police officer asked the driver, "Why were you speeding?" [The quoted material is a question]

Did the driver tell the police officer, "I was not speeding"? [The quoted material is a statement and not a question]

7. Parentheses and brackets. In general, avoid parentheses in journalistic writing and reporting. Parentheses slow readers down and require them to interpret the parenthetical material. Use square brackets inside direct quotations to clarify the meaning of acronyms or technical concepts. Brackets signify to the reader that the writer inserted the material inside the direct quote. Example:

He found a position with UNESCO [United Nations Educational, Scientific and Cultural Organization] after earning his master's degree.

SEVEN FREQUENT GRAMMAR MISTAKES

1. Its and it's. We have seen misuse of "its" and "it's" in advertisements, public signs and even highway billboards. Normally you add an apostrophe and an "s" to create the possessive form of a noun, but "its" breaks this rule. When you add an apostrophe and an "s" to "it," the result is a contraction meaning "it is." The simple "its" is the possessive form of "it." Examples:

Correct: *The company made its decision to appeal Ulrich's award on May 14.*

Correct: *It's a mistake to assume that its appeal will be successful.*

2. Sentence fragments. Every sentence requires a noun and a verb. The most frequent sentence fragments begin with subordinating conjunctions such as "although," "because" or "since." They're called "subordinating" because they create a clause that is subordinate to the main clause. Therefore, the subordinate clause isn't complete and can't stand by itself. Examples:

Incorrect: *Because she had a sunny disposition.*

Correct: *Katelin inspired friends because she had a sunny disposition.*

SIDEBAR 19.1

Popular Coordinating Conjunctions

after	rather than
although	so that
as long as	since
because	unless
before	until
even though	whenever
once	while

3. Pronoun agreement. When you use a singular noun, use a singular pronoun when you refer to it later. When you use plural nouns, use plural pronouns when you refer to them later. That's what pronoun agreement means. The most frequent problem comes from "collective nouns"— singular nouns that describe a group of people. For example, use "it" and not "they" when you refer to a company, university, store name, magazine or organization. Examples:

Incorrect: *The popular magazine announced that they will no longer accept alcohol ads.*

Correct: *The popular magazine announced that it will no longer accept alcohol ads.*

Collective Nouns Requiring Singular Verbs and Pronouns

association	family
club	group
committee	navy
company	organization
congregation	school
department	society
faculty	team

SIDEBAR 19.2

4. Possessive nouns and pronouns. The most common misuse of nouns and pronouns comes with confusing their plural and possessive forms. Both plural and possessive forms end with an "s" but the possessive form requires an apostrophe before or after the "s." Examples:

*The **committees** are meeting now.* (more than one committee)

*That **committee's** assignment is difficult.* (singular possessive)

*Those **committees'** budgeting duties are varied.* (plural possessive)

5. Unnecessary capitalization. Beginning writers are more likely to capitalize a word that shouldn't be capitalized than fail to capitalize one that should be. The most common mistake occurs when referring to a collective noun that doesn't occur as part of a proper noun. For example, most writers know to write "Oxford University" or "Sony Corporation." But when you refer to them later you should say "the university" or "the corporation" and not "the University" or "the Corporation." Both the Associated Press and Chicago style manuals follow this rule.

An unfortunate trend in business marketing and commercial writing is to capitalize words for emphasis or to give words a little extra heft. Capitalizing a word does not make it more important. It only shows you don't understand proper grammar. If you want to emphasize a word, use *italics* or **boldface**.

6. That/which/who. Always use "who" when referring to people and "that" and "which" when referring to inanimate objects or animals without names. Use "that" for restrictive clauses important for identifying the meaning of the sentence. Use "which" (with commas) for nonrestrictive clauses that amplify or illustrate the meaning. The *AP Stylebook* and dozens of online grammar sites explain and illustrate the difference between restrictive and nonrestrictive clauses. Professional journalists should have a clear understanding of them and how they affect proper punctuation.

7. Dead constructions. While not technically incorrect, dead constructions are deadly because they bore your readers to death. Dead-construction sentences begin with "it is," "it was," "it will be," "there is," "there was" or "there will be." You can usually find a way to eliminate them and start the sentence with its real subject.

THE SEVEN MOST COMMON *AP STYLEBOOK* MISTAKES

Do you write "29" or "twenty-nine"? Do you add or omit the last comma in a series such as "coffee, sugar and cream"? The *AP Stylebook* says "29 and no comma," while the Chicago and Turabian style manuals answer "twenty-nine and use the comma."

AP Stylebook and Postal Abbreviations for American States and Territories

State or Territory	AP and Chicago Stylebooks	Postal
Alabama	Ala.	AL
Alaska	Alaska	AK
Arizona	Ariz.	AZ
Arkansas	Ark.	AR
American Samoa	A.S.	AS
California	Calif.	CA
Colorado	Colo.	CO
Connecticut	Conn.	CT
Delaware	Del.	DE
District of Columbia	D.C.	DC
Florida	Fla.	FL
Georgia	Ga.	GA
Guam	Guam	GU
Hawaii	Hawaii	HI
Idaho	Idaho	ID
Illinois	Ill.	IL
Indiana	Ind.	IN
Iowa	Iowa	IA
Kansas	Kan.	KS
Kentucky	Ky.	KY
Louisiana	La.	LA
Maine	Maine	ME
Maryland	Md.	MD
Massachusetts	Mass.	MA
Michigan	Mich.	MI
Minnesota	Minn.	MN
Mississippi	Miss.	MS
Missouri	Mo.	MO
Montana	Mont.	MT
Nebraska	Neb.	NE
Nevada	Nev.	NV
New Hampshire	N.H.	NH
New Jersey	N.J.	NJ
New Mexico	N.M.	NM
New York	N.Y.	NY

(Continued)

SIDEBAR 19.3

State or Territory	AP and Chicago Stylebooks	Postal
North Carolina	N.C.	NC
North Dakota	N. Dak.	ND
Ohio	Ohio	OH
Oklahoma	Okla.	OK
Oregon	Ore.	OR
Pennsylvania	Penn.	PA
Puerto Rico	P.R.	PR
Rhode Island	R.I.	RI
South Carolina	S.C.	SC
South Dakota	S. Dak.	SD
Tennessee	Tenn.	TN
Texas	Texas	TX
Utah	Utah	UT
Virgin Islands	V.I.	VI
Washington	Wash.	WA
West Virginia	W. Va.	WV
Wisconsin	Wisc.	WI
Wyoming	Wyom.	WY

1. State abbreviations. The *AP Stylebook* doesn't follow standard ZIP code abbreviations—e.g., CA for California and OR for Oregon. Each state has its own abbreviation—e.g., Ore. for Oregon; Calif. for California; Fla. for Florida, and so on. Eight states—Alaska, Hawaii, Idaho, Iowa, Maine, Ohio, Texas and Utah—are never abbreviated.

2. Dollar signs. Use the dollar sign ($) instead of the words "dollar" or "dollars." Examples: "$10" instead of "10 dollars" and "$10 million" instead of "10 million dollars."

3. Numbers and numeral usage. Spell out numerals for nine and below (eight, five, three, etc.) but use numerals for 10 and higher. However, spell out any numerals that begin a sentence. Example: "Twenty-nine people survived the crash" instead of "29 people survived the crash." Always spell out the word "percent." Don't use the "%" sign. Always use numerals for ages and percentages.

4. Decades. Do not use the apostrophe in designating decades. Write "1990s" and "1960s," not "1990's" and "1960's."

5. Job titles. Capitalize formal titles only when they precede a name. Do not capitalize titles that follow a name, no matter how important the title sounds. Examples:

Secretary of State Dean McMillan signed the proclamation.

Dean McMillan, secretary of state, signed the proclamation.

6. Months and seasons. When using a month with a specific date, abbreviate only Jan., Feb., Aug., Sept., Oct., Nov. and Dec. Never abbreviate months with five letters or fewer: March, April, May, June and July. Spell out all months if using them alone or with just a year. The seasons—winter, spring, summer and fall—are never capitalized.

7. Farther, further and other confusing pairs. "Farther" refers to physical distance. "Further" refers to an extension of time or degree. "Affect/effect" are also confused. "Affect" is a verb, while "effect" is a noun.

CONCLUDING THOUGHTS

The 35 common mistakes we've described in this chapter are the "little mistakes." Make one and maybe no one will notice. Make two and the editor will notice. Make three and you might find yourself out of a job because readers *do notice.* "Writing is hard work. A clear sentence is no accident. Very few sentences come out right the first time, or even the third time," wrote William Zinsser in his classic book *On Writing Well.*[4] Fixing these mistakes and getting these details right will go a long way towards getting your article past the slush pile.

In a survey of hiring managers, 75 percent said it was worse for an applicant to have a spelling or grammar error on her application than to show up late or use profanity during an interview.[5] Other surveys have shown that almost half of all recruitment professionals said that more than half of the résumés they received contained grammatical errors. Good grammar and punctuation help your articles move beyond the slush pile, but they also help you find a job. Chapter 21 will give you more tips on finding that first job.

IN-CLASS ACTIVITIES

Instructor: Bring a newspaper article or draft of a story to class and give copies to all students. Students: Circle each correctly used comma and make an "X" by each wrongly used or unnecessary comma. Discuss wrongly used commas. For properly used commas, discuss which rules in the "always use a comma" section of this chapter apply to each case.

Students: Bring a copy of the *AP Stylebook* to class. In groups of two or three, discuss and identify the 10 most common AP style errors that you see in the media.

ASSIGNMENTS

Students: Bring a first draft of your most recent story assignment to class. Working in groups of two, exchange first drafts and copy edit for grammar, punctuation and AP style errors. Discuss your mistakes with each other.

Students: Find five punctuation, grammar or *AP Stylebook* errors from newspapers, magazines or websites and copy and summarize them in a written assignment.

NOTES

1   Jon Gingerich, "20 Common Grammar Mistakes That (Almost) Everyone Makes," Jan. 31, 2012. http://litreactor.com/columns/20-common-grammar-mistakes-that-almost-everyone-gets-wrong (accessed April 21, 2012).
2   "A Humorous Look at the Importance of Punctuation." www.vappingo.com/word-blog/the-importance-of-punctuation (accessed April 21, 2012).
3   Lynne Truss, *Eats, Shoots and Leaves: The Zero Tolerance Approach to Punctuation* (New York: Gotham Books, 2004).
4   William Zinsser, *On Writing Well: An Informal Guide to Writing Nonfiction*, 3rd ed. (New York: Harper & Row, 1985), 12.
5   "The Top 3 Reasons Why Grammar Matters," Nov. 27, 2009. http://falmouthinstitute.com/trisec/2009/11/top-3-reasons-why-grammar-matters (accessed April 22, 2012).

20

BEFORE YOU HIT THE "SEND" BUTTON

A CHECKLIST

KEY POINTS

- Twenty dos and don'ts for a final draft
- Recap of redundancies, qualifiers and clichés to avoid

Shhhhh. As a feature writer, you want to create *quiet* manuscripts that are free of communication noise. We're not talking about sound but about any distraction that tugs a reader's attention away from the article's content. If the noise is loud enough, the reader may concentrate on the distraction rather than on the message. Writing problems such as clumsy transitions, weak quotations, poor word choice, grammatical errors and run-on sentences qualify as communication noise. They can cause a professor to lose patience and a student to lose points. Likewise, they prompt editors to reach for their stack of rejection slips.

Too often a feature article is one draft short of an "A" if you are submitting it to a professor for a grade; or it's one draft short of acceptance if you are submitting it to an editor for publication. We suggest that, before you hit the "send" button, you should step back and review your copy as a professional evaluator does. Our 20-point checklist serves as an assessment tool to help you identify and fix common writing errors. Many of the criteria on the list are familiar because we've discussed them earlier in this book. We offer them here as a final reminder.

Feature and Magazine Writing: Action, Angle and Anecdotes, Third Edition.
David E. Sumner and Holly G. Miller.
© 2013 David E. Sumner and Holly G. Miller. Published 2013 by John Wiley & Sons, Inc.

1. Required word count. Most editors and professors specify the number of words they expect in the article packages they assign. Many writers' guidebooks give the range 1,000 to 6,000 words for articles, but that is too broad. Check the writers' guidelines of a publication to learn the recommended length. If an editor specifies 1,500 words, you can slice that number in a variety of ways—for example, a main article of 1,000 words, two sidebars of 225 words each, and an info box of 50 words. A typical magazine page accommodates about 500 words, and editors often like articles that occupy two-page or four-page spreads. Length is a good indicator of the depth an editor or professor expects.

2. Tightly focused idea. Topics that are too broad can sprout legs and take off in multiple directions. If you make the mistake of pursuing all the directions, you may end up running in circles and going nowhere. Summarize the central point of your article in one clear sentence. Include that sentence within the first three or four paragraphs of your story. The result is a billboard paragraph (or nutgraf) that points readers to what's ahead and provides a convenient stopping point if the content fails to interest them.

3. Strong lead. Ask yourself these questions: Does my lead grab reader interest? Does it set the right tone? Does it establish my chosen voice? Does it serve as a legitimate gateway to the topic? A lead paragraph that is too long (more than four sentences) can intimidate readers. A lead can be shocking, sensational, funny or deadly serious—but never boring.

4. Anecdotes. Have you included enough stories and examples that illustrate the main points? Do they add color and human interest? Reread the little stories that you've sprinkled throughout your article. Make sure you haven't used two anecdotes to illustrate one point. To qualify as an anecdote, a story needs to describe a situation and reach a conclusion. Pare your anecdotes down to their bones.

5. Smooth transitions. Look at the way you move from one point to another. Read your text out loud and listen for clumsy or abrupt "bridges" or segues. If your editor or professor allows you to use boldface subheads within the text, place them evenly and judiciously throughout your copy to move the story forward. Coherence means that the parts of a story—

facts, quotes, anecdotes, etc.—fit together in a way that flows and makes sense to the reader.

6. Quotations. Include a lively quotation from a credible source in at least every third or fourth paragraph. Direct and indirect quotations introduce people, and people add depth and color. An article without quotations tends to preach or drone. As you skim your manuscript, eliminate all bland and "cheerleader" remarks.

7. Headcount. Speaking of quotations, how many sources populate your article? How many people have you interviewed? Don't bore your readers with too few sources, but don't confuse them with too many. Everyone who is quoted in an article should bring intelligent insight to the topic. Don't add boring or meaningless words just to have a quote. Think of your sources as "voices" and strive for variety and credibility. Can you defend the presence of every source in your article?

8. Originality. Your article should cause readers to respond with comments such as "Wow, I didn't know that" or "I never heard that before" or "That's really interesting." We often read articles by students that merely recycle old news, elaborate on common sense or rehash what anyone can find by "Googling" the topic. Examine your sentences and paragraphs to determine whether they add fresh, original information to your main theme.

9. Sidebars. Editors love sidebars. Readers love sidebars. A sidebar enhances the visual appeal of a page and provides what graphic designers call a "point of entry." When readers scan pages, a sidebar catches their attention and pulls them into the package. A sidebar may offer a table, a list, a quiz, a mini-profile or a different point of view from the one expressed in the main article. Two rules to remember about sidebars: They should not contain quotes from the same sources used in the main article and their length should never exceed one-fourth that of the main article.

10. Evidence of library and online research. Have you added enough depth? Substantial, in-depth background research adds interest and gains readers. By setting a local story in a national context, you broaden its appeal and marketability. Readers will have a sense of the big picture and better understand the piece of the picture that your article explores in detail.

11. Unity. Weave the article around one central idea or main theme. As you edit the first draft, clarify your main purpose and include only ideas and concepts that fulfill that purpose. Sticking to your topic gives unity. A single purpose helps you collect and organize information economically. Unity means that a story focuses on one topic only. It gives the reader the sense that it was written for one purpose using one voice, one tense and one tone.

12. Consistent viewpoint. Viewpoint is a choice but, once established, it needs to be consistent. Make sure you've selected the right viewpoint and have maintained it. The first-person viewpoint (I) is the obvious choice for a personal essay or opinion piece; the second person (you) creates intimacy with readers; the third-person viewpoint (he or she) works well when you want to be objective. The key is to avoid switching from one viewpoint to another.

13. Consistent tone. Consider the audience you are writing for and make sure that the tone you have selected is appropriate. You might choose to sound conversational, formal, sassy, academic, witty . . . and the list goes on. Again, the key is consistency. Knowing what tone is appropriate for your article will guide you in the use of slang, sentence fragments, contractions, and so on.

14. Consistent style. If you are writing for the feature pages of a newspaper, you will probably follow the *AP Stylebook*. If you are writing for a magazine, you'll need to brush up on *The Chicago Manual of Style*. Many large publications develop their own style sheets and expect writers to adhere to the rules. Once again, the best advice is to be consistent. Don't abbreviate a word in one paragraph (Sept.) and spell it out in the next (September). Inconsistencies create communication noise that distracts readers from an article's content.

15. Clever title and cover line. Although editors may change an article's title, the writer always wants to offer a suggestion. Take a cue from the pages of the publication. Some magazines like puns, other like labels, a few want to shock. Examples of strong cover lines: *Vanity Fair* did an in-depth profile article of actress Scarlett Johansson and promoted it with the cover line "Scarlett Fever."[1] *Rolling Stone* piqued reader interest with its cover story about "The Steve Jobs Nobody Knew."[2] Your challenge is to provide a title that looks as if it fits perfectly into the publication that will receive it.

Prepare to Delete

Cleanse your copy of redundancies, qualifiers and clichés that cause editors to cringe. These wordy expressions creep into our spoken language but they have no place in our written text. One word often can do the job of two, three or four. Examples:

A majority of (most)	For the purpose of (for)
At this point in time (now)	Free gift (gift)
Brand new (new)	Gather together (gather)
Due to the fact that (because)	In order to (to)
Easter Sunday (Easter)	Came to a conclusion (concluded)
End result (result)	Mental attitude (attitude)
Exact opposites (opposites)	Past history (history)
Filled to capacity (filled)	Write a summary (summarize)

Qualifiers: If you can delete a word without losing meaning, the word is unnecessary. Get rid of it. Examples:

Completely demolished	Slightly disappointed
Little confused	Somewhat surprised
Rather important	Totally ruined
Readily available	Very obvious

Clichés: Avoid them because they display a lack of originality. Examples:

At the end of the day	Right on target
Connect the dots	Step up to the plate
Get a life	The name of the game
Out of the box	You go, girl!
Put it on the back burner	24/7

SIDEBAR 20.1

16. Few adjectives and adverbs. Pay particular attention to adverbs that you have tacked onto attributions (she said *softly*; he said *loudly*). Can you substitute one word for two (she *whispered*, he *bellowed*)? Adjectives and adverbs should never be used to inflate the word count of an article.

17. Action verbs. Watch for "is," "are," "was" and "were" verbs and see whether you can figure out a way to replace them with strong action verbs. Look for sentences beginning with the words "there is" or "there are" and rewrite them to begin with nouns and action verbs. You'll find that it's easy to rid your copy of "dead expressions."

18. Satisfying ending. Reread your article and make sure you've answered all the questions that you've raised. End with a strong quote or the wrap-up to the anecdote that you used as your lead. Don't summarize what you've already written in the body of the article.

19. Obvious purpose. Ask yourself, "What was I trying to accomplish with this feature?" Among your possible answers are: to educate, activate, motivate, commemorate, explain, demystify, inform, influence, inspire, honor, entertain, warn, persuade, argue. Now ask yourself, "Did I accomplish my purpose?"

20. Flawless mechanics. Don't rely on your computer's spelling and grammar check to get it right. It will not catch spelling errors such as using "complement" for "compliment" or "principal" for "principle" or "brakes" for "breaks." A computer can never replace a writer with a careful set of eyes and an old-fashioned dictionary by her side.

NOTES

1   Peter Biskind, "A Study in Scarlett," *Vanity Fair*, Dec. 2011, 194.
2   Jeff Goodell, "The Steve Jobs Nobody Knew," *Rolling Stone*, Oct. 27, 2011, 37.

21

CAREERS IN MAGAZINE PUBLISHING

David E. Sumner

KEY POINTS

- The magazine industry is surviving
- Business-to-business publications
- Association magazines and sponsored publications
- What about New York?
- What about a master's degree?
- Practical tips on job-hunting

News about newspapers in recent years has been bleak, and many wrongly assume that magazines share the same fate. According to a study by University of Georgia professors, full-time newsroom employees at daily newspapers declined from 62,750 in 2005 to 40,760 in 2010—a 35 percent decline. The number of paid interns at newspapers declined from 2,905 in 2005 to 1,665 in 2010.[1] A printing industry consultant recently called to ask me whether I thought magazines would still be printed 15 years from now. I told him I believed about 85 percent of all magazines will still be in print in 2027. According to my research and most other studies, magazine circulation in the United States peaked in 2000 and has declined about 8 to 10 percent since then. A large portion of that decline, however, was incurred by about four well-known magazines.[2]

Magazines remain stronger and more resilient than newspapers for many reasons, too many to discuss here. Magazines have found more ways

Feature and Magazine Writing: Action, Angle and Anecdotes, Third Edition.
David E. Sumner and Holly G. Miller.
© 2013 David E. Sumner and Holly G. Miller. Published 2013 by John Wiley & Sons, Inc.

to capitalize on digital media. Printed magazines offer a total reader experience that cannot be duplicated elsewhere. Cathie Black, former president of Hearst Magazines, told me:

> The connectivity that a reader feels with his or her magazine is one of the unique and special attributes of a magazine. We hear that over and over. A magazine also may in fact become a respite, a retreat; a place to be yourself, be inspired, aspire to be; and give you creative ideas about your home, your clothing, your life.[3]

To be sure, the magazine industry is changing: some magazines are closing, some are downsizing and some are migrating to Web-only sites. However, more new magazines were launched in 2011 than closed. Digital entrepreneurs continually create new types of sites with new content needs. For example, a former editor of the Ball State University student magazine is a writer and editor at Chacha.com, where you can obtain quick answers to almost any question. While "Content is king" is almost a cliché, readers' need for reliable information in any medium means that journalism graduates with strong writing and editing skills will find jobs.

As head of the magazine program at one of the nation's 10 largest journalism schools, I have spent more than 20 years teaching magazine writing courses and helping students find jobs in the industry. I've given dozens of lectures about how to write a résumé, improve a portfolio and search for jobs. Our graduates are working for dozens of magazines—print and online—from New York to California.

The best advice I can give is to cast a wide net and don't get fixated on working for a consumer magazine. Many students come into journalism programs with starry eyes and dreams of working for *Cosmopolitan* or *Rolling Stone*. Nicole Voges, editor-in-chief of *Healthcare Executive* in Chicago, said, "When I started my journalism degree, I thought I was going to work for *Vogue* or *Glamour* in New York City. However, those are very competitive, cut-throat kinds of jobs. They're not a place where a lot of people would feel comfortable."[4]

BUSINESS-TO-BUSINESS PUBLICATIONS

Thousands of wonderful, well-paying jobs are out there at magazines that you have probably never heard of. When most people think "magazine," they think of the typical consumer titles they see in grocery- or department-store display racks. The definition of a consumer magazine is any magazine available to the general public through subscription or single-copy sales. Yet consumer titles comprise only a third of more than 18,000 magazines published in the United States.

A business-to-business (B-to-B) magazine offers news and features to help people in specific careers and occupations become more successful at their jobs. The major difference between consumer and B-to-B magazines is how readers use their content—for business or pleasure. While consumer magazines are aimed at a group of readers with special interests, B-to-B magazine readers look to their magazines to help them excel in their careers.

Both consumer and B-to-B magazines have glossy covers, photos and well-designed pages. Both publish similar kinds of articles: profiles, dramatic stories, trends and issues, how-to, calendar-related stories and so on. Their articles employ the same principles and techniques of feature writing taught throughout this book.

Publishers and editors at most B-to-B magazines don't expect entry-level employees to have training or experience in the fields they cover. Many of them have said to me things like, "I would rather hire a journalism graduate with strong writing skills than an expert in our field and try to teach him how to write." Kathryn Keuneke is editor of *Round the Table*, the official publication of the Million Dollar Round Table, an international association of financial advisers. She started as an editorial assistant 10 years ago and quickly worked her way up to editor. She says:

> I knew nothing about the industry I was entering. It didn't matter. As the content experts, our members provided us with the information. We just had to help them present the information to each other in a polished way.[5]

Alaric DeArment, associate editor of *Drug Store News* in New York City, says he knew nothing about the drug-store industry before he took the job five years ago. But he loves the job. He says:

> One advantage is the amount of influence you can have over an industry. In many cases, your readers are top executives, big investors and political leaders. The main purpose of B-to-B media, helping companies make better business decisions, means that your articles can significantly affect how companies operate.

The biggest advantage to working at a B-to-B publication is that you acquire a much deeper level of expertise about a particular industry than you would covering the business beat at a consumer publication. It's one thing to report revenues and profits, but another to understand the company practices, industry trends and other external factors that underpin them.[6]

Chicago is a major hub for business-to-business magazines. "It's an excellent place to find a magazine job if you can look outside of the 'dream magazine job,'" says Nicole Voges.[7] Crain Communications, with 30 titles ranging from *Advertising Age* and *Autoweek* to *TelevisionWeek* and *Tire Business*, is one of the largest B-to-B publishers. Hundreds of other titles, however, are published in the greater Chicago area.

Kathryn Keuneke says:

Working here provides me with opportunities I wouldn't likely have at a consumer publication. From my first day, I was writing, editing and assisting the editor in moving the magazine through the publishing process. After five years, I became the editor of the magazine, and I have complete control over the focus and content of our 52-page bimonthly publication. You get a real education in subjects that can be very interesting and helpful in your own life.

ASSOCIATION MAGAZINES AND SPONSORED PUBLICATIONS

Association and organization magazines are published by colleges for their alumni, by religious denominations for their members by and civic and hobby associations for their members. While estimating the number of magazines in this group is difficult, 5,000 is a reasonable guess. Association magazines are published by their sponsoring organizations and associations and generally sent free as a membership benefit. They are sometimes called "sponsored publications."

AARP Magazine, which has more than 20 million subscribers, is an association magazine, not a consumer magazine. The American Association of Retired Persons sends the magazine free to all of its dues-paying members. One of the oldest magazines, *National Geographic*, is technically an association magazine. Originally created in 1888, the magazine is a "perk" for readers who "join" the National Geographic Association.

These magazines create an essential link between sponsoring associations and their members. The only contact many members have with the association or organization to which they belong is the magazine they receive. Universities rely upon their alumni magazines to maintain the goodwill, loyalty and financial support they receive from their graduates. Magazines published by civic groups, such as Kiwanis or Rotary International, serve as vital communication links between the local clubs and the international organizations.

Like B-to-B magazines, the quality and scope of the feature stories in these publications is not in any way "second rate" or inferior to those found in consumer magazines. Their editorial content does not simply contain business news but also first-rate features that keep their readers informed about interesting leaders, current events, issues and trends. The best Web gateways to association magazines are the Association Media and Publishing (http://associationmediaandpublishing.org), National Council of Nonprofits (www.councilofnonprofits.org) and Weddle's Association Directory (www.weddles.com/associations). The Internet Public Library (www.ipl.org) maintains an online directory of associations and organizations. You can also access hundreds of religious magazines through four groups representing thousands of publications: the Associated Church Press, Catholic Press Association, Evangelical Press Association and Jewish Press Association.

WHAT ABOUT NEW YORK?

If you want to work for most of the best-known consumer magazines then you almost have to move to New York City—the publishing capital of the world. The city is home to the headquarters of three of the four largest publishing companies—Hearst, Time Inc. and Condé Nast. Their combined 200 magazine titles represent most of the largest and best-known consumer magazines. (Meredith Corporation in Des Moines, Iowa, is the other of the four largest.) The advantage of working in New York is the ability to network and move easily from job to job as you progress up the career ladder. Since most companies promote from within, you can move from one magazine to another within the same company. Or you can take a job with another magazine at another company without having to move to another city. National associations such as the Association of

Seven Best Places to Look for Magazine Jobs and Internships

- www.ed2010.com (jobs and internships in the NYC area)
- www.mediabistro.com (consumer and B-to-B magazine jobs and internships)
- www.asbpe.org (American Society of Business Publication Editors)
- www.associationmediaandpublishing.org (Association Media and Publishing)
- www.careerhq.org (Center for Association Leadership)
- www.journalismjobs.com (the most-visited resource for journalism jobs)
- www.indeed.com (meta-job searches by zip code and key words)

Magazine Media, American Society of Magazine Editors and American Business Media are located in New York and offer many networking opportunities to meet people in the industry. Groups such as Ed2010.com and Mediabistro.com offer social, educational and networking opportunities for editors and writers who are beginning their magazine careers. Several local universities offer a chance to get a master's degree and take other specialized courses while you work.

New York City simply has a vibrant atmosphere full of musical, recreational and entertainment opportunities. Inexpensive public transportation makes it easy to get anywhere in the city without owning a car. Its crime rates have declined dramatically over the past 10 years. The main disadvantage, of course, is the city's cost of living. The most expensive borough is Manhattan, where apartments start at $2,000 a month. Most young people beginning their careers in New York use local Web networking opportunities to find roommates. Those working downtown often commute from less expensive residences in Brooklyn, Queens, Staten Island, the Bronx, Queens or New Jersey.

"I always suggest to journalism students to try New York," says Nichole Screws, *Esquire*'s senior fashion market editor.

If they have the support and are able to swing it, this is where the industry thrives, and there is nothing like the exposure of the national stage. In saying that, if you come and nothing is sticking, you will know when it is your time to bow out. But if you leave with years or even a summer's experience, you can go anywhere and leave a mark. Being here is simply an invaluable publishing education.[8]

WHAT ABOUT A MASTER'S DEGREE?

Many students ask whether a master's degree in journalism will help them find a job. If all other qualifications are equal, a master's degree will give you the nod over another applicant. Most master's degree programs offer few advanced skills courses such as "advanced magazine writing" or "advanced investigative reporting." Master's degree courses focus on topics such as research methodology, research statistics, media history or media law.

Some students, however, could benefit from a master's degree and gain an edge. First, master's programs are an excellent option for career-changers or those with an undergraduate degree in another major. Sometimes people seek a master's degree in journalism after spending a few years in a career they didn't enjoy. If you enter a master's program with no undergraduate courses in journalism, most universities will require you to take up to 15 hours in skills courses such as reporting, feature writing or news writing. Time spent while earning the master's degree will also allow you to get experience with an internship and work on a student newspaper or magazine.

Second, a master's degree in journalism from a prestigious university can give you an edge in getting a job, even with an undergraduate degree in journalism. Probably the most prestigious graduate programs are at Columbia, Northwestern, Syracuse, Missouri and the University of California at Berkeley. These programs admit students with undergraduate degrees in many majors. Most of the traditional Ivy League schools such as Yale or Dartmouth do not offer journalism majors at undergraduate or graduate levels.

Rebecca Berfanger, a former special sections editor at *Indianapolis Monthly*, says her master's degree definitely opened doors. After working for a Boston-area legal publication for a few years, she earned a master's from the Medill School of Journalism at Northwestern University. "It definitely opened doors for me," she said. "People usually returned my calls or e-mails, and I often got invited to informational interviews, even if they didn't have an available job at the time."[9]

Third, a master's degree in a specialized field of interest can give you a competitive edge in becoming a writer in that field. If you're interested in religion journalism, consider a master of divinity or M.A. in religion. If you're interested in business reporting, consider a master's in business administration or marketing. An M.B.A. also can give you an edge in moving up the ranks as an editor or publisher. Some journalism graduates have even earned law degrees and gone on to careers in legal writing and editing. Stephen Key, executive director of the Hoosier State Press Association (www.hspa.com), has earned both journalism and law degrees.

Fourth, a master's degree is required if you entertain any thought of teaching college-level journalism. You cannot get a tenure-track position at an accredited university without a master's degree. At the best-known schools, a Ph.D. is necessary. Most journalism faculty members today have spent five to 10 years as professional journalists before earning advanced degrees and entering the academic world. It's always easier to get graduate degrees when you're young and single instead of later in life. If you have any thought of becoming a professor, get the master's degree now.

PRACTICAL TIPS ON JOB-HUNTING

Students who succeed as writers and editors develop skills, work habits and attitudes in college that carry over into their careers. Mediocre students may take comfort in the fact that numerous studies show little correlation between grade-point average and later career success. But most of my students who succeeded as magazine editors and writers earned all A's or mostly A's in their journalism courses.

Develop good work habits

If you develop good work habits, many professors will go out of their way to help you find a job. I've often gone the extra mile to help good students find a job by making a telephone call or writing a letter. What impresses professors so that they will give you a glowing recommendation and make an extra telephone call? Here are some suggestions:

- Never be late to class.
- Don't miss a deadline or fail to turn in an assignment.

- Never miss class except for illness or a personal emergency.
- Do more work than expected or required.
- Display a teachable attitude and don't act like you know it all.

While these habits may seem like "sucking up," they are the same work habits that translate into workplace success. When asked about common mistakes she sees among interns and recent graduates, Ann Shoket, former editor of *Seventeen*, said:

> Gossiping and showing up late. When you're first coming out of school, it's so hard to understand the business world. Make sure you're modeling your behavior after the executive level instead of the other interns or entry-level staffers. Stay focused on the next level up.[10]

Ted Spiker, a journalism professor at the University of Florida, says the "hustle factor" distinguishes his most successful magazine students from others:

> The big factor that ties them all together is that they've got the ability to hustle when they report. A lot of students can write well and have good ideas, but the difference is their willingness to take the extra step to make the story succeed. Magazine editors look for the hustle factor. Are you going to settle for three sources or are you going to go for 30 until you have all the information you need?[11]

Get experience and build your portfolio

Student media experience is essential—not optional. I encourage our magazine majors to work a minimum of a year on the student magazine and a year on the daily student newspaper. Working on the magazine gives them feature writing, editing and design experience. Working on the newspaper gives them experience writing quickly and meeting daily deadlines.

Every year I conduct exit interviews with graduating seniors from the magazine journalism major. To graduate, they must have a portfolio that contains writing clips from the student magazine, the student newspaper and their internship experiences. Every year a few students bring a portfolio without any published clips—just a few articles written for their journalism classes. Without exception, no graduate without published clips finds a newspaper or magazine job.

Nichole Screws at *Esquire* says, "The best advice I can give is write, write, write. Get clips through the school paper, magazine and local online magazine. Students are lucky these days because they have a whole new medium—online—to get work published. Use it. Clips and experience are the holy grail of magazine entry."[12]

"Being involved in student media gives you an opportunity to stretch yourself. Internships confine you to a specific role or task," says Nicole Voges, editor-in-chief of *Healthcare Executive* in Chicago.

> If you are interested in doing more than one thing, say expanding your photography or design skills, it's a lot easier to break into it in student media than it is in an internship where you can't prove you have any experience. There's just more room to grow in student media. That's a very important aspect.[13]

Complete more than one internship

While most journalism students complete an internship, two or more internships will make you stand out from the crowd. You don't have to do them during the summer. Fall and spring internships are less competitive and easier to find. For every five applicants for summer internships, fall or spring internships receive one applicant. Consider a fall- or spring-semester internship, even if it means not taking classes and delaying your graduation date. Graduates with two internships get the best-paying jobs more quickly.

"Some of my best magazine students have done four or five internships by the time they graduate," says Larry Stains,[14] director of the magazine journalism program at Temple University. His former students are now working at *People*, *Entertainment Weekly*, *Harper's Bazaar* and other well-known consumer magazines in New York City.

"The most successful students have a good balance of internships," says Ted Spiker at the University of Florida. "They have some local magazine experience and they have interned at a big one to see how the inside of a big magazine works. They've also worked on the local newspaper and obtained daily reporting experience."[15]

An unseen advantage of internships is the networking opportunities. "The skill I wish they would teach more in journalism school is the art of networking. Being able to make and maintain relationships in the magazine industry is key to breaking in and staying. Whom you know is a huge advantage," says Nichole Screws from *Esquire*. "Once a relationship is started . . . maintain it by staying in touch. Write an occasional note, remind them about you. If they show interest in your career, update them on internships and job changes," she advises.[16]

Take advantage of social networking

Social media sites such as LinkedIn.com offer unlimited chances to network and stay in touch with people. They help you locate people who have attended the same university, lived in the same city or worked at the same places you have. "They don't substitute for the personal connections, but they do help you nurture and enhance the connections you have," says Nicole Voges from *Healthcare Executive*. "Take your LinkedIn profile and take advantage of the personalized URL that you can request. It isn't an online Rollerdex. But it's an opportunity for communication and easy access to people you have connected with in your work," says Voges.[17]

Decide what you want and pursue it

When you start the job search, which should be in your junior year, the first thing to do is decide exactly what you want to do and where you want to do it. *What Color Is Your Parachute: A Practical Manual for Job Hunters and Career Changes* by Richard Bolles is the world's best-selling job-hunting book.[18] Originally published in 1970, the 40th edition was published in 2012. It has sold 8 million copies in 12 languages, averaging 20,000 copies per month in sales.

Deciding what you want and pursuing it aggressively is the central tenet of Bolles' advice, which he based on extensive research. Sidebar 21.2 contains Bolles' five best and five worst ways to find a job.

Journalism professors and recent graduates interviewed for this chapter consistently echo Bolles' advice. "My most successful students have a persistent and unshakeable goal and desire to get to where they want to get to. They have a single-minded determination and never give up," says Larry Stains at Temple University.[19] Determination is more important than talent, he says. "They may not be the best writer; they may have less talent. But the key factor in their success is determination."

Best and Worst Ways to Find a Job

In *What Color Is Your Parachute: A Practical Manual for Job Hunters and Career Changes*, Richard Bolles offers "five best ways to find a job" and "five worst ways to find a job." His tips are based on documented research and echo advice given by recent graduates and professors quoted in this chapter.

Five best ways to find a job

- asking for job leads from family, friends, professors or anyone you know (33 percent success rate)
- knocking on doors of any company that interests you, whether you know it has a vacancy or not (47 percent success rate)
- using the Yellow Pages to find companies that interest you in cities where you want to work (69 percent success rate)
- with a group of friends, using the Yellow Pages to find companies that interest you (84 percent success rate)
- the creative approach: decide exactly what your skills are, where you want to work and what you want to do and pursue your goal relentlessly in any way possible (86 percent success rate)

Five worst ways to find a job

- using the Internet (10 percent success rate)
- mailing out résumés at random to employers (7 percent success rate)
- answering ads in trade and professional journals (7 percent success rate)
- answering local newspaper ads (5 to 24 percent success rate)
- going to employment agencies and search firms (5 to 24 percent success rate)

Write an original cover letter

The cover letter offers a great chance to display your creativity and writing skill. Your letter should display knowledge of each magazine you apply to and explain how your talents can serve its interests. Talk about how your skills can help this magazine or publishing company. Don't send the same boiler-plate cover letter to every company you contact. Don't talk about why you want the job or what it will mean for your career. Don't paraphrase your résumé in a cover letter.

"Never send a generic cover letter that begins with 'to whom it may concern,'" says Nichole Screws from *Esquire*. "A cover letter is your first chance to impress the editors with your passion for working where they work. Be specific, cite examples and anecdotes and show creativity. Prove that you've read the magazine, at least a few issues, and start with something that will keep them reading past hello," she says.[20]

Lauren Gelman, features editor for health at *Reader's Digest*, says, "When you're mass applying to multiple jobs a day, remember to be careful and give due diligence to each application. Research the publication thoroughly and have a very clear understanding of what it's about, who the reader is, what makes it unique and why you want to work there."[21]

"The cover letter offers a perfect opportunity to show you can capture the tone of the magazine. If you do a lot of homework on the company, you can show that in the cover letter. You have the chance to produce the kind of writing they are looking for," says Adam Bornstein.[22]

Make telephone calls and visits

Richard Bolles, author of *What Color Is Your Parachute*, estimates that 80 percent of all job vacancies are not advertised. All companies prefer to fill vacancies without having to go through the time and expense of advertising for three reasons. First, advertising their vacancies can bring hundreds of applications, and they don't want to spend time sifting through and replying to each one. If they can get a few strong applicants through word-of-mouth referrals and unsolicited applications, then there's no need to advertise. Second, résumés and cover letters don't reveal intangible qualities such as honesty, reliability and initiative and can cover up character deficiencies such as substance abuse or a criminal record. If an employer can get enough qualified applicants through word-of-mouth referrals and unsolicited applications, again, why advertise? Third, public advertising of jobs puts employers at risk of lawsuits if rejected applicants feel they've been discriminated against for any number of reasons.

Therefore, even if you don't feel adept at networking, a phone call or e-mail to the right editor at the right time can get your foot in the door before everyone else's. Lauren Gelman from *Reader's Digest* says informational interviews can make a big impression:

> People love to help students and are usually willing to spend some time on a desk-side informational interview. Make a list of all the publications or companies you'd love to work for and e-mail a couple of editors introducing yourself and asking for an informational interview. You'll learn a little bit about their job and what the publication looks for in pitches from writers or potential staffers, and you'll have a contact to follow up with down the road. Even if it doesn't pan out to anything right away, you'll still have made a face-to-face contact and have gotten your name out there, putting yourself in a more valuable position should something open up later.[23]

"Everyone is going to have a cover letter, résumé and clips," says Adam Bornstein. "The biggest thing you can do to get noticed is your willingness to show up or place a phone call. You can only see so much about my personality on a piece of paper, but personal contact can make a huge difference."[24]

In conclusion, if you want to become a magazine writer or editor, then don't settle for a career choice that merely offers a paycheck. Follow your heart's passion. Read and write every day. Fill your mind with great ideas while you follow your dream. When you begin applying for jobs, you may get dozens of "no" answers, but remember it only takes one "yes." The oldest, simplest advice is still the best: Never give up.

NOTES

1   "2010 Surveys of Editors and News Directors," The Cox Center, University of Georgia, 2011. www.grady.uga.edu/annualsurveys (accessed April 27, 2012).
2   David E. Sumner, "American Magazine Winners and Losers 2001 to 2010," International Conference on Communication, Media, Technology and Design, Istanbul, Turkey, May 9–11, 2012.
3   Quoted in David E. Sumner, *The Magazine Century: American Magazines Since 1900* (New York: Peter Lang Publishing, 2010).
4   Telephone interview with David E. Sumner, April 5, 2012.
5   Telephone interview with David E. Sumner, Aug. 13, 2008. Updated correspondence April 27, 2012.
6   E-mail to David E. Sumner, April 18, 2012.

7   Telephone interview with David E. Sumner, April 5, 2012.

8   Telephone interview with David E. Sumner, Sept. 3, 2008. Updated correspondence April 27, 2012.

9   Interview with David E. Sumner, April 19, 2012.

10   Kristin Granero, "Chat with an EIC: *Seventeen*'s EIC, Ann Shoket." www.ed2010.com/2008/08/chat-eic-seventeen-s-eic-ann-shoket (accessed Aug. 20, 2008).

11   Interview with David E. Sumner, Aug. 8, 2008.

12   Telephone interview with David E. Sumner, Sept. 3, 2008. Updated correspondence April 27, 2012.

13   Telephone interview with David E. Sumner, April 5, 2012.

14   Telephone interview with David E. Sumner, Aug. 12, 2008. Reconfirmed via e-mail May 1, 2012.

15   Interview with David E. Sumner, Aug. 8, 2008.

16   Telephone interview with David E. Sumner, Sept. 3, 2008. Updated correspondence April 27, 2012.

17   Telephone interview with David E. Sumner, April 5, 2012.

18   Richard Bolles, *What Color Is Your Parachute: A Practical Manual for Job Hunters and Career Changes*, 40th ed. (Berkeley, Calif.: Ten Speed Press, 2012).

19   Telephone interview with David E. Sumner, Aug. 12, 2008. Reconfirmed via e-mail May 1, 2012.

20   Telephone interview with David E. Sumner, Sept. 3, 2008. Updated correspondence April 27, 2012.

21   Telephone interview with David E. Sumner, Aug. 12, 2008. Updated correspondence April 27, 2012.

22   Telephone interview with David E. Sumner, Aug. 13, 2008. Reconfirmed via e-mail April 27, 2012.

23   Telephone interview with David E. Sumner, Aug. 12, 2008. Updated correspondence April 27, 2012.

24   Telephone interview with David E. Sumner, Aug. 13, 2008. Reconfirmed via e-mail April 27, 2012.

Appendix

SHOPTALK: A GLOSSARY OF MAGAZINE LINGO

action verbs Verbs that describe tangible action taken by people or things. Nonaction verbs are linking verbs such as "is," "are," "was," "were" and "be."

action A person, entity or phenomenon changing from one place or situation to another. Feature articles that contain description of change are more appealing than those without any action.

active voice A form of verb structure in which the subject of the sentence is the principal actor in the sentence. In the passive voice, the subject is the recipient of the action.

actor Story sources directly involved with the event or issue that a story describes. Actors may be victims, perpetuators or participants in some other way.

all rights Allows the publisher to publish the article in its magazine, put it on its website or digital editions, or publish portions in another magazine it owns or in a subsequent book with a collection of articles. The writer gives up any opportunity of selling or reusing the material.

American Society of Magazine Editors The primary professional association in the United States for editors of major consumer magazines.

anecdote A true story used to illustrate the larger theme of a story. Anecdotes contain one or two central characters and some dialogue or quotations, and occur in a specific time and place.

angle The specific approach that you take toward covering a broad topic. Think of an angle like a small slice of a large topical "pie." Strong angles reveal fresh, original information.

Feature and Magazine Writing: Action, Angle and Anecdotes, Third Edition.
David E. Sumner and Holly G. Miller.
© 2013 David E. Sumner and Holly G. Miller. Published 2013 by John Wiley & Sons, Inc.

annual report   A publication produced every year by a company or nonprofit organization explaining its significant accomplishments and financial activity for the previous year. These reports often contain some biographical information on key officers and board members.

article package   Separate but related elements that cover a topic in a comprehensive way. In addition to the main story, these elements might include sidebars, data boxes, graphics and illustrations.

attribution   Words that identify a speaker as the source of information. Most news articles use forms of the verb "said" ("said Jones," "says Smith"). In a feature story the writer has the freedom to use other verbs of attribution ("explained Jones," "insisted Smith").

author's bio   Two or three sentences about the author's background that appear at the conclusion of an article. Often called a "bionote."

billboard paragraph   A paragraph usually placed immediately after the lead that tells in a nutshell what an article is about. Newspaper journalists call it the "nutgraf."

breaking news   Newsworthy events that are unfolding right now. The reporter's challenge is to collect and verify the facts and relay them to readers quickly and without embellishment.

business-to-business media   A term describing companies that produce magazines, tabloid newspapers, newsletters, websites and trade shows serving people who work in specific jobs, careers and professions. Their main purpose is to provide information that serves the professional needs of their readers.

cheerleader quotations   Predictable and shallow observations that add little substance to an article. Examples: "She is a very nice person"; "Everyone likes him."

cinematic storytelling   The use of video, audio, interactive graphics, maps and data visualization within long-form stories. These stories appear on interactive reading devices such as eReaders and tablet computers.

clips   Published samples of articles. Often writers include clips of their previous work when they approach editors with ideas for future articles.

closing date   The deadline for submission of all materials, including advertisements, scheduled for a particular issue of a magazine.

coherence   The unity of a story resulting from a logical organization of the facts, anecdotes and quotations that comprise it. The component parts fit together in a way that makes sense to the reader.

collector blog   Sometimes referred to as "beat blogging," this type of blog gives writers the opportunity to create posts that pull together the "best of" links for particular topic areas and provide context for each.

common knowledge   Information that's available from several published sources and, therefore, not protected by copyright. Common knowledge falls into many categories such as art, geography, science, history, music, medicine and technology.

complication   The central problem encountered by the central character in a story. The process of solving or overcoming the complication forms the plot for the story.

conflict   Disagreement on issues or events by affected parties, such as labor and management, customers and owners, or faculty and administration.

contributing editor   A title sometimes given to writers who frequently write for a publication but are not on the full-time staff. They get first preference for story assignments.

controlled circulation   Free subscriptions offered by business-to-business publishers to targeted readers with key management or decision-making responsibilities in their companies or organizations.

controversy   A prolonged, intense debate about a public issue without an immediate or easy solution.

conventional wisdom   The most commonly held opinions and attitudes about various issues. Many creative and original articles call into question the conventional wisdom about the topics they address.

conversationalist blog   This news-driven type of blog allows magazines to respond to the daily news flow through quick response posts. These blogs often have multiple authors.

cover line   Short, catchy descriptions of articles that appear on a magazine's cover and try to capture the casual reader's attention.

creator blog   Author-driven blogs in which writers create original, dedicated content built around their long-form projects. This home base creates a space for authors to speak directly to readers.

critic blog   This topic-driven type of blog focuses on one specific topic area (e.g., science) and allows writers the opportunity to respond to those working in the same field.

dead construction   A lifeless pronoun-verb combination at the beginning of a sentence, such as "there is," "there are," "there was," "there will be," "it is," "it was," "it will be."

demographics Vital statistics about readers such as age, education level, geographic location, employment, gender, political and religious leanings, number of children, hobbies and interests.

departments Sections of a magazine published on a recurring basis and covering the same general types of topics in every issue.

description Details about a person's appearance, clothing or surroundings that help reveal the person's character and personality.

dialogue Direct quotations of conversation between two people that occurred at a specific time and place. Dialogue differs from quotes that simply involve the reporting of reflections and observations from one person.

direct quotation Exact words spoken by an interviewee, placed within quotation marks and included in the body of an article. ("I grew up in the South during the turbulent 1960s," said Jones.)

dramatic story A true story that describes how a central character or characters encounter a complicating situation that they fight to overcome.

editorial formula The combination of types of articles used by a magazine on a regular basis. For example, some magazines may publish three news stories, two feature profiles and four standing columns in every issue.

editorial packages A feature article plus its sidebars, hotboxes, graphics and other related elements.

evergreen topics Article topics and ideas that publications revisit once a year or more and that readers are always interested in knowing about. For example, weight loss is an evergreen topic at many women's and fitness magazines.

expert or voice of authority An interviewee who, through virtue of job title, experience or education, is a credible source of information about a particular topic.

exposition Factual material in a story that explains needed background or context. Expository writing usually lacks people or action and should be limited.

fair use Section 107 of the U.S. Copyright Code, which defines four legal criteria determining whether intellectual property may be "fairly" used without permission. All intellectual property, including any online Web content, is governed by fair use laws. Even if covered by fair use, the source of any quoted material must be cited by writers. See www.copyright.gov for more information.

feature article   A term used mostly by newspaper journalists to describe stories that aren't "hard news." Magazine journalists use more specific categories such as profiles, how-to, travel, nonfiction narratives, inspirational and so on, all of which may be called "features."

first reader   Often an intern or editorial assistant who opens unsolicited manuscripts and screens them according to quality. If an article is publishable, the first reader directs it to the attention of an editor.

first serial rights (first rights)   Legal rights sold to a publisher giving it the first opportunity to publish the article. After the article is published, writers retain the right to sell unlimited reprint rights to other publishers.

gang query   A letter of inquiry written by a freelancer that proposes more than one story idea to an editor.

hook, introduction, lead   The opening sentences or paragraphs of an article, designed to capture readers' attention and interest.

indirect quotation   Words spoken by an interviewee but not placed within quotation marks. (Jones said that he grew up in the South during the turbulent 1960s.)

in-flight magazine   A sponsored publication published by an airline and available at no cost to passengers on the airline's flights.

intangible how-to article   Self-help articles that often lead to internal changes rather than the creation of some object that you can see and touch. Example: "How to Feel More Content."

intellectual property   Any work by a writer, musician, artist, sculptor or computer programmer capable of commercial use or distribution. Original creators hold legal rights to the reproduction, distribution, public performance or public display of their work. They also have the right to sell part or all of their ownership.

interactive media   A broad description of digital media that stretches from the addition of hyperlinks on a webpage to nonlinear navigation in touch-screen environments. The essence of the definition deals with asking readers to choose what action to take to push forward the reading experience.

inverted pyramid   A way of organizing an article; the writer places the most important material first and then arranges subsequent information in descending order of importance.

investigative reporting   Stories that report deceit, fraud or dishonesty on the part of corporate, government or public officials. After publication, they usually result in public controversy.

issue   A phenomenon or development that poses a risk or danger to the public or some segment of the population. Since some issues may benefit some population segments and hurt others, the solutions are debatable.

keywords   Words and phrases that emphasize the main theme of an article. Keywords should be used frequently enough to allow search engines to rank them highly in Web searches.

kill fee   An amount of money that an editor pays a writer to cancel an assigned article. Typically a kill fee is at least 20 percent of the amount the magazine agreed to pay the author for a published article.

lead time   The number of weeks or months required by a publication's staff to produce an issue. Most monthly magazines work on a three-to-six-month lead time.

linking verbs   Forms of "to be" verbs such as "is," "are" and "was" that link a subject to a similar object. Writers should use linking verbs as infrequently as possible.

list article   A brief article that contains practical information presented in a 1–2–3 format.

listserv   An electronic special-interest newsletter subscribed to by people interested in that topic. Any subscriber can send e-mail questions or comments to all of the other subscribers.

loaded words   Words that convey the writer's opinion toward a topic or a person.

luggage paragraph   A catchall for information; the writer dumps an assortment of facts into one paragraph, often making it long and confusing.

masthead   Often positioned near a magazine's table of contents, it lists editors and other staff members affiliated with a publication.

narrative   A story with a chronological structure that proceeds from one event to the next.

National Magazine Awards   The most prestigious awards given in the U.S. magazine industry. The annual competition is sponsored by the American Society of Magazine Editors.

New Journalism   A writing genre that developed during the 1960s, later called "literary nonfiction." Its distinguishing characteristic is the use of fiction techniques—especially narrative, dialogue, description, scene-by-scene reporting—in nonfiction reporting.

news feature   A broadly used term that includes articles about trends, conflicts, investigative reporting and other issues that are not "hard news."

news peg   A current or recent event related to the topic that you are writing about; a news peg gives timeliness to a feature article.

news values   Certain characteristics of news and feature stories that make them interesting. The most common news values are novelty, conflict, magnitude, impact, tension and humor.

newsgroup   Online discussion group on topics of special interest that anyone can read and contribute to. They differ from listservs, which have subscription-only access. Newsgroups can be accessed using Google's "group" function.

niche   The narrowly defined content and readership that characterizes most magazines. While most magazines serve a narrow niche within a national audience, most newspapers serve a wide niche of ages and interests in one city or region.

nutgraf   See billboard paragraph.

on speculation   These words, often included in a query letter, indicate a writer's willingness to submit an article without any guarantee that the editor will accept it for publication.

on the record   A comment intended for publication; an off-the-record comment is meant to help the writer understand something but is not meant for publication.

one-time rights   One-time rights are sold to several different publications, giving them the right to publish the article simultaneously. Syndicated columns appearing in many newspapers are usually sold with one-time rights.

open-ended question   A question that cannot be answered with "yes" or "no" and that strives to elicit an interviewee's insights.

organization magazine   A magazine published by an association, company, university, religious group or other organization for its members. Sometimes called a "sponsored magazine" or "sponsored publication," its goal is to publish news and features about the organization and promote its goals and views.

parallel structure   The use of the same verb tense, phrase and clause structure in sentences and paragraphs.

partial quotation   Part of a sentence, spoken by an interviewee and placed within quotation marks. (Jones said he grew up in the South "during the turbulent 1960s.")

participant   Someone with first-hand experience in dealing with the subject you are writing about. Participants will be "experts" by virtue of their experience.

passive voice   A form of verb structure in which the subject of the sentence is the recipient of the action from another object in the sentence.

plot   The problem or complication in a story that the central character(s) must solve. A good plot also creates tension and helps keep the reader interested and involved.

primary source   The originating source for specific news and information. Primary source material has not been published or interpreted through other writers.

profile article   A feature that looks in depth at one person.

pronoun agreement   The use of singular pronouns to refer back to singular nouns, and plural pronouns to refer back to plural nouns.

public domain   Written material not protected by copyright that anyone may use. Copyrighted material expires 70 years after the death of the author in the United States. Anything published by the U.S. government is (with some exceptions) in the public domain.

query letter   A letter written to the editor of a magazine that proposes the details of a story idea and explains the writer's qualifications to write it.

regional correspondent   A writer responsible for generating articles from a specific geographic part of the country. These contributors live in the region and usually work out of their homes.

reprint rights   The formal term is "second serial rights," which give a publication the opportunity to reprint previously published material. Most publications purchase reprint rights if the original publication's readership doesn't overlap with their own.

resolution   In a dramatic story, the outcome of the central character's effort to solve the complication, which may involve happy or sad endings.

rhythm   Variety in the movement or pace of writing. Strong rhythm results from varied sentence and paragraph length with frequent use of action verbs and active voice.

round-up article   An article containing several persons' points of view on a common topic, often packaged as separate mini-profiles. Example: "Why I Home School My Kids—Five Families Share Their Experiences."

run-on sentence   Two complete sentences incorrectly separated by a comma and not a period or conjunction.

scene-by-scene reporting   A description of the unfolding scenes of a narrative as it moves from one event to another.

scholarly journals   Journals whose content deals with academic disciplines and subdisciplines whose authors are typically college professors. Articles are based on original research and must be approved by a peer-reviewed panel of other scholars prior to acceptance.

secondary source   A secondary source is a "second-hand" source that stands between the reader and the originating source. Articles appearing in newspapers, magazines and websites are usually secondary sources.

service journalism   Articles written to directly help readers in their everyday lives. Service journalism articles may provide practical help in improving readers' health, recreation, finances or careers. "How-to" articles are a special type of service journalism that focuses on completing a specific, immediate task.

shadowing   A research technique that has the writer accompanying a subject as the subject goes about his day. The writer observes the subject in a variety of circumstances.

shelf life   The length of time that a topic or an issue of a publication remains pertinent.

short   Interesting, informative and intentional nonfiction items of various lengths.

sidebar   Lists or pieces of related information presented outside the main body of the article in a separate space. Editors like sidebars because they attract readers' attention and serve as an entry-point into the article.

single-copy sales   The opposite of subscription sales, this term refers to newsstand sales of a publication.

snapshot   A tightly focused, brief look at a person.

special collections   Noncirculating documents held by libraries that often serve as useful information for journalists and researchers. Public officials and celebrities often donate their correspondence and documents to libraries for their special collections.

spin doctors   Writers and public-relations persons who manipulate information to support their points of view.

split anecdote   A story that is cut in half and separated by paragraphs containing other information. Often the first half of the anecdote serves as an article's lead and the second half brings the article to a conclusion.

spreadsheet   A computer program that allows users to enter data and text in rows and columns and perform numerous statistical calculations on the data. Understanding spreadsheets and how to do numerical reporting can advance a journalist's career.

standing column A regular feature that is present in every issue of a publication. The name of the column doesn't change, and it usually appears in the same place and is written by the same writer.

structure How the parts of a story—such as facts, quotes and anecdotes—are put together in the most clear, logical and easy-to-read way for the reader.

style A broad term describing the combination of voice, viewpoint, rhythm and tone in an author's writing.

style manual A guide to proper use of writing falling outside normal rules of grammar. Commonly used style manuals are the *AP Stylebook, Turabian Guide* and *Chicago Manual of Style*. Some magazines write their own style manuals.

subsidiary rights A term used in book publishing. Subsidiary rights include all other rights such as movie or television rights, foreign editions, book-club rights, audio-book editions and electronic rights.

summary lead An article's opening sentences that answer the essential questions about an event: who, what, where, when, why and how.

support interview A supporting source of information to a profile or narrative centered around one individual; support interviews add depth and insight to the profile or narrative.

talking points Key information that an interviewee is determined to work into an interview regardless of the questions asked.

tangible how-to article An article that leads to the creation of something that can be seen and touched.

tear sheet A page torn from a publication that contains a sample of your writing.

tension The introduction of an unsolved problem at the beginning of a story that writers use as a way of attracting and sustaining readers' attention.

tone The writer's attitude displayed in an article, which may be humorous, satirical, light-hearted, heavy, sarcastic, whimsical, persuasive, argumentative, self-deprecating, disparaging or respectful.

trade magazine A magazine whose main purpose is to provide useful information to practitioners of the various professions and trades; also known as business-to-business publication.

transition   Words that serve as a "bridge" or a segue to move an article from one point to the next.

trend   A phenomenon that is increasing or decreasing in frequency. Trends always have a quantifiable dimension and can occur in politics, pop culture or any field of interest.

unity   Keeping the focus on a single angle in an article while using a consistent viewpoint, verb tense, voice and tone.

viewpoint   The role the author takes in writing an article. The first person makes frequent use of the "I" viewpoint, while the second person uses the "you" viewpoint frequently. The third person uses primarily "he," "she" or "it" viewpoints.

vlog   Short for "video blog."

voice   How writers reveal their personality and identity in their writing style.

writer's block   A "condition," claimed by many writers, when words don't flow and sentences don't find their way quickly onto paper or the computer screen.

INDEX

Feature and Magazine Writing: Action, Angle and Anecdotes, Third Edition.
David E. Sumner and Holly G. Miller.
© 2013 David E. Sumner and Holly G. Miller. Published 2013 by John Wiley & Sons, Inc.